THE GOSPEL OF
Matthew

The Crowning
of the King

G. Steve Kinnard

THE GOSPEL OF MATTHEW

The Crowning of the King

ipi

The Gospel of Matthew – The Crowning of the King
©2004 by G. Steve Kinnard

Printed in the United States of America
08 07 06 05 04   1 2 3 4 5

ISBN: 0-9745342-4-2

Published by
Illuminations Publishers International
1190 Boylston Street
Newton, Massachusetts, MA 02464
www.ipibooks.com

ipi

To my dad,
Glen E. Kinnard,
and in loving memory of my mom,
Anne Witherow Kinnard,
who, simply put,
were the two greatest parents
a kid could ever have.

Contents

Acknowledgements

To my family, Leigh, Chelsea, and Daniel, thank you for your constant love and support.

To the New York City Church of Christ, thank you for the honor of serving you, with Leigh, for more than twenty years now. Special thanks to my friends in the Hudson Valley sector of the church for your encouragement.

To the eldership of the New York City Church of Christ, thank you for your support of my writing and of the teaching ministry over the years.

Special thanks to Dr. Douglas Jacoby, a trusted friend and advisor (and the smartest man I know) who read through the text and made many valuable suggestions.

To Kelly Petre and the staff at Discipleship Publications International, thank you for your help with the manuscript.

To Toney C. Mulhollan and the staff of Illumination Publishers International, thank you for editing and publishing this book.

Preface

Oh! For a closer walk with God,
   A calm and heavenly frame;
A light to shine upon the road
   That leads me to the Lamb!

Where is the blessedness I knew
   When first I saw the Lord?
Where is the soul-refreshing view
   Of Jesus and his word?

What peaceful hours I once enjoyed!
   How sweet their memory still!
But they have left an aching void
   The world can never fill.

Return, O holy Dove, return,
   Sweet messenger of rest;
I hate the sins that made thee mourn,
   And drove thee from my breast.

The dearest idol I have known,
   Whatever that idol be,
Help me to tear it from thy throne,
   And worship only Thee.

So shall my walk be close with God,
   Calm and serene my frame;
So purer light shall mark the road
   That leads me to the Lamb.

> *"Walking with God"* by William Cowper (1731-1800)

I. Why another book on Matthew?

You might be asking, why another book on the life of Jesus? Why another book on the gospel of Matthew? Why? Why? Why? How many books on Matthew are there already? Dozens, perhaps hundreds. And that's just in English. Why one more? I have written this book because I wanted to write a practical commentary on Matthew that was scholarly in approach, yet practical in scope. Most commentaries are either one or the other.

The commentary I wanted to write is like a submarine. A submarine is able to dive deep and is also able to maneuver across the surface of the water. Such a commentary digs deep into the text and also speaks directly to our hearts. Most scholarly commentaries go deep into word studies and background material, without ever surfacing to speak to the heart, while the practical commentaries mostly stay on the surface without exploring the depth of the Scriptures. In this book, we will attempt to do both. We will explore the meanings of words. We will look at the first century background behind the text. At points, we will see what other commentators say about certain verses. I will also share sermons, lessons, and practical points, and provide material that can be used for personal devotional times.

II. My translation

I began my study of Matthew by translating the gospel from Greek into English. Translators usually approach the Bible in one of two ways, to provide either the literal equivalent or the dynamic equivalent. The literal equivalent is the word-for-word translation of the text. It is not possible to translate literally word for word, because the translation would be nonsensical to the English reader, but the hope is to stay as close to the original text as possible. The advantage of this method is that the translation follows the original text very closely; however, the translation is often difficult to read.

The translator using a dynamic equivalent approach attempts to translate the text idea for idea rather than word for word. The advantage is that the translation will be far more readable than a literal equivalence translation. The major disadvantage is that the translator can plant ideas in the text that are not really there. In this book, I use the dynamic approach to translation. I try to make sure the idea that is stated in the original comes across in the English.

III. My exegesis

Exegesis is the process of acquiring meaning from the text. Whenever we read, we have to interpret what is written. To begin, we will delve into the meaning of Greek words and sometimes the Hebrew/Aramaic behind the Greek, as is done in literal equivalent translation. But we will not stop there, for understanding the words of the Scriptures is critical, but it is not the whole story. We cannot get to the truth of the Scriptures unless we can make sense of those words. To do that, we will go behind the text to discover the first century setting of the text, as is done in preparing a dynamic equivalent translation.

Since the setting of the Gospels is so different from our world today, we have to travel back in time to understand the text. For example, who were the Pharisees and how were they different from the Sadducees? What was the attitude of the Jews towards the Romans in the first century? Jesus lived most of his life in Galilee; what was Galilee like in Jesus' day? To better understand the text, we will consider such questions of historical, geographical, economic, and cultural background.

Once the task of determining the meaning of the text based on the first century setting has been done, we can apply that meaning to our day and time. We can make the Scriptures practical for our lives today. If we try to apply the Scriptures without first discovering the rich and complex meaning of the text, looking at the text from both the literal and the dynamic equivalent perspective, then we run the risk of misapplying them.

IV. How to use the book

I suggest that you study the Gospel of Matthew beginning with chapter one and working your way through to the end. Although it is possible to hopscotch back and forth within the book, Matthew is presenting a linear argument, demonstrating that Jesus is the Christ, the King. The best way to understand his argument is to follow it through the book.

V. If you have questions

I welcome your feedback and questions about this book. I don't know if I will be able to respond to every communication, because of time constraints and because I am sure I will not have all the answers. But I will try. Please address e-mail correspondence to stevekinnard@mac.com.

Introduction
to Matthew's Gospel

When we open our New Testament, we find a man looking at us who, although not a professional revolutionist has been the cause of many revolutions, and who, although not a disturber of the peace, has repeatedly turned the world upside down. He is not numbered among the radicals because in his radicalism he outstrips them all. He dares to reverse all human standards; confounds the wise by things, which are foolish; and confounds the mighty by the things which are weak. He has much to say about authority and power, and it is his claim that he can make all things new.

Charles Edward Jefferson, **Jesus the Same**

The Gospel of Matthew is the first Gospel, in fact the first book, in our New Testament. Because of this, Matthew is often the first book of the New Testament that people read, and it is the first introduction to the life of Jesus for many people. This in and of itself makes Matthew an important book, and one that we should study.

There are many other reasons why Matthew is important. It is a long book. It has twenty-eight chapters (four more than Luke and as many chapters as Acts). It is one of three synoptic gospels, meaning its content is similar to Mark and Luke. Matthew's gospel is the most quoted New Testament book in Christian writings of the second century. It is the only gospel to give us the longest discourse (sermon) of Jesus–the Sermon on the Mount. It is the only gospel to mention the church (the *ekklesia*). It is the most Jewish of the Gospels. It and John are the only gospels written by one of the twelve apostles of Jesus who were eyewitnesses of his ministry.

I love each of the Gospels for different reasons. I love Mark because I believe it was the first gospel that was written and circulated. Mark's gospel is concise and compact. It has Jesus moving from one scene to the next like Flash Gordon in the comics. I love Luke because he took Mark's gospel and expanded on it, making it intelligible to the Greek world. Luke emphasizes the historicity of the life of Jesus. He also includes many events that speak of the compassion of Jesus and his love for the poor. I love John because it is so different from the Synoptic gospels (Matthew, Mark, and Luke). John's gospel is the easiest to read. It reads more like a novel with each chapter dealing with a specific event in Jesus' life. John is easy to grasp and easy to get your arms around.

But I also love the Gospel of Matthew. Having spent a year of my life in Jerusalem, Israel/Palestine, I love the Jewish nature of Matthew's gospel. He brings ancient Palestine to life. I love his lengthy portrayal of Jesus. I love the way he ties in the Old Testament with the life of Jesus. He makes it clear that Jesus is the fulfillment of prophecy. He declares beyond doubt that Jesus is the Christ, the Messiah. He does this for a Jewish audience, while pointing out that God has included the Gentiles in his mission. Matthew is bold, clear, inspiring, and readable. No wonder the early church placed this gospel before the others, indeed placed it first in the New Testament canon.

This introduction will give background information concerning the Gospel of Matthew. We will consider the following questions:

I.   What is a gospel?
II.   Why were the Gospels recorded?
III.   How do we interpret the Gospels?
IV.   Who wrote the Gospel of Matthew?
V.   When and where was Matthew written?
VI.   To whom was it written?
VII.   What was the purpose of Matthew's gospel?
VIII.   What early church needs were met by the Gospel of Matthew?
IX.   What are the characteristics of Matthew's gospel?
X.   What makes Matthew's gospel distinctive?
XI.   What structure does Matthew use to outline his gospel?
XII.   Additional ideas concerning Matthew's gospel.
XIII.   My abbreviated outline.
XIV.   My expanded outline.
XV.   Who was Matthew?

I. What is a gospel?

Here then we find the supreme mission of the Christian minister: It is to help men to fall in love with the character of Jesus. The Bible is an invaluable book chiefly because it contains a portrait of Jesus. The New Testament is immeasurably superior to the Old because in the New Testament we have the face of Jesus. The Holy of Holies of the New Testament is the Gospels because it is here we look directly into the eyes of Jesus. We often speak of the Gospel: What is it? Jesus!

–Charles Edward Jefferson, **Jesus the Same**

The word gospel (*euangelion* in the Greek) means "good news, the report by the herald of a king." In the Ptolemaic period just before the birth of Jesus, *euangelion*, the gospel, was proclaimed when a king was born and especially when he ascended the throne. Even earlier, *euangelion* meant the fee paid to the messenger who brought reports of good news to a general in battle. The Christians adopted this term and applied it to Jesus, their king. They proclaimed *euangelion* to announce his ascension to the throne of God. The early Christians enriched the idea of *euangelion* with the Jewish concept of the Living Word. For the Jew, the word was never just a report or a story; it was always the living and active word of God (Hebrews 4:12). The New Testament writers used the term "gospel" to mean the living word of preaching Christ as king. The gospel writers were not journalists or historians recording an everyday story; they were believers heralding the birth and ascension of the King of the Universe. A gospel is not a biography in the sense that we use the word today. It is a tract designed to promote faith in Jesus, a man the writers knew to be like no other (Luke 1:2-4, John 20:31).

Luke makes this clear at the beginning of his gospel, when he writes:

> *Many have undertaken to draw up an account of the things that have been fulfilled among us, just as they were handed down to us by those who from the first were eyewitnesses and servants of the word. Therefore, since I myself have carefully investigated everything from the beginning, it seemed good also to me to write an orderly account for you, most excellent Theophilus so that you may know the certainty of the things you have been taught. (Luke 1:1-4, NIV).*

The gospel writers were concerned that an orderly, historical account of Jesus' life be circulated.

Many modern scholars express doubt about the historicity of the Gospels comparing them to rabbinic midrash or commentary. D.A. Carson answers these criticisms, by writing:

> We conclude that the evangelists, including Matthew, intended that their Gospels convey historical information. This does not mean they intended to write dispassionate, modern biographies. But advocacy does not necessarily affect truth telling: a Jewish writer on the Holocaust is not necessarily either more or less accurate because his family perished at Auschwitz. Nor is it proper in the study of any document professedly dealing with history to approach it with a neutral stance that demands proof of authenticity as well as proof on a lack of authenticity.[1]

The gospel writers were writing historical tracts that promoted the mission of Jesus. The gospels were not strict biography. They were part memoirs, part theological treatises, part biography, part sermon, part doctrinal teaching, part profession of faith, part encouraging letter, and part homage to the Lord. Along with strict adherence to the truth, they were presentations of the good news that Jesus is the Messiah, the Son of God, and Immanuel, who came to save the world from sin.

II. Why were the Gospels recorded?

1. The early Christian community believed that Jesus was going to return quickly. As time passed and his Second Coming had not yet occurred, the need was felt to record the testimony of the ministry of Jesus. This historical record of Jesus' life and ministry kept the memory of Jesus alive as the eyewitnesses of Jesus passed away.

2. As more people became Christians (especially those outside of Palestine who were unfamiliar with the life of Jesus), there was a need to collect the stories of Jesus to educate the disciples.

3. Very early in the ministry of the church, false teaching about Jesus became commonplace. Gnostics, who denied that Jesus was God in the flesh, began circulating false teaching about Jesus. The Gospels were correctives to these false ideas about Jesus.

4. As the early church grew, there was a need to provide material that could be used in worship services. The Gospels could be read in the worship of the early church as a means of encouragement.

III. How do we interpret the Gospels?

The Gospels are of a different genre than the writings of Paul or the Book of Revelation. When we read the Gospels, we should recognize the differences between the Four Gospels and the other books of the New Testament. Here are some guidelines for interpreting the Gospels:

1. Jesus spoke in Aramaic/Hebrew. Since the Gospels were recorded in Greek, we are at best one step removed from the actual words of Jesus. We must attempt to go behind the Greek and understand the Jewish context. Since Matthew was written for a Jewish audience, he helps us to grasp the Jewishness of the message of Jesus more than the other Gospels.

2. Look at the Gospels at two levels.
   • The historical concerns of who Jesus was and what he did.
   • Retelling the story of Jesus for the needs of the church.

3. Understand the historical context of the Gospels and the time in which they were written.

4. Understand the forms that Jesus used in his teaching: proverbs, similes and metaphors, poetry, questions, and irony.
5. When interpreting an individual pericope, an individual story:
   • Think horizontally. Consider how the story is used in the other Gospels.
   • Think vertically. Consider the historical context of the story.

IV. Who wrote the Gospel of Matthew?

The Apostle Matthew wrote the Gospel of Matthew. The early Church Fathers attest to this. Papias, an elder in the early church who wrote around AD 130 states, "Matthew composed the *logia* (words, teachings) in the Hebrew tongue and everyone interpreted them as he was able."[2] Not only does Papias declare that Matthew wrote the gospel, but he notes that it was written in Hebrew. Matthew's work is very Semitic in nature. The more we understand the first century Jewish mind, the better we will understand the Gospel of Matthew.

Irenaeus, another early church father, in AD 202 wrote, "Now Matthew published also a book of the gospel among the Hebrews in their own dialect, while Peter and Paul were preaching the gospel in Rome and founding the Church."[3]

Ignatius of Antioch also quotes from Matthew, making note that the Gospel was written from Antioch. Origen states that Matthew, once a tax collector and afterwards an apostle of Jesus Christ, wrote the First Gospel, and that it was prepared for the converts from Judaism and published in the Hebrew language.[4]

Some scholars suggest another interpretation to Papius' statement concerning Matthew. They say that *logia* doesn't have to mean the entire Gospel of Matthew, but that Matthew could have written some of the sayings of Jesus and then another writer or school of writers constructed the Gospel around those sayings. But the other church fathers took Papius' statement as saying that Matthew composed the Gospel. There seems to be no adequate reason for rejecting the apostle Matthew as the author of the First Gospel.

V. When and where was Matthew written?

Most scholars date the writing of Matthew to around AD 80 to 85, some time after the temple was destroyed in AD 70. Since Matthew 24 contains very exact details concerning the destruction of the temple, modern scholars feel it had to be written after the temple was destroyed. These scholars do not believe in predictive prophecy, or that Jesus could have predicted the destruction of the temple in such detail; therefore, the gospel must have been written after AD

70. If you believe in predictive prophecy, then you can easily date Matthew's gospel before AD 70.

I would date it around the year AD 66. D.A. Carson, author of an excellent two-volume commentary on Matthew, writes:

> First, we do not know when Mark was written, but most estimates fall between AD 50 and 65. Second, on this basis most critics think Matthew could not have been written until 75 or 80. But even if Mark is as late as 65, there is no reason based on literary dependence why Matthew could not be dated AD 66. As soon as a written source circulated, it is available for copying.[5]

I agree with Carson's assessment here.

Most scholars believe that Matthew used Mark's Gospel as a source, and that Matthew shared a common source with Luke, often called the Q source. This was in addition to his own material, possibly his own records of Jesus' teachings, material referred to as the M source.

Two places are usually mentioned as the site where Matthew was written:

1. Palestine is the most traditional; the Gospel is very Jewish in its background and this lends weight to its having been written in Palestine.

2. Scholars like B. H. Streeter and Merrill Tenney have suggested Antioch in Syria.

Merrill Tenney writes:

> The place of the writing could be Antioch. This first Gospel was probably the favorite of the Syro-Jewish church. Furthermore, the church at Antioch was the first to have a markedly Gentile constituency that spoke Aramaic and Greek. It may, therefore, have been composed some time between AD 50 and 70 and have been circulated by those who worked in and from the church of Antioch.[6]

The church in Antioch, Syria was almost as Jewish as the church in Palestine. Even the Gentiles there would have spoken Aramaic. Our first evidence of anyone using the Gospel of Matthew comes from Ignatius of Antioch. He was an elder/bishop over the church in Antioch at the beginning of the second century. Peter was closely associated with the church in Antioch. Peter is highlighted throughout Matthew's gospel. Antioch was a pillar church in the first century. Some scholars estimate that the church in Antioch grew to 20,000 members. I believe this to be the most likely site of origin for Matthew's Gospel.

VI. To whom was it written?

It is certain that the gospel was written to an audience with a Jewish background. Matthew uses the Old Testament to speak of Jesus as the direct fulfillment of Old Testament prophecy. He opens by stating that Jesus is the "Son of David, the Son of Abraham." Why mention David first? Matthew wanted to emphasize the kingship/ messiahship of Jesus. This would have been lost on a Gentile audience.

Jesus uses many Jewish phrases and expressions without explaining them. He speaks of *korban* and *raca*, ceremonial hand washing, whitewashed sepulchers, and the traditions of the elders. He brings up rabbinic disputes between the schools of Hillel and Shammai without specifying what is meant. David Hill, a New Testament scholar, writes in the introduction to his commentary on Matthew, "Matthew's Gospel is written from a Jewish Christian standpoint, in order to defend Christianity, to make it acceptable to Jewish-Christian readers, and to prove that Jesus is the Messiah of the Jews."[7]

VII. What was the purpose of Matthew's Gospel?

1. Apologetics: To convince Jewish readers that Jesus is the Messiah, the son of the living God.
2. Fulfillment formulas: Matthew uses "this was done to fulfill" throughout his gospel. He is demonstrating that the life of Jesus is direct fulfillment of Old Testament prophecy.
3. Infancy narrative. Matthew defends the birth of Jesus as legitimate.
4. Resurrection: Matthew describes the bribery of the guard, and shows that Jesus' body was not stolen. This is a defense of the bodily resurrection of Jesus.
5. Matthew displays the church as the true Israel.
6. Matthew demonstrates that Jesus came to fulfill the law.
7. Matthew shows that being Jewish will not save you.
   - 3:9-10 God can make Jews from stones.
   - 10:1-ff. Jesus sends the twelve to the lost of Israel; Israel is lost.
   - 27:25 The blood of Jesus is on Jewish hands.
8. The righteous life is the indication of true faith.
   - 7:15-28 Not everyone who says, "Lord, Lord" will enter heaven. The one who does the will of God will enter heaven.
   - 13:24-ff. The Parable of the Weeds.
   - 22:1-14 The Parable of the Wedding Garment = symbol of good deeds.
   - 25:24-30 The Parable of the Talents.

• 25:31-46 The Parable of the Sheep and Goats.

Matthew says you can't work your way into heaven, but there is no way to get there if you don't work. A gift as great as salvation requires an appropriate response. Let's suppose you were crossing the street to grab a pizza and a runaway truck plows right toward you. If someone pushed you out of the way at the last moment and takes the hit for you, what would you do? Would you continue into the pizza parlor to eat your pizza? Would you forget the event by the next day? More than likely, you would live with this moment the rest of life. You would feel that you had been given a new lease on life. Most people would try to think of a way to repay such an act of heroism. This should be our response to the cross as well.

VIII. What early church needs were met by the Gospel of Matthew?

1. It was used to teach and instruct the early disciples about the life of Jesus and discipleship.
2. Matthew provided material outlining the motivation for and the objective of the outreach of the early church to both Jews and Gentiles. Even today, Matthew 28:18-20 stands as the rallying cry for the evangelization of the world.
3. As the early church grew more distant from Jesus, Matthew's gospel provided material that would remind the church about the life and mission of Jesus. Matthew records the events of his birth, baptism, early ministry, healing stories, parables, teachings, and suffering.
4. His gospel also would have strengthened the hearts of the early disciples as they faced persecution. Jesus promised that his disciples would be persecuted, and he was persecuted himself. Matthew lets the early church know that if they will hold onto their faith in spite of opposition, then they will be blessed.

IX. What are the characteristics of Matthew's Gospel?

1. Concise in structure.
2. Messianic in tone, proving that Jesus is the Messiah.
3. Although a very Jewish gospel, Matthew opens the church to those outside of Judaism (Matthew 28:18-20). The faults of Judaism are not passed over lightly.
4. It is ecclesiastical, being the only gospel to mention the church.
5. It is eschatological, concerned with the study of last things/the end of time. Matthew's Gospel has the longest section on the destruction of Jerusalem and on the coming of Jesus at the end of time.
6. Matthew uses 90% of Mark, which takes up about 50% of

Matthew.

27% of Matthew is from "Q" = the source common with Luke.

22% of Matthew is from "M" = Matthew's own source

It is clear that most of Matthew is gleaned from the author's own experience and memory of walking with Jesus.

7. Matthew uses over 60 quotes from the Old Testament.

1. Direct quotes

2. Formula quotations = "this was done that it might be fulfilled through the prophet saying..." These are used approximately 40 times.

8. Didactic, useful for teaching. Matthew emphasized Jesus as Teacher. His gospel contains the longest block of teaching material found in the Gospels, The Sermon on the Mount (chapters 5-7). The teaching discourses of Jesus comprise three-fifths of Matthew's material.

X. What makes Matthew's Gospel distinctive?

1. The term "kingdom of heaven" appears 33 times. Only 5 times does Matthew speak of the kingdom of God.

2. The visit of the Magi.

3. The flight to Egypt and the massacre of the infants.

4.   The incident at the crucifixion where the ground shook, tombs opened, and holy people went into the city.

5. The bribery of the tomb guards after the resurrection.

6. The miracle of the two blind men.

7. The story of the dumb demoniac.

8. The story of the coin in the fish's mouth.

9. The longest single discourse of Jesus, Mt. 5-7.

10. The only gospel to mention the church.

XI. What is the underlying structure of the Gospel of Matthew?

1. It is possible to find several different outlines that elucidate the themes of Matthew's gospel. We could follow the pattern of Mark's gospel and use a geographical outline for Matthew. For example:

Introduction	Mt. 1:1-4:11
Ministry in Galilee	Mt. 4:12-13:58
Wider Ministry in the North	Mt. 14:1-16:12
Towards Jerusalem	Mt. 16:13-20:34
Confrontation in Jerusalem	Mt. 21:1-25:46
Passion and Resurrection	Mt. 26:1-28:20

2. B.W. Bacon, who wrote a commentary on Matthew, has suggested a five-fold structure based on the concept that Matthew is presenting a new Torah (the five books of Moses). Bacon outlined Matthew in this fashion:

There are five narrative sections and five discourse sections. Each teaches something about the kingdom.

a. The New Law, the law of the kingdom of God.
Narrative (Galilean ministry)   3:1-4:25
Teaching (Sermon on the Mount)   5:1-7:29

b. Christian discipleship.
Narrative   8:1-9:34
Teaching   9:35-10:42

c. The meaning of the kingdom.
Narrative   11:1-12:50
Teaching (Parables)   13:1 -52

d. The Church.
Narrative   13:53-17:27
Teaching (order, discipline, and worship)   18:1-35

e. Judgment.
Narrative (Controversies in Jerusalem)   19:1-22:46
Teaching (judgment on the Pharisees, apocalyptic teachings) 23:1-25:46

The proclamation of the kingdom. Jesus sends out the 72. (10:5-42)
The extension of the kingdom. Seven Parables. (Matthew 13)
The fellowship of the kingdom. Humility. (Matthew 18)
The consummation of the kingdom. Eschatology. (Matthew 24-25)

3. The New Testament scholar, J.D. Kingsbury, suggests a threefold division of the Gospel:
a. The person of Jesus as Messiah and Son of God (1:1-4:16).
b. The proclamation of Jesus' message (4:17-16:20).
c. The suffering, death, and resurrection of the Messiah and Son of God (16:21-28:20).

XII. Additional ideas concerning Matthew's Gospel
1. Although Matthew is longer than Mark's gospel, the narrative material that Matthew has in common with Mark is shorter than in

Mark's account. This shows that most of the expansion in Matthew's Gospel is from material not given in Mark.

2. Matthew emphasizes both Jesus' teaching and his actions.

3. The scripture references scattered throughout Matthew's Gospel show the historical events of Jesus' life that fulfill Old Testament prophecy.

4. The Hebrew gospel of Matthew circulated first. It began in the late 60s' in Syria, or possibly in Galilee or Judea.

5. The gospel has a definite Jewish character to it:
- Jewish customs are familiar to everyone.
- The debate concerning the law is key throughout the gospel.
- The observance of the Sabbath is a central idea.

XIII. My abbreviated outline

Part One
The Birth and Preparation of Jesus (1:1-4:16).

Part Two
Ministry in Galilee. The Sermon on the Mount (5:1-7:29).

Part Three
Ministry in Galilee. Miracles, Ministry, and Messianic Activity (8:1-12:50).

Part Four
Ministry in Galilee. Parables and People (13:1-16:20).

Part Five
Private Ministry in Galilee. Preparing the Hearts of the Disciples (16:21-18:35).

Part Six
Ministry in Judea. Turning to Jerusalem (19:1-23:39).

Part Seven
Ministry in Judea. Teaching about the Future (24:1-25:46).

Part Eight
The Death and Resurrection of Jesus (26:1-28:20).

XIV. My expanded outline

Part One–The Birth and Preparation of Jesus (1:1-4:16)

1:1-1:17	The Genealogy of Jesus the King
1:18-25	The Birth Narrative–Immanuel
2:1-12	The Visit of the Magi
2:13-23	The Escape to Egypt, the Massacre of the Infants, and the Return to Nazareth
3:1-12	John the Baptist
3:13-17	The Baptism of Jesus
4:1-11	The Testing of Jesus
4:12-17	Jesus Begins his Ministry in Galilee

XV. Who Was Matthew?

The name Matthew means, "gift of God." Matthew, also known as Levi, was a tax collector whom Jesus called to be an apostle (Matthew 9:9-13, 10:3). He probably sat at a tollbooth located on the road between Capernaum and Bethsaida beside the Sea of Galilee. This booth marked the division between the territory of Herod Antipas in the south and Herod Philip in the north. Everyone who passed by this booth was taxed for use of the roads.

Tax collectors were notorious. They were considered thieves and were hated. Their pay was usually based on the surplus system: whatever was taken in excess of the tax, they got to keep. Since the tax money went to the Roman Empire, they were considered to be Roman sympathizers. Jesus broke social norms by calling a tax collector to be in his circle of disciples. Jesus apparently included two revolutionaries in his Twelve, Simon the Zealot and Judas Iscariot. If so, then they would have been the sworn enemies of anyone like Matthew. They would have literally been at each other's throats. But Jesus called them to follow him, and he forged unity between them. Matthew became a valuable part of Jesus' ministry.

Matthew would have been an educated man. His gospel could be the result of keeping records of the journeys and teaching of Jesus.

R.H. Gundry, in his commentary on Matthew, writes that the Apostle Matthew was a note-taker during the earthly ministry of Jesus, and that his notes provided the basis for the bulk of the apostolic gospel tradition. He comments on Matthew's ability to be a scribe for Jesus:

> As an ex-publican, whose employment and post near Capernaum on the Great West Road would have required and given a good command of Greek and instilled the habit of jotting down information, and perhaps as a Levite, whose background would have given him acquaintance with the Old Testament in its Semitic as well as Greek forms, Matthew the Apostle was admirably fitted for such a function among the unlettered disciples.[8]

Matthew was well fitted for his role as writer of the Gospel of Jesus Christ. Perhaps Jesus called him precisely for this purpose.

Recommended Books
on Jesus of Nazareth

Andrew G. Hodges, *Jesus: An Interview Across Time* (1986).

Brad H. Young, *Jesus: The Jewish Theologian* (1995).

Bruce Barton, *The Man Nobody Knows* (1925).

Charles Edward Jefferson, *Jesus the Same* (1908).

David Bivin and Roy Blizzard, Jr., *Understanding the Difficult Words of Jesus: New Insights From a Hebraic Perspective* (1994, Revised Edition).

David Flusser, *Jesus* (1997).

D. James Kennedy and Jerry Newcombe, *What if Jesus Had Never Been Born?* (1994).

Harry Emerson Fosdick, *The Man From Nazareth: As His Contemporaries Saw Him* (1994).

Jim Bishop, *The Day Christ Died* (1957).

Jim Bishop, *The Day Christ Was Born* (1957).

John R. W. Stott, *Christ the Controversialist* (1970).

Leslie D. Weatherhead, *A Plain Man Looks at the Cross* (1945).

Mary Ellen Ashcroft, *The Magdalene Gospel: What If Women Had Written the Gospels?* (1995).

Neil R. Lightfoot, *Lesson From the Parables* (1965).

Philip Yancey, *The Jesus I Never Knew* (1995).

Endnotes

[1] D.A. Carson, *The Expositor's Bible Commentary with the New International Version* (Grand Rapids, Michigan: Zondervan Publishing House, 1995), pp. 10-11.

[2] As quoted in Donald Guthrie's *New Testament Introduction* (Downers Grove, Ill., Inter-Varsity Press, 1970), p. 33.

[3] Ibid. p. 39.

[4] Ibid.

[5] Carson, pp. 20.

[6] Merrill C. Tenney, *New Testament Survey, Revised.* (Grand Rapids: Wm. B. Eerdmans Publishing Co., 1985), p. 19.

[7] David Hill, *The New Century Bible Commentary: The Gospel of Matthew* (Grand Rapids: Eerdmans Publ. Co., 1972), p. 40.

[8] R. H. Gundry, *Matthew: A Commentary on his Literary and Theological Art* (Grand Rapids: Eerdmans, 1982), p. 26.

1

The Birth and Preparation of Jesus
Matthew 1:1–4:16

Suppose we hear an unknown man spoken of by many men. Suppose we were puzzled to hear that some men said he was too tall and some too short; some objected to his fatness, some lamented his leanness; some thought him too dark, and some too fair. One explanation would be that he might be an odd shape. But there is another explanation. He might be the right shape. Perhaps (in short) this extraordinary thing is really the ordinary thing; at least the normal thing, the centre.

–G. K. Chesterton, British writer and critic

The Genealogy of Jesus the King (1:1–17)

1:1An account of ancestry of Jesus Christ/Messiah, the son of David, the son of Abraham.
2Abraham was the father of Isaac,
Isaac was the father of Jacob,
Jacob was the father of Judah and his brothers.
3Judah was the father of Perez and Zerah by Tamar.
Perez was the father of Hezron,
Hezron was the father of Aram.
4Aram was the father of Aminadab,
Aminadab was the father of Nahshon,
Nahshon was the father of Salmon.
5Salmon was the father of Boaz by Rahab.
Boaz was the father of Obed by Ruth.
Obed was the father of Jesse.
6Jesse was the father of David the King.
David was the father of Solomon by Uriah's wife.
7Solomon was the father of Rehoboam.
Rehoboam was the father of Abijah.
Abijah was the father of Asaph.
8Asaph was the father of Jehoshaphat.
Jehoshaphat was the father of Joram.

Joram was the father of Uzziah.
⁹Uzziah was the father of Jotham.
Jotham was the father of Ahaz.
Ahaz was the father of Hezekiah.
¹⁰Hezekiah was the father of Manasseh.
Manasseh was the father of Amos.
Amos was the father of Josiah.
¹¹Josiah was the father of Jechoniah and his brothers at the time of the exile to Babylon.
¹²After the exile to Babylon,
Jechoniah was the father of Salathiel.
Salathiel was the father of Zerubbabel.
¹³Zerubbabel was the father of Abiud.
Abiud was the father of Eliakim.
Eliakim was the father of Azor.
¹⁴Azor was the father of Zadok.
Zadok was the father of Achim.
Achim was the father of Eliud.
¹⁵Eliud was the father of Eleazar.
Eleazar was the father of Matthan.
Matthan was the father of Jacob.
¹⁶Jacob was the father of Joseph, the husband of Mary, who bore Jesus called the Christ/Messiah.
¹⁷So all the generations from Abraham to David are fourteen, from David to the deportation to Babylon are fourteen, and from the deportation to Babylon to the Christ/Messiah are fourteen.

The translation that appears at each section is by G. Steve Kinnard[1]

Genealogies were important to the first century Jews. A review of the use of genealogies in the Old Testament will show this. Being a priest required proof of one's lineage. Today it seems strange to begin a book with a genealogy, but in the first century this was common.

The opening and closing of the genealogy in Matthew's Gospel demonstrates what he wished to prove—that Jesus is the Messiah or Christ, and the King. He begins by saying that Jesus is the "son of David, the son of Abraham" (Matthew 1:1). Why mention David before Abraham? Because Matthew wants to emphasize that Jesus is of the lineage of David, a descendant of David and a king in the order of the great King David. Notice in the following verses how many ways in which Matthew makes his point that Jesus is the Christ, the son of David (emphasis mine):

- 1:1 – "A record of the genealogy of Jesus Christ"
- 1:1 – "The son of David"

- 1:6 — "Jesse the father of King David"
- 1:6 — "Father of King David. David was the father of Solomon." (David is mentioned twice. He concludes generations 1–14 and begins generations 15–28.)
- 1:6–16 — The lineage follows the royal line of King David.
- 1:16 — "Of whom was born Jesus, who is called Christ"
- 1:17 — "Fourteen generations in all from Abraham to David, fourteen from David to the exile."
- 1:17 — "And fourteen from the exile to the Christ"

He closes the genealogy by saying that Jesus is "called Christ." Matthew's message is clear — The Messiah has come, the King of Israel has ascended the throne of David, and that Messiah is Jesus of Nazareth. Matthew crowns Jesus as King.

Have you ever wondered why Matthew and Luke use two different genealogies to trace the lineage of Jesus? It is because they were emphasizing two different aspects of the nature of Jesus. Luke was writing to a predominately Gentile audience who did not really care that Jesus was the son of David. Therefore, Luke traces the line of Jesus through Joseph beginning with Jesus, "the son of Adam, the Son of God." The Gentile mind could appreciate Jesus being a descendant of our common ancestor Adam and "the Son of God."

Matthew traces his line through the kings of Israel, giving a royal or official genealogy of Jesus, which would satisfy the Jewish mind. This line would not necessarily pass from the father to the son, but would travel through the family line. Therefore, the names do not have to match precisely. Matthew uses a verb for "beget" (*gennao*) which does not necessarily denote a genetic connection (see 1 Corinthians 4:15 and Philemon 10). We must realize that the real purpose of the genealogies is to make a point, not to simply recount the family tree.

Matthew traces the lineage of Jesus through Mary's husband, Joseph. Even though Joseph was not the physical father of Jesus, legally, he was his father. Matthew 1:1–16 traces the genealogy through Joseph, who was a descendant of the great King David. Therefore Jesus was a legal descendant of King David. Matthew makes this point very clearly. When we compare the family lists in Matthew and Luke (Luke 3:23–38), we can see that the lists split after King David. Matthew lists Jesus as descending through Solomon while Luke lists him coming through Nathan (both were children of Bathsheba). Which list is right? Both are. Matthew traces the lineage through the official/legal lines tracing Jesus to King David, through the family line and through the Kings of Judah. Luke traces Jesus' lineage through the actual physical descendants. David Hill comments, "The considerable differences between the two genealogies may be accounted for by the view that Luke provides a pedigree of actual descent, while Matthew gives the throne succession."[2]

However, some scholars claim Luke's genealogy follows Mary's line, but this is unlikely for two reasons: First, Luke mentions it as being Joseph's line; and second in the Old Testament the lineage of a person was traced through the male descendants. Matthew gives us the official genealogy and Luke the literal genealogy.

1:1 Matthew's Gospel opens with the words, *biblos geneseos*, which means "a book of the generations," indicating the importance of genealogies in early Jewish thinking, as noted above. Before Matthew does anything else, he must establish the lineage of Jesus. He mentions "son of David" before "son of Abraham" to emphasize Jesus' Messianic nature. Yet mentioning both stresses that Jesus is a true king and a true Jew. "Jesus" is the Aramaic equivalent of the OT Hebrew name "Joshua" meaning "Savior." "Christ" is the Greek equivalent to "Messiah" or the "Anointed One." This first verse is loaded with theological meaning: Matthew is establishing at the beginning of his Gospel that he will demonstrate throughout that Jesus is the promised Messiah of the Jews.

2-6 Interestingly, four women, all of them mothers, are mentioned in Matthew's genealogy. Three of these were likely non-Jewish, and the fourth, Bathsheba, was married to a Gentile. Tamar was a Canaanite, Rahab was a Canaanite, Bathsheba was the wife of a Hittite, and Ruth was from Moab. This illustrates that even before Jesus was born, God was drawing to him people who were outside of Israel, a central theme of Matthew. These non-Jewish women played a key role in the salvation of Israel. It's encouraging to see that God chooses ordinary people to do extraordinary things.

The mention of these women also demonstrates the sovereignty of God—he worked in strange and unexpected ways to preserve the line of the Messiah.

7-12 Matthew follows the genealogy of 1 Chronicles 3:10-17 and Ezra 3:2. He omits three kings (Ahaziah, Joash and Amaziah), showing that Matthew is giving a selective genealogy, which emphasizes the royalty of Jesus. He is not interested in exact detail. He abbreviates and selects the names he feels are important to mention. In Hebrew the phrase "the father of" can also mean "the grandfather of" or even "the uncle of" or "a relative of."

Matthew lists the father of Jotham as Uzziah (1:9). Many believe that this is a mistake because in 2 Kings 15:1-7 and in 1

Chronicles 3:12, Azariah is mentioned as the father of Jotham. But in 2 Kings 15:32 and 34, Uzziah is called the father of Jotham. Both are right: Azariah and Uzziah are the same person. Just like in the New Testament, Peter and Simon are the same person and Paul and Saul are the same person. In fact, many OT characters were known by two names: Gideon/Jerubbaal, Abijam/Abijah, Eliakim/Jehoiakim. Matthew chooses to list the name of Uzziah in his genealogy. He could have just as easily selected Azariah.

16 In Luke 3:24 Heli is given as the father of Joseph. Was it Heli or Jacob? (1:16) Perhaps Heli died and Joseph became the adopted son of Jacob. Or perhaps Heli was the physical father of Joseph, and he was the brother of Jacob. In the Hebrew, Joseph would still be listed as the son of Jacob, though he was his uncle. If the second is true, then this demonstrates Matthew's desire to trace the royal lineage of Jesus instead of the literal genealogy.

17 Matthew's use of the number fourteen here (1:17) demonstrates his tendency to arrange items in lists. Perhaps he chose the number fourteen because the numerical value of David's name in Hebrew is fourteen. That he uses three lists of fourteen makes the genealogy easier to remember. We need to remember that his purpose is theological, not historical. He mentions David twice in his summary: "from Abraham to David" and "from David to the exile to Babylon." This again emphasizes the Messianic nature of Jesus.

Since there are actually only thirteen names in the list between the captivity and Christ, did Matthew make a mistake? No, for Jeconiah is counted in both lists because he lived both before and after the captivity.

The Birth Narrative — Immanuel (1:18–25)

¹⁸The birth of Jesus Christ took place like this. His mother Mary was engaged to Joseph. Before they came together as a married couple, she was found to be pregnant by the Holy Spirit. ¹⁹Joseph, her husband, was a man of character, and he did not want to expose her publicly, so he planned to divorce her secretly.

²⁰When he decided to do this, an angel of the Lord appeared to him saying, "Joseph, son of David, do not be afraid to take Mary as your wife, for she is pregnant by means of the Holy Spirit. ²¹She will bear a son, and you will name him Jesus; for he will save his people from their sins." ²²All this happened to fulfill the word of the Lord through the prophets, saying:
²³Behold, the virgin will be with child and

> *Will give birth to a son,*
> *And they will name him Immanuel*
> *Which means, 'God with us.'*
> 24*When Joseph woke from his sleep, he did as the angel of the Lord commanded him and he took her as his wife. They had no marital relations until she bore a son, and they named him Jesus.*

Matthew's story of Jesus opens and ends with the same thought. It opens here with the pronouncement that the child born to Mary should be named Immanuel—which means "God with us." It closes in Matthew 28 with this child, having now finished his mission on earth, saying to his disciples, "I will be with you to the end of the age" (28:20). The story of Jesus is the story of God's desire to be with us. God sent Jesus into the world to let us know that he wants to be with us. If we feel distant from God, it is not God's fault—he has gone to great lengths to let us know that he wants to be with us.

The fact that Jesus was never called "Immanuel" in the Gospels demonstrates that this name was more of a title or role that he was given than an actual name. He literally was "Immanuel"—"God with us." As John 1:14 says, "The Word became flesh and made his dwelling among us." Jesus was God living among humanity.

18-19 If Joseph and Mary were only engaged to be married, then why did he have in mind to "divorce her" privately? Because in the first century engagements were taken more seriously than today, Joseph needed a certificate of divorce to separate from Mary. An engagement was a binding contract between families. It usually lasted one year. To sever the engagement took a certificate of divorce. Therefore, when Mary was discovered to be with child, Joseph decided to divorce her. Not wishing to publicly shame her, he opted for a private divorce in the company of two witnesses at which time Mary would be given a certificate of divorce.

20 An angel of the Lord appears to Joseph in a dream and tells him to take Mary as his wife. Angels are the messengers of God. In the Old Testament God often spoke to men through angels and through dreams. At the direction of God's spirit, Joseph took Mary as his wife. This must have taken great faith on his part. Joseph and Mary are both great examples of people who listened to the voice of God and obeyed his will.

21 The child is to be called "Jesus," which is the Greek form of the Hebrew word "Yoshua" or "Joshua," meaning "God saves." Matthew explains this with the phrase—"he will save his people from their sins."

22-23 The nature of the virgin birth of Jesus underscores the fact that his birth was not ordinary. Scholars have tried to get around the fact that Matthew used the word "virgin" to describe Mary here. They have tried to go back to Isaiah 7:14 and show that the word in Hebrew can mean "young woman" as well as "virgin." But Matthew quotes from the Septuagint, the Greek Old Testament, where the word *parthenos* can only mean "virgin." This was no ordinary birth. In fact, nothing would be ordinary about this child. This would be the most extraordinary person to ever walk the earth. Could you expect anything less of the King of Kings?

Most scholars believe that Isaiah 7:13–14 is a dual fulfillment prophecy. It was talking about the future restoration of the physical kingdom of Israel to greatness, and it was talking about a future spiritual kingdom of Israel.

> *Then Isaiah said, "Hear now, you house of David! Is it not enough to try the patience of men? Will you try the patience of my God also? Therefore the Lord himself will give you a sign: The virgin will be with child and will give birth to a son, and will call him Immanuel." (Isaiah 7:13–14, NIV)*

The Hebrew word, *almah*, can mean "a young maiden or a virgin." Isaiah applied the prophecy to an immediate historical time under King Ahaz. In the time that it took for a "young maiden" or "virgin" to conceive a child and raise him to the age of knowing right from wrong, God would deliver his people from two powerful kings that they feared. He also had in mind a Messianic prediction: a virgin would be with child who would deliver the world.

Matthew uses a fulfillment prophecy here. This is also called a "reflective quotation" because there is a New Testament, mirror-like reflection of the fulfillment of an OT prophecy. These will be used often in Matthew nine times in all (2:15, 17, 23; 4:14; 8:17; 12:17; 13: 35; 21:4; 27:9; compare 26:56). Each quotation follows a narrative— the quotation is used to highlight the event as a fulfillment of OT prophecy. This is one of several ways in which Matthew emphasizes the Messianic nature of Jesus.

24-25 The text mentions that Joseph did not have union with Mary until after the birth of Jesus. This underscores her virginity when Jesus was born. It also implies that after the birth of Jesus, Joseph and Mary had a normal, healthy marital relationship. The brothers and sisters of Jesus (Matthew 12:46) were the product of this relationship. The Bible does not teach a doctrine of the "perpetual virginity" of Mary, a tradition that is not to be found in the scriptures.

The Titles and Names of Jesus Used in Matthew

Son of David—emphasizes the kingship of Jesus
Son of Abraham—connects Jesus to the long line of Jewish faithful
Immanuel—means "God with us" in Hebrew and supports the idea of the incarnation
Jesus—"Joshua" in Hebrew, which means "Savior"
Christ—the Messiah or the Anointed One
Lord—in Greek, *kurios*, which means "ruler" or "master"
King of the Jews—emphasizes the kingship of Jesus

The Visit of the Magi (2:1–12)

²:¹*After Jesus was born in Bethlehem of Judea, in the days of King Herod the Great, Magi from the East arrived in Jerusalem. ²They asked, "Where is the child who has been born King of the Jews? We saw his star at its rising and we have come to worship him."*

³*When King Herod heard this, he was disturbed and all Jerusalem with him. ⁴He assembled all the chief priests and scribes of the people and inquired of them where this Messiah was to be born.*

⁵*They answered him, "In Bethlehem of Judea, for it is written in the prophets:*

⁶*And you Bethlehem, in the Land of Judah,*
Are by no means least among the rulers of Judah.
From you will come a ruler
Who will shepherd my people, Israel."

⁷*Then Herod secretly called for the Magi and learned from them the time when the star appeared. ⁸He sent them to Bethlehem saying, "Go and search for the child, and when you discover him, report this to me so I may come and worship him."*

⁹*After hearing the King, they set out following the star which they had seen at its rising until it stopped over the place where the child was. ¹⁰Seeing the star had stopped, they had great joy. ¹¹When they entered the house, they saw the child with his mother, Mary, and they bowed down and worshiped him. They opened their treasures and offered him gifts of gold, frankincense and myrrh. ¹²Having been warned in a dream not to return to Herod, they returned to their country by another road.*

This passage gives us many interesting facts about the birth of Jesus. Some of them demonstrate how we need to pay close attention to the details of the Bible, making sure we are not placing tradition over the Bible. For example, when was Jesus born? The Bible mentions that Jesus was born during the reign of Herod the Great. Since Herod died in 4 BC, Jesus must have been born sometime before 4 BC. How could Jesus have been born "BC," before Christ? Good question. As it turns out, the early historians made a mistake! They started the modern calendar at least four years too late.[3]

Notice that the Magi came upon Jesus and Mary in a house, not a stable (1:11). The Nativity scene with the shepherds and the Magi all bowing before Jesus might be beautiful on our Christmas cards, but it is not Biblically accurate. Jesus was a small child (Herod singled out children two and under to be killed in Bethlehem — he was probably around two), not a baby when the Magi offered their gifts to him. This places the birth of Jesus around 6 BC.

Who were these Magi? Were they part of a secret order like the Masons? Did they worship the stars and practice magic arts? Were they the original "Men in Black" who traced extra-terrestrial events? It seems that they were part of a Persian priestly caste that studied astrology as a sophisticated science. We do know that although astrology is prohibited in the Old Testament, first century Judaism was influenced by it. I have visited ruins of synagogues in Palestine that were decorated with the signs of the zodiac.

The Magi could have traveled from Arabia or Babylon to search out Jesus. Although the Bible does not mention the significance of each gift, gold may have been given to honor Jesus as a king, incense to honor him as a priest, and myrrh to honor the death that he would die for humanity. We know that there were three gifts, but we do not know how many Magi were present — the Bible does not say. A late sixth century AD Armenian Infancy Gospel names them as Melkon (Melchior), Belthasar and Caspar. Once again, we must be careful to not let tradition cloud our view of the Bible.

Although some scholars have attacked the historical probability that the Magi would have made this journey to Jerusalem, there is no reason to doubt that the event is historical. In 66 AD, Parthian Magi traveled all the way to Rome to visit the Emperor Nero. Also it is unlikely that the early church would have circulated this story if it were not true because the early church opposed astrology.

In this passage describing the visit of the Magi, R. T. France notes several themes given here that Matthew will develop later in this chapter and later in his Gospel:

1. The fulfillment of scripture
2. Jesus as the "true" king in contrast to King Herod
3. The parallelism between Jesus and Moses
4. Jesus as the Messiah of all the nations[4]

2:2 Many attempts have been made to locate a natural phenomena that would explain the occurrence of the star that led the Magi to Jesus. The phrase "in the east" could be better rendered "at its rising." Some have suggested that it was the alignment of Saturn and Jupiter (Kepler fixed the date as 7 BC in the sign of Pisces). Others suggest that it was a comet (Halley's comet traveled through the area in 12 or 11 BC). Still others connect it to a nova (a star which has exploded, giving off great brightness). This would help scholars lock in on an exact date of the birth of Jesus. Yet, such attempts have proven fruitless. The appearance of the star was a supernatural phenomenon produced by God. It was probably not the alignment of the planets over Bethlehem or a passing comet that moved over the city. Instead, God sent the star in the same way that he sent a fish to swallow Jonah. The Magi noted the special nature of the star and followed it to Bethlehem. That they came to worship (*proskuneo*) the child could mean they came to pay him homage.

2-3 King Herod was born in 73 BC. He became governor of Galilee in 47 BC., and through crafty political alignment with Caesar Augustus, he was appointed King of Judea in 40 BC. That King Herod was disturbed at the news of a child-king fits well with what we know about him historically.

5-6 Matthew gives his second fulfillment formula here. He quotes from Micah 5:2, although the text differs from the Hebrew. Matthew could either be using another source or just paraphrasing the scripture. He uses the phrase "land of Judah" instead of "Ephrathah." Since both refer to the same place, he is not changing the meaning of the verse. Perhaps this was a common paraphrase in his time.

Also, Matthew says that Bethlehem is "not the least," while Micah said it is "little." It is little, but it is also not the least. Matthew is saying the same thing as Micah, but he places the emphasis in a different spot. Bethlehem was an insignificant little village located a few miles south of Jerusalem. Its population in the first century is estimated to have been approximately three hundred people. In the Bible it is mentioned as the place (1) near which Jacob buried Rachel; (2) where Ruth met Boaz; and (3) where David was born. Bethlehem also connects Jesus to King David since both of them were born there.

The insignificance of Bethlehem's size is contrasted with the fact that the most significant event in the history of humanity up to that point occurred there.

Finally, in 2:6 Matthew adds a phrase to the end of the quote from Micah ("who will be the shepherd of my people Israel") which is a paraphrase of 2 Samuel 5:2. To combine one scripture with another was a common rabbinic tool that other NT writers used. For example, Mark combined Isaiah 40:3 with Malachi 3:1 in Mark 1:2-3.

In the Hebrew, *Bet Lechem*, means a "house of bread." Shepherd fields surround Bethlehem. This rocky, hilly terrain is best suited for raising livestock. This was true in David's day and is still true today.

7 "Then" (*tote* in Greek) is Matthew's favorite word. He uses it ninety times in his Gospel!

11 To place gifts at the feet of the child represents submission. Travelers in the East were known for bringing gifts when approaching a superior.

Jesus' Early Years (2:13-23)

13When they left, an angel of the Lord appeared to Joseph in a dream saying, "Get up, take the child and his mother and flee to Egypt. Remain there until I tell you, for Herod desires to kill the child."

14So he got up and took the child and his mother by night and left for Egypt. 15They stayed there until Herod died that the word of the Lord might be fulfilled through the prophet, which says, "Out of Egypt I called my son."

16When Herod realized that the Magi had tricked him, he was enraged. He sent orders to kill all the children in Bethlehem and her region who were two years old and under, according to the time he had learned from the Magi. 17Then the word of the prophet Jeremiah was fulfilled, saying:

18A voice was heard in Ramah,
Wailing and much morning,
Rachel weeping for her children.
She refused to be comforted
Because they are no more.

19After Herod died, an angel of the Lord appeared in a dream to Joseph in Egypt 20saying, "Get up and take the child and his mother and return to the land of Israel. For the ones who desired his life are dead." 21He got up and took the child and his mother and returned to Israel. 22But when he heard that Archuleus was ruling over Judea instead of his father Herod, he was afraid to go there. After being warned in a dream, he went to the district of Galilee. [23]*He went and lived in a town called "Nazareth." Thus the word of the prophets was fulfilled, "He will be called a 'Natzorean.'"*

The search by the Magi for Jesus prompted another search led by Herod the Great. Herod was an Idumean that had been appointed as king by the Romans. He feared that a legitimate Davidic heir could usurp his throne. Would Herod have ordered the deaths of the children in Bethlehem? Although there is no evidence outside the Bible that records this order, it does fit in with the Herod's character. He was a suspicious egomaniac who constantly fretted over his throne. He rebuilt the temple of Jerusalem in an attempt to make the Jews feel as if he was a good Jew and a good ruler. He had six different palaces that also served as forts in case he needed a quick escape from Jerusalem. One of these palace/forts was the Herodion, located just outside the town of Bethlehem. It is believed to be his burial place. Perhaps Herod retreated to this fort to oversee the slaughter of the children in Bethlehem. If so, he could have personally heard the laments of the mothers over their babies coming from the valley below.

13-14 After the Magi left, the Lord appeared to Joseph in a dream telling him to escape from Bethlehem to Egypt. Egypt would have been a natural place to flee because it was a Roman province outside the jurisdiction of Herod. In 40 AD, Philo of Alexandria mentioned that Egypt had a million Jews living there. The sovereignty of God is implicit in this story: he is taking care of the child who would later take care of the sins of the world.

15 After the death of Herod the Great, Joseph returned to Judea. Matthew saw this as a fulfillment of Hosea 11:1: "When Israel was a child, I loved him, and out of Egypt I called my son." This is a reference to the Exodus from Egypt. How can Jesus' return from Egypt be a fulfillment of Hosea 11:1? As God delivered the children of Israel out of bondage, he will deliver all humanity out of their bondage to sin through Jesus.

16 Herod decided to kill the boys that were two years old and under. It is most likely that Jesus was at least two years old by this time.

17-18 Matthew connects the mourning in Bethlehem with mourning in Jeremiah's time over the deportation of God's people, either by the Assyrians in 722 BC or the Babylonians in 586 BC (Jeremiah 31:15). God's people had suffered greatly in history, but their suffering was not over. However, one has come who will ease the pain of God's people — Jesus will ultimately wipe away every tear.

First Century Insights ℭ℞

Palestine Under Herod the Great

After Octavian defeated Pompey for control of the Roman Empire, he gave himself a new name: Caesar Augustus (27 BC). At about the same time in Palestine, Herod was purging the land of all his opponents. He married Marianne who was of the lineage of the Hasmoneans which gave him the appearance of continuing the Hasmonean dynasty. Later he killed his wife Marianne and their two sons, Alexander and Aristobulus, for fear of their Hasmonean blood. The NT account, which describes the murder of infant boys two years and younger for fear that one was a future king, fits the historical depiction of Herod the Great (Matthew 2:16).

Herod ruled both Judea and Galilee. He was over both Jews and Gentiles. He wanted to be accepted as a Jew by the Jews and as a Gentile by the Gentiles. For the Gentiles he rebuilt their cities, adding gymnasiums, theaters and pagan temples. For the Jews he rebuilt their temple and enlarged it, giving it the form it had in Solomon's day. It became known as Herod's temple. In spite of rebuilding the temple, many Jews hated Herod because he was a ruthless tyrant and a friend of Romans and pagans.

Herod accomplished much during his reign. He built Sebaste on the site of the destroyed city of Samaria. He built Caesarea on the coast. He constructed Antonia, a strong citadel in Jerusalem, which looked down upon the temple courts. He built Masada on the top of a mountain in the Dead Sea. Masada was a great fortress, which later became the spot of a tremendous battle between the Romans and the Jews. It became a symbol of Jewish perseverance and determination.

During his reign, both Jesus and John the Baptist were born. When Herod died, he passed his kingdom on to three sons, whom he had not killed:
- Archelaus who ruled over Judea, Samaria, and Idumea
- Herod Antipas who ruled over Galilee and Perea
- Philip who ruled over the territory northeast of the Jordan

19-23 After the death of Herod, many of the Jews who had fled Judea now felt as if it was safe to return. The Qumran sect, whose center was destroyed in 31 BC, also returned after Herod's death. In a dream Joseph was informed that it was safe for him to return to his homeland.

After the death of Herod, his territory was divided into three parts and given to his three sons: Archelaus, Antipas and Philip. Of the three, Archelaus was the most inept ruler. He was the most hated and his reign was the briefest. In 6 AD a petition was sent to Augustus in Rome asking for the removal of Archelaus. The Romans agreed with the populace and exiled him to Gaul, replacing him with a Roman governor. Thus, in the time of Jesus, Roman procurators (governors) ruled over Judea, Samaria and Idumea (Luke 3:1). History tells us that Joseph had good reason to fear when he heard that Archelaus was reigning over Judea.

Matthew mentions that Jesus' return to Nazareth was a fulfillment of prophecy. The only problem is this prophecy cannot be found in the Old Testament! Perhaps this is why Matthew uses the vague wording "said through the prophets." It is possible that he is not quoting a direct prophecy, but a tradition that was carried through the prophets that the Messiah would be called a Nazarene. It is also possible that the designation was a play on the Hebrew word for "branch" (*netser*) that was another way of referring to the Messiah (Isaiah 11:1).

John the Baptist (3:1-12)

3:1In those days John the Baptist appeared, preaching in the wilderness of Judea, 2saying, "Repent, for the kingdom of heaven is fast approaching." 3This is the word spoken through Isaiah the prophet:

The voice of one crying in the desert
'Prepare the way of the Lord
Make his paths straight.'

4John clothed himself in garments of camel's hair with a leather belt around his waist. His diet was locusts and wild honey. 5The people of Jerusalem and all Judea and all the region of the Jordon were going to him, 6and he baptized them in the Jordon River as they confessed their sins.

7When he saw many of the Pharisees and Sadducees coming for baptism, he said to them, "You nest of vipers, who warned you to flee from the coming wrath? 8Produce fruit worthy of repentance. 8Don't think you can say to yourselves – Abraham is our Father. 9For I tell you, God is able to make children of Abraham from these stones. 10Already the ax is at the root of the tree. Every tree that does not produce good fruit is cut down and cast in the fire.

11"I baptize you in water for repentance, but the one coming after me is mightier than I. I am not worthy to carry his sandals. He will baptize you in the Holy Spirit and fire. 12His winnowing fork is in his hand and he will clear his threshing floor. He will gather his wheat in the granary, and the chaff he will burn with unquenchable fire."

Although he does not appear in many chapters in the story of Jesus, John the Baptist is one of the major figures. He comes on the scene like the prophets of old to prepare the way of the Lord. Along the way, he preaches repentance, baptizes the multitudes, rebukes the Pharisees and Sadducees, and points people to Jesus — only to become skeptical of Jesus in his last days. John's life deserves our attention because we can learn many spiritual lessons from this great prophet.

3:1 "In those days" is a way to say the days in which Jesus was living in Nazareth. In fact, almost thirty years pass between chapters 2 and 3.

"The Baptist" was the title given to John because baptism was the distinguishing mark of his ministry. He could also have been called "John the Preparer" because he prepared the way for Jesus. Or "John the Bringer of Judgment" because he was getting the people ready for judgment. Or "John the Preacher" because he was preaching in the wilderness.

The Greek word for "preach" is *kerusso*. It means, "to proclaim the proclamation of the king." It emphasizes the legal and official nature of the proclamation. The message itself is what gives the herald confidence. He comes as a representative of the king.

Tradition says that John was born at Ein Kerem, a small village southwest of Jerusalem. He preached in the Desert of Judea. The Desert of Judea is a large expanse of barren land that is located just east of Jerusalem and continues to the Jordan River. John was located close to the Jordan because it was the primary source of water in the Judean wilderness. When I lived with my family for a year in Jerusalem, our back window looked out upon the Judean wilderness. I often sat at my window imagining the "voice in the wilderness" that prepared the way of the Lord.

2 The message of John was clear and concise: "Repent, for the kingdom of heaven is near." This message has three components:

(1) "*Repent.*" Repentance is from the Greek word *metanoeo* which means "to change" — a change in thinking, attitude, mind and way of living. It means "to turn about, to turn around." In military terms it is the order "about face." For example, if you were walking one direction and you "repented," you would turn around one hundred and eighty degrees and begin walking back the way you came. Fritz Rienecker notes, "The primary sense [of repentance] in Judaism is always a change in a man's attitude toward God and in the conduct of life."[5] Therefore, a change of attitude without a change in conduct is not repentance. Additionally, R. T. France writes

Repent means more than "be sorry" or even "change your mind";
it echoes the Old Testament prophets' frequent summons to Israel
to return to God, to abandon their rebellion and come back into
covenant-obedience.[6]

(2) *"The kingdom of heaven."* Matthew prefers this designation
to "kingdom of God" because it avoids the name of God, which better
suits a Jewish audience. "The kingdom" encompasses the rule of God
in heaven and on earth. In the Old Testament the kingdom or rule of
God is almost synonymous with the Gospel writers' expression "the
age to come," a time of perfect righteousness.

(3) *"At hand."* Personally, I follow Albright and Mann and
translate this phrase as "fast approaching."[7] John the Baptist preaches
the imminence of the kingdom: it is so close that you must now repent
and get ready for it.

3 Matthew uses his fulfillment formula to say that John is the
fulfillment of Isaiah 40:3, "a voice of one calling in the desert."

4-6 John's clothing and diet are as unique to our Western ears
as his message was to the people of his day. He wore clothes
made from camel's hair and his diet consisted of locusts and wild
honey. Locusts were an ordinary part of the diet of desert people
in ancient times and today because they are a good source of many
vitamins. Non-domesticated bees in the desert produced wild honey.
John's diet and clothing reveal that he was an ascetic. They also
connect him with the prophets of Israel, specifically Elijah, who also
wore camel's hair and preached in the wilderness (2 Kings 1:8).

All the residents of the countryside came to hear John's
preaching. He then baptized them as they confessed their sins.
Albright and Mann write concerning John's baptism,

> It (John's baptism) incorporated a man or woman into the covenant
> people of the Messiah, conceived as one with the Israel of the Old
> Covenant, and at the same time it was a token of repentance and
> instrument of pardon.[8] (Words in the parenthesis are mine).

If their definition is correct, then there was not much difference
between the baptism of John and the baptism of Jesus as practiced in
Acts. The former looked ahead to the death, burial and resurrection of
Jesus, and the latter looked backed at it.

7 The Pharisees and Sadducees were two sects of the Jews that
controlled much of the religious environment in and around Je-

First Century Insights ೞ

Essenes

The Essenes (100 BC–100 AD) are not mentioned in the New Testament. They were an extreme group of Pharisees who gave up on changing the rabbinic Judaism of Jerusalem and opted to move near the northwestern corner of the Dead Sea to form a community. This sect became known as Qumran.

The Essenes separated themselves from society, living a simple, ascetic life of hard work. They practiced celibacy, communistic communalism, baptism for ritual cleansing and vows of secrecy. Sources reveal that approximately four thousand people joined this movement. Scholars often associate John the Baptist with the Essenes. For example, Albright and Mann write, "There seems no question that John took over the practice of baptism, including the emphasis on repentance, from the Essences, but gave it a far more profound meaning."[9]

But we need not insist that John adopted the practice of baptism from the Essenes. All the Jewish sects of that day practiced cleansing by ritual immersion in water. Hundreds of *mikvaot* (pools for ritual cleansing, singular *mikveh*) have been discovered in the Holy Land by archaeologists. Also, the Essenes were baptized over and over again as a purity rite. John's baptism was a one-time immersion.

rusalem. It would be natural for them to show up at John's baptism to see what John was preaching. John welcomes them with harsh words: "you brood of vipers." These sects would be the opponents of the kingdom throughout Matthew's Gospel. John asks them, "Who warned you to flee from the coming wrath?" indicating the judgment that was to come.

8 To prepare for the coming judgment, they—and—we—must produce fruits of repentance. In other words God wants to see changes in our character and our action.

9-10 The Jews claimed their rights to the kingdom as a result of their descent through Abraham. One rabbinic story has Abraham waiting at the gates of *Gehenna* to rescue any Jew that might be consigned to its punishment. However John the Baptist lets the Jewish elite know that this claim will not avail them of entrance into the kingdom. God will not look at a person's bloodline, but at the heart. God could raise up children of Abraham from stones. John is saying there is no privilege to be gained from being Abraham's children. God will judge the heart of every person. This must have seemed a radical new teaching to the Jewish leaders.

First Century Insights ❧

Life in Nazareth

So, Joseph goes to Nazareth, a small backwater town in the northern province of Galilee. It is estimated that in Jesus' day, Nazareth was populated by not more than one hundred twenty to one hundred fifty people (some say as few as six to twelve families lived there). Certainly everyone in the village knew each other; many of them were related. The town is not mentioned in any source outside the Bible until the fourth century AD. Nazareth was an out of the way place—not the kind of place that jumps to mind for raising a king. Ironically, as we shall see, people in Nazareth believed they were raising kings—Messianic kings.

What was it like for a boy to grow up in a carpenter's home in Nazareth in the first century? The carpenter's trade was a respected one. The word for carpenter could have referred to a woodworker or stonemason. Jesus, as the eldest son, would have been expected to follow in his father's footsteps and learn the trade. Great expectations would be placed upon him to be a reliable businessman and provide for the family if something should happen to their father. Greater pressure would have been placed on Jesus than on the other children, as the oldest male child.

Between the ages of seven and thirteen, Jesus would have been given the opportunity to study the Torah. At synagogue he would learn how to read and write, and he would learn about the law of God, an opportunity not afforded to girls.

Living in a poor village in rural Galilee would not allow for many niceties in life. The day would begin before sunrise and would end shortly after sunset. The summer would be warm with long working hours. The winters would be cold and rainy with short days and long nights. The Gospel writers say that it was during this time that Jesus learned responsibility—he "grew in wisdom and statue, and in favor with God and men" (Luke 2:52).

Some scholars believe that Nazareth was a village established by a sect of Jews called the "Natzoreans" from the Hebrew word *netzer* meaning "branch." This was a Messianic community that gathered together to await the coming of the Messiah. Isaiah 11:1 reads, "A shoot will come up from the stump of Jesse; from his roots a Branch *(netzer)* will bear fruit." Thus a tribal clan who believed themselves to be "Davidids," descendants of David, gathered in this small village, expecting the Messiah to come from their midst. They did not realize that a king was being raised there, a king who learned the carpenter's trade from his father, a king whom they would reject, and a king who would be derided by those outside of Nazareth: "Can anything good come from there?" (John 1:46).

John preached that the ax was already at the foot of the tree, meaning that the time for the coming of the kingdom was imminent. People must change now and be ready for it. This also meant that the Jewish dispensation was coming to an end.

11 John announces that one mightier or stronger than he is coming, which refers to force. Jesus will initiate greater changes than John whose baptism is for repentance; the baptism of Jesus gives the Holy Spirit.

John considers himself unworthy to even *carry* the sandals of Jesus. Mark and Luke mention "untie" the sandals. This was the task of a slave in the Greco-Roman world. A rabbi could ask his disciple to do anything for him except one thing—he could not ask him to untie his sandals. He could ask him to cook him an egg if he was hungry or get him a drink if he was thirsty. But untying his sandals was considered too demeaning. John would have gladly untied and carried Jesus' sandals, but he did not feel worthy to do it—this is how much greater Jesus is than John.

Jesus' baptism would be with the Spirit and fire. The Spirit was the gift of Jesus' baptism (Acts 2:38), and fire means that it would purify our lives or take our sins away. Spirit and fire are also used as symbols of judgment throughout the New Testament.

12 Jesus would also come with judgment. He would separate the wheat from the chaff, the unrighteous from the righteous.

The Baptism of Jesus (3:13–17)

¹³Then Jesus went from Galilee, to be baptized by John in the Jordan. ¹⁴But John tried to prevent him saying, "I have need to be baptized by you, and you come to me?"

¹⁵But Jesus answered, "Permit it now. For it is proper for us to fulfill all righteousness." So he consented.

¹⁶Jesus was baptized, and just as he came up out of the water, behold, the heavens were opened, and he saw the Spirit of God descend as a dove and alight upon him. ¹⁷And a voice from the heavens said, "This is my Son whom I love; in him I am well pleased."

Jesus journeys from Galilee to be baptized by John in the Jordan River. This begins Jesus' public ministry. His baptism is "to fulfill all righteousness." After his baptism God puts his seal of approval on Jesus declaring, "This is my Son, whom I love; with him I am well pleased."

50 — The Gospel According to Matthew

**Practically Speaking** ᖀ

Searching for Jesus

The God of power, as he did ride
In his majestick robes of glorie
Resolv'd to light; and so one day
He did descend, undressing all the way.
—George Herbert, British poet

The shepherds searched for Jesus to honor him (Luke 2:8–20). The Magi searched for Jesus to worship him. Herod the Great searched for Jesus to kill him. Today people are still searching for Jesus. Where will they find him? Will they find him in the divided, fragmented denominational religious world? Not likely. Will they find him in the tattered, demythologized teachings of modern theological scholarship? Not hardly. Will they find him in the pseudo-religious pandering of new-age religion? Not at all. Will they find him by looking at your life as a disciple who follows the teachings of the Bible? Let's hope so.

People searched for Jesus two thousand years ago, and they are still searching today. They can find him by reading the Bible, but most people don't read the Bible. I believe it was the theologian Augustine who hundreds of years ago said, "The only Bible that most people will ever read is the Bible lived out in your life." The most likely place today

13-14 When Jesus comes to be baptized by John, John recognizes that he is the Messiah. He protests baptizing Jesus and instead asks to be baptized by Jesus. John is probably requesting the Holy Spirit baptism mentioned above.

15 Jesus instructs John that he must baptize him because they must "fulfill all righteousness." This has been a troubling phrase. We know that Jesus was sinless and did not need baptism for repentance—he had nothing to repent of. So what does he mean here? The key phrase is "to fulfill all righteousness." In the context, Jesus is submitting to John's baptism because it is the right thing to do. Righteousness (*diakaiosune*) is described by Rienecker as:

> The righteousness of life through obedience in accordance with the divine will. Jesus acknowledges the standard of righteousness as valid and affirms the fact he must establish it as the will of God in the kingdom.[10]

Since others need the baptism of John, Jesus, as an example, identifies with the people and submits to this baptism. He lives in solidarity with his community. He will follow God's standard of righteousness throughout his life and also expects his followers to hold to it. He will not call others to do what he will not do. Therefore, Jesus is baptized to fulfill all righteousness.

16 The heavens are opened and God's Spirit descends as a dove. The words "he saw" seem to imply that Jesus was the only one to see this. But later, God pronounces, "This is my Son," implying that others could also hear the proclamation.

17 God's voice will ring out twice in the Gospel of Matthew–once here and once at the transfiguration. Both times he testifies that Jesus is his Son, underscoring the importance of these events. It establishes that Jesus is the true Messiah who was sent from God.

The Testing of Jesus (4:1–11)

^{4:1}*Then Jesus was led by the Spirit into the wilderness to be tested by the devil. ²After fasting forty days and forty nights, he was hungry. ³The Tempter came and said to him, "If you are the Son of God, speak and these stones will become bread."*

⁴Jesus answered, "It is written,

> *Man does not live by bread alone,*
> *but by every word that proceeds*
> *from the mouth of God."*

⁵Then the Slanderer took him into the holy city and he stood on the pinnacle of the temple. He said to him, "If you are God's Son, cast yourself down, for it is written,

> *He will command his angels concerning you,*
> *and on their hands they will lift you up,*
> *so that you will not dash your foot on a stone."*

⁷Jesus answered him, "Again, it is written,

> *Do not test the Lord your God."*

⁸Again the Devil took him to a very high mountain and showed him all the kingdoms of the world and their glory and he said to him, ⁹"I will give you all this if you bow down and worship me."

¹⁰Then Jesus said to him, "Go away, Satan, for it is written,

> *Worship the Lord your God,*
> *and serve only him."*

¹¹Then the Devil left him, and suddenly angels came and met his needs.

First Century Insights ∞

Pharisees

The largest and most influential group among the sects of first century Judaism was the Pharisees (around six thousand members in Judea). Their origin dates back to the time of Hyrcanaus I. The word "Pharisee" means "separate or separated one"—they felt they were to be separate from the common people.

Pharisees placed great emphasis on oral traditions, which were laws that had been established outside the written code of the Old Testament. The goal of their sect was to build a hedge around the law so that the law would never be broken. They believed that on Sinai God gave Moses a body of rules orally, and Moses passed them on to Joshua and then to the elders, prophets, and the men of the Great Synagogue. In their minds, they were the "Keepers of the Traditions."

The Pharisees believed in a bodily resurrection after death. They also believed in angels and spirits and a punishment after death for the unrighteous. They relied upon the Divine providence of God, but they put an undue importance in the oral law.

In summary, the Pharisees believed in:

1. God's control of the lives of men
2. The resurrection of the body and a reward for piety
3. A world of angels and demons (a real spirit world)
4. A two-part scripture system: (1) the written Scripture and
   (2) the oral traditions of the rabbis

The Pharisees also had their own traditions on how to live a life faithful to the Judaism to which they were devoted. Their internal rules were sectarian with an emphasis on ritual purity, food tithes and Sabbath observances. They were admired by the people and functioned at least some of the time as a social and political force against foreign and Hellenized Jewish leaders (those Jewish leaders who were sympathetic to Greek language and culture). Many were very educated in the law and some were politically powerful.

During Jesus' day, two leading schools among the Pharisees existed. Hillel led the moderate school, and Shammai, the conservatives. These groups basically agreed with each other in many areas, but small disagreements regularly occurred. One area of disagreement centered on divorce. Hillel approved of divorce, saying a man could divorce his wife for any reason, great or small, including if he met someone he liked better or if his wife had burned breakfast. Shammai said that the only reason for divorce was adultery.

In this life, we often go from times of spiritual ecstasy to times of trial and despair. Jesus goes from his baptism, when the heavens open with the voice of God, to the desert area to be tempted by Satan. Life is full of mountaintop experiences and seasons in the desert valley. Part of discipleship is learning how to weather both.

How did Jesus handle facing Satan in the desert? Each time Satan tempted him, Jesus answered him with a scripture. To handle temptation, we must know God's word. The Psalmist said, "I have hidden your word in my heart that I might not sin against you" (Psalm 119:11). By storing the word in our hearts, we are guarding against Satan entering there. This is one reason it is important not only to study the Bible, but also to memorize Scripture. When was the last time you set out to memorize a portion of the Bible? Set a goal right now to memorize a certain amount of Scripture this month. For example, you could make a list of your greatest temptations and find and memorize one scripture that will strengthen you for each. By doing this, you will be guarding your heart against Satan's attacks.

4:1 Since God does not tempt us, how is it that his Spirit leads Jesus into temptation? The word translated "tempted" in the NIV can also be translated "tested," and it is the preferred rendering here. God doesn't tempt us with evil (see James 1:13–15); however, God does test us. For instance, he tested Abraham by asking him to sacrifice his son Isaac. The simple fact is, without testing, we will not grow. Testing is good. The Spirit prepares Jesus for his ministry by leading him into the wilderness to be tested by Satan.

2 Jesus fasts for forty days and forty nights. This parallels the other great lawgiver, Moses, who fasted for forty days. Fasting often precedes great spiritual decisions. Jesus prepares himself to begin his ministry by fasting.

3 The Greek word *diabolos* can be translated as "deceiver, slanderer, devil or the diabolical one." The Septuagint usually translates this word as "Satan." He has been known by many names throughout history: Lucifer, Beelzebub, Satan and the Devil. He is described in the Bible in real terms—not as fiction or fantasy. He is the father of lies and can twist Scripture to his own advantage. He is the chief opponent of God. The Hebrew writer informs us that Jesus was "tempted in every way, just as we are," and for this reason he understands our weaknesses (Hebrews 4:15). But none of us has been tested or tempted to the degree that Jesus was—we have not had to battle Satan face to face. Oh, yes, we must remember that Jesus was tempted, but he did not sin. Every time Jesus was tempted, he passed the test.

"If you are the Son of God" (4:4,6): the "if" does not express doubt, because Satan knows that Jesus is God's Son. It could also be translated, "since you are the Son of God."

He tests Jesus by asking him to use his power for self-gratification, to satisfy his physical hunger.

4 Jesus answers Satan by quoting scripture, demonstrating the best way to fend off temptation and sin. Jesus quotes Deuteronomy 8:3 from the Septuagint. This passage teaches that every trial of Israel, even her hunger in the Sinai wilderness, was a lesson that God used to teach her dependence on him. Jesus is affirming this in his use of this passage. He is saying that he is not sustained by bread but by being obedient to the Father.

Jesus is asked to use his power in a way that is not consistent with his mission. While he is on the cross, he faces the same words, "If you are the Son of God...." The test is the same—will Jesus trust in God or use his power to handle this situation on his own? He had to learn to trust his Father; he had to learn obedience through suffering (Hebrews 3:5–6).

We must learn to trust God in the same way. Recently, a mom in our ministry shared with me the joy of her son being baptized. She confessed how difficult it was for her when she was a young disciple to let go and trust the teen ministry workers who were helping her son. She wanted to be personally in control of every aspect of her son's life, but she had to learn to let go and trust God. As she learned to give God control, peace entered her life. She shared with me how wonderful it was to learn to trust him like never before.

5-6 Next the devil takes Jesus into Jerusalem to the top of the pinnacle of the temple. Many scholars believe this to be the highest tower of the temple complex—the southeastern tower, which rose about a hundred and eighty feet above the ground. Satan quotes Scripture to his own advantage here, demonstrating that just quoting scriptures does not necessarily show a right heart. He quotes Psalm 91:11–12, which says that God will give special protection for those who are in his care. Satan implores Jesus to jump off the pinnacle and claim the special protection promised him by God.

7 Jesus again answers the devil by referring to a scripture: Deuteronomy 6:16, "Do not test the Lord your God as you did at Massah." This harkens back to a time when Israel tried to get God to prove his presence with a miraculous sign. Jesus reiterates that it is not right to ask God to prove his care through miraculous events.

First Century Insights ᑫ

Sadducees

The Sadducees considered themselves the "Sons of Zadok," a priest of God (1 Kings 2:35). The origin of the Sadducees goes back to John Hyrcanaus I. The Sadducees wanted to follow the Greek culture with the Romans instead of revolting. Because of their tolerance of the Romans, the Romans favored the Sadducees in their dealings with the Jews. They were the wealthy, social elite. Only a thousand existed in Judea in the first century.

Theologically, the Sadducees accepted only the Pentateuch, the first five books of the Bible, as their Scripture. They rejected the bodily resurrection, angels and the spirits. They went strictly by the written law and rejected the oral traditions. They approached the Pentateuch literally. While the stronghold of the Pharisees was the synagogue, the stronghold of the Sadducees was the temple.

The beliefs of the Sadducees can be summarized as follows:

1. Individual freedom (God is distant)
2. No resurrection
3. A rejection of the spirit world
4. Scripture consisting only of the written law (the Pentateuch)

8-9 The devil next takes Jesus to a very high mountain. Traditionally, the site of this testing is a mountain overlooking Jericho, the Jordan Valley and the Dead Sea. Here, Jesus would have had a panoramic view, looking south toward Egypt and east toward Mesopotamia, the oldest and greatest civilizations of history. Just like when Moses stood on Mt. Nebo and looked over into the Promised Land, Jesus now stands on a mountain and looks at the great kingdoms of the world. Satan is tempting Jesus with power—the power to rule the world. He is offering a shortcut to full authority: worship of his enemy.

10 Jesus again battles Satan by quoting a verse. Deuteronomy 6:13 commands Israel to worship God alone. To worship Satan was out of the question. Only God deserves allegiance and praise.

In comparing Matthew's account of the temptation of Jesus with Luke's account, there is a slight variation (see Luke 4:1–13). Matthew and Luke both mention that Jesus was first tempted to turn stones to bread. As compared to Matthew's Gospel, Luke inverts the last two temptations: the kingdoms of the world are second and the pinnacle of the temple is third. Why is this? Most scholars believe that

Practically Speaking ☙

The Example of John

One of my favorite Bible characters is John the Baptist. He carries on the great prophetic tradition of Elijah, Isaiah and Jeremiah. What can we learn from John? Plenty. Here are some of the lessons that I have learned from looking at John the Baptist. See if you can think of others.

(1) **John lived a radical life (3:4).** John lived in the desert of Judea, a hot, sun-parched wilderness southeast of Jerusalem. He dressed in a camel's hair garment and ate locusts and wild honey. Material possessions meant little to John the Baptist. His life was devoted to his mission: to prepare the way for the Lord. When people look at the way we are living, would they say that we are living on the edge? The prophetic life is a radical life. Are you consumed by the mission or by materialism? How radical is your lifestyle? John's life was not characterized by comfort or selfishness.

To go into a wilderness today with a camel's hair garment while eating locusts and wild honey would be radical, but it would not be effective. We can be radical in different ways. We can decide to be the most loving parent any child has ever known. We can decide to be the most honest employee a boss has ever seen. We can decide to be radically evangelistic or radical students of the Word or radical men and women of prayer. To be radical we must set ourselves apart from the mediocrity of the world. Certainly, as disciples, we must find ways to be radical men and women for God.

(2) **John preached a strong message (3:1).** The message of John was one of repentance. John taught people that they must give up sin because the kingdom was near. This tough message drew people to John. Some believe that if we challenge people, they will leave. This was not true with John. Like John, we have to be willing to preach a strong message. Are we willing to tell people what they need to hear? If we don't tell them, who will?

(3) **John touched the lives of others (3:5–6).** People came from Jerusalem and all Judea to hear John. They responded by confessing their sins and by being baptized in water. John's message touched their hearts. One goal of being a disciple is to make other disciples. Right now, whose life are you touching with the gospel? Are you studying the Bible with anyone? Are you reaching out to anyone who has shown interest in the church? What are you going to do today to share your faith with someone?

(4) **John was willing to stand up for his convictions (3:7–10).** Not everyone responded joyously to the message of John. The Pharisees and Sadducees, who were leaders of the Jews, opposed John and his message. It seems as if jealousy drove them to oppose John who did not cower at their opposition. Instead, he unmasked their hypocrisy by calling them "a brood of vipers." He was willing to weather the storm of opposition because of his convictions.

Today, when we take a stand for God, we can expect opposition—from co-workers, from school friends, from our parents, from our spouse, or from network television or local newspapers. In fact, we will never be friends with the world (James 4:4). Are you ready to weather the storms of persecution? Will you stand against opposition?

(5) **John was humble (3:11–14).** Remember that in the Jewish tradition, a rabbi could ask his pupil to do anything for him except put on or take off his sandals. John the Baptist states that if Jesus were to ask him to take off his sandals, he would gladly do it. Yet John considered himself unworthy of such a task because he understood the greatness of Jesus. He was willing to make himself less so that Jesus might be greater (John 3:30). He took himself out of the picture and encouraged people to focus on Jesus. This is the heart of a disciple. Do you have a humble heart? Ask your three closest friends if you are a humble person and see how they respond. "God opposes the proud, but gives grace to the humble" (James 4:6). Are you growing in humility?

Matthew is more concerned with chronology and that Luke selects a more topical approach by listing the temptations climactically—expressing the climax that he wants to highlight. He uses the simple conjunction "and" to link the temptations, while Matthew uses the words "then" and "again." This suggests that Luke is not concerned with the sequential order of events.

Jesus Begins His Ministry in Galilee (4:12–17)

[12]When Jesus heard that John had been arrested, he returned to Galilee. [13]He left Nazareth and made his home in Capernaum by the Sea in the region of Zebulun and Naphtali, [14]in order that the word of the prophet Isaiah might be fulfilled:

[15]Land of Zebulon and land of Naphtali
by the way of the sea, across the Jordon,
Galilee of the nations —
[16]The people who live in darkness
Have seen a great light;
And on those living in the land and shadow of death,
A light has dawned.

[17]From that time Jesus began to preach, saying, "Repent, for the kingdom of heaven is fast approaching."

Jesus begins his ministry in the northwestern corner of the Sea of Galilee between the towns of Capernaum, Bethsaida and Corazim. This has been called the "evangelical triangle." because the bulk of Jesus' ministry in Galilee occurred between these three towns. Capernaum became the home base of Jesus' ministry. It was a town of some one thousand residents located in the territory of Herod Antipas, right on the Sea of Galilee, and was a small, humble fishing village.

The message of Jesus' ministry was the same as that of John: "Repent, for the kingdom of heaven is near [at hand, fast approaching]." The dawn of the kingdom had arrived. As King, Jesus would usher God's kingdom into the world. These were exciting times.

12 You might notice that the phrase concerning John's arrest and imprisonment is in the passive voice—"had been arrested." Many scholars call this "the divine passive," implying that God himself was the one that arrested John.

At the arrest of John, Jesus departs (withdraws) to the region of Galilee. His ministry in Galilee officially begins at this time. His departure to Galilee might simply be because of personal preference. But it might infer that since John was rejected in the south, Jesus would now go north to a place that had not heard the message of salvation.

13 Jesus leaves Nazareth and makes his home in "Capernaum by the Sea." Capernaum in the Hebrew is *Kafer Nahum*, which could be translated as "village of Nahum" or "village of comfort." Capernaum becomes Jesus' hub during his ministry in Galilee. A military outpost of the Romans was located there in order to collect tax revenues from the fishing industry. Rome's view was that it was leasing out the Sea of Galilee to the local fishermen. Since the Roman troops lived in better conditions than the locals, the residents must have felt tremendous enmity toward the soldiers. Understanding this background helps us recognize how unusual it would have been for a centurion to have received the respect that the Gospel writers gave the centurion of Capernaum (Matthew 8:5-13, Luke 7:1-10).

Also, the apostle Peter lived in Capernaum with his mother-in-law. His move to Capernaum was probably economically motivated, since as a fisherman, he would then be next to towns that were famous for preserving fish for transport. In Magdala, the home of Mary Magdalene, they preserved fish by smoking them, and Taricheae was known for its pickling industry. Additionally, by living in Capernaum, Peter would have escaped paying a border tax that was required each time he came from Bethsaida (his hometown) to Capernaum. Herod Antipas had set up this tollbooth to the consternation of the people. (Incidentally, Matthew may have been collecting taxes there when he received his call from Jesus.)

Archaeologists have discovered houses that date from the first century in Capernaum. One house is traditionally identified as the house where Peter lived with his wife and mother-in-law. After

Jesus healed her, she must have loved having him in her home.

Additionally, archaeologists have uncovered the synagogue at Capernaum. Although its columns date later than the first century, its foundation dates to the time of Jesus. It was here in this synagogue that Jesus drove out the evil spirit from a demoniac, as recorded by Luke and Mark. When the people heard his teaching and saw his miracle, they exclaimed, "What is this? A new teaching — and with authority! He even gives orders to evil spirits and they obey him"(Mark 1:27). The crowds noticed something radically different about Jesus.

On a personal note, *Kafer Nahum* is one of my favorite places to visit in the Holy Land. When I am there, I know I am walking where Jesus walked. The ruins of the village help me understand what life in first century Galilee was like. This humble, unpretentious first century fishing village was the hub of Jesus' ministry in Galilee. Today its ruins remind us of the humble, unpretentious Rabbi who chose to make this village his home. It may lie in ruins, but the Rabbi is still alive, and his teachings are still changing the lives of people all over the world.

14-16 Matthew paraphrases Isaiah 8:22–9:1, keeping the meaning of the passage without directly quoting it. He also may have been quoting from a Palestinian translation that is no longer in existence. D.A. Carson writes:

> The point of the quotation is clear enough. In despised Galilee, the place where people live in darkness (i.e., without the religious and cultic advantages of Jerusalem and Judea), the land of the shadow of death (i.e., where the darkness is most dense; cf. Job 10:21; Ps. 107: 10; Jer. 13:16; Amos 5:8), here the light has dawned (v. 16). "Dawned" *(aneteilen)* suggests that the light first shone brilliantly here, not that it was shining brightly elsewhere and then moved here.[11]

Jesus honored Galilee as the land where he began his ministry. He would minister there for three years — teaching in its synagogues, preaching the good news, and healing various diseases.

The Call and the Crowds (4:18–25)

18Walking by the Sea of Galilee, he saw two brothers, Simon called Peter and his brother Andrew. They were casting nets into the sea, for they were fishermen. 19He said to them, "Come, follow me, and I will make you fishers of men." 20Immediately, they left their nets and followed him.

21Going on from there, he saw two other brothers, James the son of Zebedee and John his brother. They were in a boat with Zebedee their father, preparing their nets. He called them. 22Immediately, they left the boat and their father and followed him.

²³*And he went into the whole region of Galilee, teaching in their synagogues and preaching the good news of the kingdom and healing every disease and every sickness of the people.* ²⁴*And reports of him spread into all of Syria, and they brought to him all who were sick with various diseases and suffering severe pain, and demoniacs, epileptics and paralytics, and he healed them.* ²⁵*Large crowds followed him from Galilee and the Decapolis (the ten cities), Jerusalem, Judea and across the Jordan.*

Jesus called his first disciples, Peter and Andrew, while they were fishing on the Sea of Galilee. He gave them a new vocation — instead of being fishermen, they were to be fishers of men. The immediacy of their response demonstrates three facts. First, they must have had prior knowledge of Jesus. Why would they drop everything and follow Jesus unless they knew who he was? They must have been some of the disciples of John that were mentioned in Matthew 3. Second, the call to discipleship deserves an urgent, immediate response. When Jesus calls, we must answer and answer quickly. Third, the call also required a sacrifice. Peter and John left their nets, their livelihood, to follow Jesus. James and John left their father and their family business to follow him. Jesus does not expect everyone to abandon his or her family to follow him. However, if family becomes a stumbling block to our walk with God, our walk with God must be the priority.

The ministry of Jesus consisted of teaching, preaching and healing. News spread quickly about this amazing teacher. Crowds from the north, south and east of Galilee came to see Jesus. His ministry began with immediate, outstanding results. Would you expect anything less from the King of Kings?

18 The net that Peter and Andrew were using would have been thrown over their shoulders and would become a circle when it was cast out into the sea. Fishermen still use this type of net on the Sea of Galilee today. Early in the morning, you can see fishermen who have waded out into the water casting this net.

19-20 "Come, follow me" is the call of a rabbi to his pupils. The students were to stay in constant attendance of the rabbi and learn everything he had to teach them. They were to listen and learn — often being adept at remembering his exact words. The followers of Jesus were urged to do more than just listen and learn. They were to take an active part in his ministry: they were to be fishers of men.

First Century Insights ◌

The Sea of Galilee

The Sea of Galilee is fully surrounded by a ridge, making for a breathtaking first glimpse. It sits like a beautiful blue gem in the middle of a lush valley.

It is also called the Sea of Tiberius (after the city of Tiberius), Lake Genneserat (after the region), and the Sea of Kinnereth (which means "harp," since it is harp-shaped). This is where Jesus walked on the water, calmed the storm and spent most of his ministry, preaching to the villages that surround its shores. This is the sea where Peter, Andrew, James and John fished for a living and where Peter walked on the water while the other disciples sat in a boat.

The Sea of Galilee is more than what we usually think of as a lake and less than a sea. It is about fourteen miles north to south and seven miles east to west and sits seven hundred feet below sea level, in the bottom of the Rift Valley. It is fed from the north by the Jordan River and empties again into the Jordan in the south, which then travels some seventy miles south, ending in the Dead Sea.

I remember the first time I saw the Sea of Galilee—I literally cried. Geography can change over time, but I knew that the Sea of Galilee was virtually the same sea that Jesus had looked upon when he delivered the Sermon on the Mount. I was overcome by emotion. Now I have seen the Sea of Galilee more than a dozen times. I've had picnics on her shores with my family, swam in her waters and sailed across her in boats.

But, every time I see the Sea of Galilee, I am overcome by emotion. I cry because she represents the day-to-day ministry of Jesus to me: his patience as he trained his twelve disciples along her shores and his love for people as he made the lame walk and the blind see. Here Jesus cast demons out of the demoniac and helped his disciples catch a miraculous haul of fish. I love the Sea of Galilee!

Some events that occurred around the Sea of Galilee:
- The calling of Jesus' first disciples (Mark 1)
- The cure of a man with palsy (Mark 2)
- The miraculous catch of fish (Luke 5)
- The Sermon on the Mount (Matthew 5–7)
- The miracle of the loaves (Matthew 14)
- The post-resurrection appearance of Jesus to his disciples (John 21)

Simon Peter and Andrew were the first set of brothers called by Jesus. They were originally from Bethsaida, which could be translated "Fishtown," and was just across the Jordon River from Capernaum on the northern tip of the Sea of Galilee. Herod the Great gave this territory to his son Herod Philip. The city took on a Greek and Roman flavor under Herod Philip's rule. Today archaeologists have uncovered the ruins of ancient Bethsaida, finding fishing hooks, lead weights and curved needles for mending nets.

21-22 The second set of bothers Jesus called was James and John, the sons of Zebedee. Jesus would change their name to the Sons of Thunder. They were mending their nets, either getting ready to go fishing or coming in from a night of fishing. In other words, they were at work. They were in business with their father, Zebedee, but Jesus calls them to a new work—to go into business with his Father. James and John leave their nets, their father and their business to follow the rabbi.

23 The three participles—teaching, preaching and healing—summarize the Lord's work in Galilee. R. T. France writes:

> Jesus' ministry is summarized under three headings: teaching in their synagogues (i.e. biblical exposition, as in Lk. 4:16ff), preaching the gospel of the kingdom (i.e. public proclamation, as in 4:17), and healing, in which the power of the kingdom of heaven was actually brought into operation (cf. 12:28); John had preached the same message, but in Jesus' ministry what for John was future became present.[12]

Today our ministry should have the same elements as the ministry of Jesus. Are we teaching the precepts of the Bible, preaching the good news of kingdom, and seeing his power heal the hurt in people's lives? In which of these elements are we the weakest? Let's restore the ministry of Jesus.

The synagogue was a building where Jews gathered to read the Torah and to learn about the law. Scholars are unsure of the exact origins of the synagogue, but its rise is usually associated with the time of the Babylonian captivity (the sixth century BC). While the Jews were in captivity in Babylon, they had to learn to exist apart from the temple in Jerusalem. Since they could not offer sacrifices, the reading and study of the Torah became central in their gatherings. After 200 BC, synagogues began to appear in Palestine. Each village could have a synagogue.

24-25 The location "Syria" refers to the area north of Israel, usually including the area of Phoenicia. The Romans considered all of Palestine within the region of Syria. Although many Jews lived in this area, the references to Syria and to the Decapolis (the Ten Cities in the NIV footnote) represent the response of Gentiles to the ministry of Jesus.

The healing ministry of Jesus is divided into three categories which sometimes overlap: (1) the demoniacs; (2) epileptics and those having seizures; and (3) the paralyzed. That Jesus could heal "all types" of diseases displays his power and authority over sickness.

Endnotes

[1] The translation at the beginning of each section of Matthew is the author's own translation from the USB Greek New Testament, Third Edition.

[2] Hill, p. 76.

[3] Albright and Mann note, "Unfortunately, the system of dating events in the Christian era, which we have inherited, was constructed by Dionysius Exiguus at the beginning of the sixth century. He assumed wrongly that the date of Jesus' birth was 753 A.U.C. (ab urbe condita), i.e., 753 years after the founding of the city of Rome. Herod died four years before that, in 749 A.U.C.; hence we say he died in 4 BC. Actually, if we assume the accuracy of the events described, then the latest date for the birth of Jesus must be 4 BC (the year Herod died), and it may well have been as early as 9 BC." See W. F. Albright and C. S. Mann, *Matthew, The Anchor Bible, vol. 26.* (Garden City, Doubleday, 1971), 23.

[4] R. T. France, *Matthew, Tyndale New Testament Commentaries* (Grand Rapids: Eerdmans, 1985), p. 80.

[5] Fritz Rienecker, *A Linguistic Key To The Greek New Testament,* edited by Cleon L. Rogers (Grand Rapids: Regency Reference Library, 1976) p. 8.

[6] France, p. 90.

[7] Albright and Mann, p. 25.

[8] Ibid, p. 25.

[9] Ibid, p. 25.

[10] Rienecker, p. 14.

[11] D. A. Carson, p. 117.

[12] R. T. France, pp. 104–105.

2

Ministry in Galilee
The Sermon on the Mount
Matthew 5:1–7:29

I ndeed, if we consider the unblushing promises of reward and the staggering nature of the rewards promised in the Gospels, it would seem that Our Lord finds our desires, not too strong, but too weak. We are half-hearted creatures, fooling about with drink and sex and ambition when infinite joy is offered us, like an ignorant child who wants to go on making mud pies in a slum because he cannot imagine what is meant by the offer of a holiday at the sea.

–G. K. Chesterton, British writer and literary critic

The Sermon on the Mount represents Jesus' longest discourse in the Gospels. In Matthew it is the first of five blocks of discourse, with each block ending with the same formula: "when Jesus had finished saying these things…" The five blocks of discourse material are as follows:

1. The Sermon on the Mount (Matthew 5–7)
2. The Instruction of the Twelve (Matthew 10)
3. Parables About the Kingdom (Matthew 13)
4. Life in the Christian Community (Matthew 18)
5. Teaching About the Future (Matthew 23–25)

The Sermon on the Mount is the greatest sermon and the greatest ethical discourse ever given. It is the bedrock of the church. Jesus gathers a prospective community and tells them his ideals. He uses the text of the Old Testament as a foundation for it, repeating the phrase "you have heard that it was said…but I tell you" as a formula to expound upon and clarify the teaching of the Old Testament for his new community. This was a common practice among rabbis. The role of the rabbi was to give "midrash" — commentary on the Scripture. However, Jesus' commentary does not take away from the authority of the Scripture, but rather heightens it. As his followers, we must also have great respect for the Bible today.

Traditionally, the setting of the Sermon on the Mount is a hillside looking out over the Sea of Galilee. The particular site has since been named the Mount of the Beatitudes. It is a grassy field that slopes down toward the water. Although we are uncertain exactly where the sermon was delivered, it is likely that it was close to the city of Capernaum.

Matthew records the Sermon on the Mount, and Luke records the Sermon on the Plain. Many scholars teach that neither represents a historical portrayal of an event. Some teach that these two accounts contradict each other. But Jesus was an itinerate preacher—he could have preached several sermons in different locations that contained some, all or more than the material in the Sermon on the Mount.

The Beatitudes—The Blessings (5:1–12)

5:1When Jesus saw the crowds, he went up on the mountain, and after he sat down, his disciples came to him. 2Then he began to teach them, saying:

3"Fortunate are the humble in spirit, for theirs is the kingdom of heaven.

4Fortunate are those who mourn, for they will be comforted.

5Fortunate are the meek, for they will inherit the earth.

6Fortunate are those whose who hunger and thirst for righteousness, for they will be filled.

7Fortunate are the merciful, for they will receive mercy.

8Fortunate are the single-minded, for they will see God.

9Fortunate are the peacemakers, for they will be called the children of God.

10Fortunate are those who are persecuted because of righteousness, for theirs is the kingdom of heaven.

11"Fortunate are you when people insult you and persecute you and speak all kinds of evil against your falsely because of me. Rejoice and be glad, because your reward is great in heaven. For they persecuted the prophets before you in the same way."

Before Jesus delves into practical instructions for his community, he begins by talking about their attitudes, their hearts. This is where a relationship with God begins. Jesus wants his followers to have the right attitude about following God, so he gives them beatitudes—the "be-this–attitudes". According to Webster's dictionary, the word "beatitude" comes from the Latin *beatitudo*, from *beatus*, meaning "a state of utmost bliss."

The word "blessed" (*makarios*) can also be translated "happy." I follow Albright and Mann and translate *makarios* with the word "fortunate." They comment, "The word in Greek was used in classical times of the state of the gods in contrast to men."[1] The Greeks believed their gods to exist in a plane above the world that was superior to the world. You see this belief expressed in the philosophy of Plato. Their gods were fortunate in this way. When we adopt the attitudes of the beatitudes, we elevate ourselves above the earthly existence of this world. We enter into a spiritual realm that calls us higher. In this way, those who follow the beatitudes are fortunate.

As Christians, we are fortunate because God has favored us by allowing us to have a relationship with him. Do we feel favored? Do people around us know that we are favored and happy? I remember one of my favorite preachers once telling his audience, "If you're happy to be here today, then notify your face." Our happy, vibrant attitude should distinguish us as disciples. We are on a serious mission, but our relationship with God needs to keep us happy and content. We are the fortunate ones. But this does not mean that we should fake happiness. The world is an incredibly tough place. Bad things happen to disciples too. Jesus doesn't expect us to walk around all the time with a silly grin on our faces. He does expect us to face our struggles with faith. This faithful acceptance of even the difficult matters of life, will separate the disciple of Jesus from the non-disciple. And at times, it is even possible to keep a happy, positive, faithful attitude in the midst of a difficult circumstance.

1-2 Jesus sat down to teach, which was typical for teachers in synagogues.

3 "Blessed [happy, fortunate] are the poor [humble in spirit], for theirs is the kingdom of heaven." What does it mean to be poor in spirit? The word usually translated "poor" can also mean "afflicted" or "humble." Spiritual poverty is our recognition of our need for God. This is where happiness starts. If we do not see our need for God, then we will never come to him.

Also, the poor are desperate. I have had the opportunity to travel to several Third World countries and have seen intense physical poverty. I will never forget the eyes of a young girl that I saw in Calcutta, India. She must have been around ten or twelve years old at the time. She was standing outside our car with twenty or thirty other children. She had an old, faded dress that was so worn and threadbare that you could see right through it. Her hair was matted with dirt. She was so thin that her skin was stretched tautly against her bones. Her ribcage was visible through the threadbare dress. She reached out her hands, cupped together like a drinking cup, hoping for a handout. I will never forget the look in her eyes — sheer desperation. She was not just begging for some change or for a bowl of soup. She was begging for her life. This is poverty and desperation.

How desperate are we to have a relationship with God? To begin with, we must recognize how pitiful and poor we are without him in our lives—spiritually speaking, we are nothing. If we are desperate, we will do anything to have a relationship with God. We will study, repent, pray, come to all the church services and seek out help from others. Is there desperation in the way we seek out God? Only the spiritually poor will receive heaven. Are we poor in spirit?

4 "Blessed are those who mourn, for they will be comforted." This beatitude contains a paradox: how are those who mourn happy? They are happy because they know that their mourning over their sins will be replaced by an overwhelming since of joy and contentment. Spiritual poverty leads to repentance. And when we repent, we hurt over the pain that our sin has caused God, others and self. But once we confess our sin, God is quick to forgive; he turns sadness to joy.

The OT book of Hosea is a vivid illustration of God's willingness to forgive. God tells Hosea to marry a prostitute named Gomer. Hosea takes her into his house and takes care of her and loves her. But she turns her back on him and returns to prostitution. Hosea does not give up on Gomer. He searches for her, declares his love to her, and accepts her back into his home and his heart. Like Hosea, God searches us out, declares his love for us, and welcomes us back into his home and his heart. If we repent of our sin, then God is quick to forgive. Therefore, mourning is turned to laughter.

5 "Blessed are the meek, for they will inherit the earth." Some would claim that Jesus was wrong on this point. They would say that we live in a dog eat dog world and that the meanest, toughest dog wins every time. They would say the meek will not inherit anything and that they are cannon fodder for the power brokers. These people are wrong, however. They are wrong because they do not understand what Jesus meant when he spoke of meekness.

Meekness does not mean wimpiness, frailty or passivity. Jesus is not speaking of groveling to anyone with a rough, gruff voice. For Jesus, meekness is power under control. The word "meek" (*praus*) suggests gentleness and self-control. D. A. Carson writes about meekness:

> In general the Greeks considered meekness a vice because they failed to distinguish it from servility. To be meek toward others implies freedom from malice and a vengeful spirit. We must acknowledge our own bankruptcy (vs. 3) and mourn (vs. 4). But to respond with meekness when others tell us of our bankruptcy is far harder. Meekness therefore requires such a true view about us as will express itself even in our attitude toward others.[2]

Meekness does not come easily. It goes against what we are taught by the world. To become meek, we must look to Jesus.

Jesus exemplified meekness in his own life. He was the kind of person who could huddle up with children for a laugh or drive thieves and moneychangers from the temple courts. He was just as comfortable in the house of the poorest widow or the palace of the king. He could have called ten thousand angels to save him from the cross, but he bowed his head in submission and died for the sins of humanity. He had power under control. This type of meekness inherits the earth. This type of meekness means thinking before answering, praying before responding, and asking, "What would Jesus do?" in every situation. This type of meekness garners the respect of other people. Jesus, the meek King of kings, was willing to stretch out his arms and be nailed to a cross, suspended between heaven and earth, for the sins of humanity.

6 "Blessed are those who hunger and thirst for righteousness, for they will be filled." Not many of us in the First World know hunger, real hunger. We say we are hungry when we have a craving for sugar or caffeine, but have we ever really been hungry? We sometimes put ourselves through self-imposed times of hunger by fasting, and by so doing can begin to experience a bit of what hunger is really all about. I once fasted for twenty-one days on just water. No food, no juice, no cokes, only water. For the first few days, I felt sick, not hungry, because of all the withdrawal pain from food and sugar and chemicals like caffeine. At about day nine or ten, I began to feel hungry. My sense of smell was heightened. I would salivate at the mere mention of food. It was not so much that I wanted a big meal, but I wanted a taste, a sliver of meat, a kernel of popcorn, a taste of Coke or a pinch of salt. Hunger produces an intense desire to grab any morsel of food and eat it. Hunger (like poverty) implies desperation.

I usually translate righteousness as "right living." When we are righteous, we are focused on doing everything right. We want even the least little detail to be right. We would not dare to exaggerate our stories to make them a bit more dramatic or glamorous. We watch the speed limit, buckle our seat belts, and stop at every stop sign. We fill out our taxes properly, reporting everything that needs to be reported. Then God will fill us with confidence because we know that we are doing the right thing. When we know we are living right, we feel full, content and at peace. This is God's plan of righteousness.

Throughout the Bible, God's call to righteousness or to "right living" happens within the context of his covenant community. This means that God's call to righteousness is based on us having a right relationship with him. Jesus continues this idea by giving the Sermon on the Mount to a community of people. Righteousness or "right living" follows having a right relationship with Jesus. Jesus reaches out to us to begin that relationship. He then empowers us to continue in that relationship with "right living."

7 "Blessed are the merciful, for they will be shown mercy." To receive mercy, we must give mercy. The Greek work for merciful is *eleamon*. It can also mean sympathetic. To have mercy means to be filled with compassion or pity for someone. Sometimes we have pity on people because we understand that they have suffered an incredible hurt. But we can also pity someone because we fear that except for the grace of God we might end up in his or her situation. Jesus expects his disciples to have compassionate hearts. He expects us to empathize with others. If we are going to receive mercy, then we must be merciful.

8 "Blessed are the pure in heart, for they will see God." Only the pure hearted will see God. We usually think of purity as an absence of lust, especially sexual lust; but the term means so much more. Purity in the Bible means single-mindedness. Dietrich Bonhoeffer, in his excellent book, *The Cost of Discipleship*, answers the question "Who is pure in heart?" by writing:

> Only those who have surrendered their hearts completely to Jesus that he may reign in them alone. Only those whose hearts are undefiled by their own evil, and by their own virtues too. Only they will see God, who in this life have looked solely unto Jesus Christ, the Son of God. For then their hearts are free from all defiling phantasies and are not distracted by conflicting desires and intentions.[3]

Purity is the ability to keep our focus on God and not let our eyes wander over to the distractions of the world. When God is our focus, then everything else in life is in the proper perspective. Soren Kierkegaard, the Danish philosopher, wrote a book entitled *Purity of Heart Is to Will One Thing*. Kierkegaard emphasizes that purity must incorporate a single-minded focus on God. What are your greatest distractions in life? How do these distractions keep you from focusing on God? How can you rid yourself of these distractions so that you can be keenly focused on God?

9 "Blessed are the peacemakers, for they will be called sons of God." It is rare in this life to find someone who keeps peace. It is even more rare to find someone who makes peace. "Peace" in the Hebrew is *shalom*. This is the word of greeting meaning "Hello" or "Goodbye."

But it means much more. It means wholeness in life. When we greet others by saying *shalom*, we are telling them that we want them to experience "life to the full." Jesus came to give this type of fullness in our lives (John 10:10). As his disciples, we are to pass this full, abundant life onto other people. Are you a peacemaker? Do you share your full life in Jesus with other people? The people who share the life that they have found in God with others will be called children of God.

10-12 "Blessed are those who are persecuted...for theirs is the kingdom of heaven." Once again, we have a paradox—how can the persecuted be happy? Happiness does not come from suffering—Jesus was not a sadist or a masochist. Happiness comes from knowing that just as Jesus and the prophets were persecuted, persecution places us in the company of men and women throughout history who were willing to stand up and do what was right. To be persecuted for righteousness means that someone must have noticed that we were doing something right. Living like Jesus will get us noticed. And not everyone will like it. Some will try to hurt us for it, but we can endure the pain of isolation, humiliation or intimidation by looking to Jesus and to the prophets who were persecuted before us. We do not take delight in the persecution—and we should never bring persecution on ourselves—but we delight in the fact that we have been included with Jesus and the prophets.

Following Jesus demands suffering. It may be self-inflicted (making a sacrifice for the kingdom), or it might be inflicted upon us (someone persecutes us for following Jesus). Most of us who live in America do not have to worry about suffering being inflicted on us. But in other parts of the world, our brothers and sister do endure suffering inflicted by others because of their stand for righteousness. Either way, every time we suffer, we connect ourselves with the cross of Jesus. Bonhoeffer writes,

> The cross means sharing the suffering of Christ to the last and to the fullest. Only a man thus totally committed in discipleship can experience the meaning of the cross. The cross is there, right from the beginning, he has only got to pick it up; there is no need for him to go out and look for a cross for himself, no need for him deliberately to run after suffering. Jesus says that every Christian has his own cross waiting for him, a cross destined and appointed by God. Each must endure his allotted share of suffering and rejection.[4]

If we never sacrifice, never suffer, never put ourselves out for the kingdom, then we are disconnected from the cross. To be connected with the cross implies sacrifice.

Salt and Light (5:13–16)

[13]*"You are the salt of the earth, but if salt loses its saltiness, how is it able to become salty again? It is good for nothing, except to be thrown out and trampled under men's feet.*

[14]*"You are the light of the world. A city built on a hill is not able to be hidden. [15]Neither do men light a lamp and place it under a bushel, but on a stand, and it shines to all who are in the house. [16]Let your light so shine before men that they may see your good works and glorify your Father in heaven."*

13 We are to be like salt. In the first century salt served at least three purposes. (1) It was used as a spice to flavor food. Like salt, we must bring the flavor of Jesus to the world. (2) Salt was also used as a preservative. Before refrigeration, meat was salted to keep it fresh. As disciples, we must see ourselves as preservers of all that is good. (3) Salt was used as fertilizer. It was mixed with the soil to help plants grow. Like salt, we help things grow.

But if salt loses its saltiness, it is good for nothing. Technically, salt cannot become unsalty, but it can become spoiled by containments. In the first century bad salt was thrown on the roads and on the flat rooftops, where it would harden with the soil and be trampled under foot. Disciples are to make a difference in the world around them. What are you doing to change the part of the world where you live? Do people sense something distinctive about your way of life? We need to be the salt of the earth.

14-16 Furthermore, we are to be "the light of the world." God has designed our eyes to require light to be able to see. As Christians, we are to be the spiritual light that allows the world to see spiritual truths. The light of our example will expose lies and darkness and show people what they need to change. We are to be conspicuously different in this world. How bright is your light?

Jesus and the Law (5:17-20)

[17]*"Do not think that I have come to destroy the Law or the Prophets have not come to destroy but to clarify the true meaning of Scripture. [18]I tell you truthfully, until heaven and earth pass away, not one letter or one stoke of a pen will pass from the law until all is accomplished. [19]Therefore, whoever breaks one of the least of these commandments and teaches others to do the same, he will be called least in the kingdom of heaven. Whoever does and teaches these commandments, he will be call great in the kingdom of heaven. [20]For I tell you, unless your righteousness exceeds that of the scribes and Pharisees, you will not enter the kingdom of heaven."*

First Century Insights ❧

The Canon

The word "canon" means "a rod or measuring stick." Theologically speaking, it is the set of scriptures that measure up to the standard of being God's inspired word. The Jewish canon is made up of three divisions:
  1. *Torah*—the five books of Moses; also known as the Pentateuch
  2. *Neviim*—the collection of prophetic writings and the historical books
  3. *Ketuvim*—the wisdom literature and the psalms
Take the first letter from these three words to form *Tanakh* or the Jewish Bible today. "The Septuagint" was the translation of the Hebrew Old Testament into Greek. Its name comes from the Latin for "seventy," the approximate number of men who worked on it. Legend says that seventy-two scribes worked for seventy-two days to complete it. However, it was actually translated and collected between 250–150 BC. The Septuagint became the Bible of the early church and is usually identified by the abbreviation LXX, the Roman numeral for seventy.

17-20 Jesus did not "come to abolish the Law or the Prophets (which to the Jewish mind meant the writings of the Old Testament)...but to fulfill (*pleroo*) them." The word *pleroo* can mean "to complete," but it can also mean "to clarify." I believe the second meaning fits better with this context. Jesus came to heighten our understanding concerning the law. Throughout this section he uses the formula, "you have heard that it was said...but I say to you." Jesus takes ethical statements from the Old Testament and reinterprets them, showing the deeper, more radical heart behind them.

In this first example, our righteousness must surpass the righteousness of the Pharisees (a lay group having stringent oral laws that were scrupulously kept) and the scribes (the experts, teachers of the law). As disciples we must not only keep the letter of the law, but also the heart of it. Jesus is about to heighten our perception of the law in six particular areas: anger, murder, divorce, oaths, retaliation and love of enemies.

But when Jesus came to fulfill the law, he also had in mind that he would fulfill it through his own life. All the OT laws and the teaching of the prophets find their fulfillment in Jesus. Paul says in Romans 8:3-4, "For what the Law could not do, weak as it was through the flesh, God did: sending his own Son in the likeness of sinful flesh and as an offering for sin, he condemned sin in the flesh, so that the requirement of the Law might be fulfilled in us, who do not walk according to the flesh but according to the Spirit." The law stands until heaven and earth pass away because Jesus now stands as the Messiah, the completion of the law. He has heightened it, "heartened" it, clarified it, lived it out, personified it and fulfilled it.

Anger (5:21–26)

²¹*"You have heard that it was said of the ancients, 'Do not murder, and whoever murders will be liable to judgment.' ²²But I say to you that everyone who is angry with his brother is liable to judgment. Whoever says to his brother, 'Raca,' is liable to the council. Anyone who says, 'Fool,' is liable to the Gehenna of fire.*

²³*"Therefore, when you bring your gift to the altar, if you remember your brother has anything against you, ²⁴leave the gift before the altar and first go and reconcile yourself with your brother.*

²⁵*"Settle the matter quickly with your adversary on the way to court, or he may deliver you to the judge and the judge to the officer, and he will throw you in prison. ²⁶I tell you the truth, you will not get out until you have paid the last penny."*

21-26 It was said, "Do not murder," but Jesus says to not be angry with our brother. The focus here goes from the act of murder to the heart behind the act. If lies, hatred, prejudice and anger are rooted out, then we can stop murder.

Furthermore, we are not to insult our brother. *Raca* and *moros* both generally mean, "fool." But the word *raca* is more of a slur on a person's intelligence, while "moros" is more of an attack on his character.

To be "subject to judgment" refers to being judged by God, because no legal court will find a person guilty of anger.

Gehenna refers to the Hinnon Valley just south of Jerusalem. In the Old Testament this valley was notorious for being a place where sacrifices—even child sacrifices—were made to the god Molech. By NT times, the Hinnon Valley had become a garbage dump where a fire continually burned. This reference became synonymous with hell, the place of torment, "where the fire never goes out" (Mark 9:43).

Jesus gets to the root of the problem of anger. We must not blame others, and we need to take the first step toward reconciliation. He tells us we must be reconciled with our adversaries. This should be an urgent action: "Do not let the sun go down while you are still angry" (Ephesians 4:26). Do you have something against a brother or a sister that is eating at you? Take care of this matter. Do it quickly. Jesus says that relationships are important matters. They must be taken care of and guarded as precious gifts.

First Century Insights ☙

The Sanhedrin

The word "Sanhedrin" literally means "a sitting down with." It is often used in Greek literature to refer to city councils or meetings of city officials. In Jerusalem, this group of Pharisees and Sadducees was made up of seventy Jewish elders, plus the high priest, who oversaw it. The members of the Sanhedrin included priests, elders, scribes and leading citizens. The Roman government gave the Sanhedrin authority over the province of Judea in all political, judicial and legislative matters, except for the death penalty.

The Jewish population looked upon the Sanhedrin as the authority over Jewish people everywhere. The Sanhedrin was considered the highest legislative body of the Jews, the supreme court and grand jury, the council of the Pharisees, and the final decision making voice in *halakic* (legal) questions. Over the years the makeup and the power of Sanhedrin varied widely. Its power was often limited or magnified by the current ruler of the land.

In the Gospels, the Sanhedrin finds Jesus guilty and condemns him to death, but then hands Jesus over to the Romans to be crucified.

As an aside, Matthew includes the saying of Jesus that refers to the sacrificial system in Jerusalem. This must mean that he wrote his Gospel before the destruction of the temple in Jerusalem in 70 AD.

Adultery (5:27–30)

[27]*"You have heard that it was said, 'Do not commit adultery.'* [28]*I say to you — 'everyone who looks at a woman in a lustful manner has already committed adultery with her in his heart.'"*

[29]*"If your right eye scandalizes you, tear it out and cast it from you. For it is better to lose one of your members than your whole body be cast into Gehenna.* [30]*And, if your right hand scandalizes you, cut it off and toss it away for it is better to lose your hand than your whole body be thrown into Gehenna."*

27-28 It was said, "Do not commit adultery," but Jesus essentially says, "Do not lust after another person." In fact, he goes on to say that to lust after someone is to commit adultery in your heart. Here, Jesus heightens the ethic of moral purity in his community. To guard ourselves against adultery, we must not lust. We need to consider lust as "bad" as adultery. Since sin begins in our minds, we must control what we put in our minds.

29-30 Jesus also gives a new, radical way of dealing with sin in our lives. He says, "If your right eye causes you to sin, gouge it out and throw it away" (5:29). Is Jesus here advocating self-mutilation? Some have taken this literally (like Origen who castrated himself), but Jesus did not mean for us to take this literally. If he had, we would have some interesting Sunday services with most of us missing various body parts. No, Jesus is using a figure of speech call hyperbole, an exaggeration. Jesus is heightening our awareness of sin to say that if something is causing you to sin, then distance yourself from that temptation. If every time you go by a certain street corner you are tempted to purchase drugs, then find another route home. If certain movies cause you to struggle with lust, then stay away from those movies. If certain friends make you stumble, then find some new friends. Get radical about sin — it is the standard of Jesus!

Divorce (5:31–32)

[31]"It was said, 'Whoever divorces his wife must give her a certificate of divorce.' [32]But I say to you, 'Everyone who divorces his wife, except for marital unfaithfulness, makes her commit adultery, and whoever marries a divorced woman commits adultery.'"

31-32 Jesus sensitizes us toward divorce by saying that divorce is only accepted in the case of marital unfaithfulness (*porneia*). Jesus is speaking to his covenant community here, and he expects them to follow this standard. God does say, "I hate divorce" (Malachi 3:6), but he allowed divorce in Moses' day. Many will come into the kingdom having gone through divorce and remarriage. Paul states that they should be received in whatever state they find themselves in when they enter the kingdom (1 Corinthians 7). But for those who are already Christians, we should see that marriage is for life. Jesus is attempting to get those in his community to have a serious attitude about their marriage vows. If you are married, you should never joke about or threaten your spouse with divorce. God has made us "one flesh," and we will remain that way until death. Jesus does give this exception: if one partner leaves God and commits adultery, the other partner is free to remarry. We could raise many questions here based on situations in which people leave the church, divorce and then come back to the church. These matters should be considered individually. But the general teaching of Jesus is to say that God wants us to take our marriage vows seriously.[5]

Oaths (5:33–37)

33"Again you have heard it said by the ancients, 'Do not swear falsely, but keep your oaths to the Lord.' 34I say to you, Do not swear at all: neither by heaven, which is God's throne; 35neither by the earth, which is his footstool; or by Jerusalem, which is the city of the great King. 36Do not swear by your head, because you are not able to make one hair white or black. 37Let your word be 'yes, yes' or 'no, no' — anything exceeding this is from the Evil One."

33-37 In the Old Testament, the taking of oaths was not prohibited. But if a person took an oath, he was expected to keep it. Jesus is not necessarily speaking against taking oaths, but against those who would take an oath and not keep it.

In the Jewish mind there were all types of different oaths that could be taken. Some oaths were considered more serious and binding than others. Some were too serious and should never be invoked. Jesus cuts through this pecking order and gets to the heart of the matter: Be honest and live up to your word. Jesus tells his community to refrain from taking oaths. He says to let your "yes" be "yes" and your "no" be "no." In other words, do not lie — always be truthful.

Does this mean that we should not take an oath in court? Although Jesus does not address this matter specifically here, he does say that people in his community do not need to take oaths because we are going to be honest. Many religious groups have used this verse to refuse to take an oath in a court of law (the Anabaptists and Jehovah's Witnesses). But Jesus testified under oath (Matthew 26:63–64), and Paul took oaths (Romans 1:9; 2 Corinthians 1:23). To take an oath in court is not wrong; it is just redundant. We were "sworn in" to tell the truth, the whole truth and nothing but the truth when we became disciples.

Retaliation (5:38–42)

38"You have heard it said, 'An eye for an eye and a tooth for a tooth.' 39But I tell you, Do not resist an evil person. But if anyone strikes your right cheek, turn the other to him. 40If someone wants to sue you for your tunic, give him your outer cloak as well. 41If someone forces you to go one mile, go two with him. 42Give to everyone who asks, and do not refuse anyone who wants to borrow from you. Love your enemies."

38-42 In the movie *Clear and Present Danger*, the United States wants to get tough with drug barons in South America by making them pay for running drugs in the United States. A policy of reciprocity is put before the president. For every evil the drug barons inflict on others, they will receive swift, equal retribution. This is what the non-Christian world understands: You hit me; I'll hit you back. This is OT justice, but Jesus makes a radical turn here. He says that we should resist inflicting evil on others, even if they deserve it. However, we need to keep in mind that Jesus is speaking to his community here, those who will later form his church. He is teaching them how they need to act toward one another as his followers. To take these principles and apply them to situations outside the community of Jesus is going beyond what he expects. We must pray about and be wise in our practical application of these verses.

In general, when problems arise within the church, they should be worked out within the church. When problems occur outside the church, we can appeal to the legal-justice system where we live. Here, Jesus uses four illustrations of how we are to treat others.

(1) One of the most difficult sayings in the Bible reads, "If someone strikes you on the right cheek, turn to him the other also" (5:39). To strike someone on the cheek was considered an insult, like slapping someone across the face with a glove in the nineteenth century. When insulted, how should we act? We should not insult the person back or return evil for evil. This is difficult, but it is the only way that we can live together in peace. If a Christian physically hits us, we should not hit them back, but we can report them to the proper authorities.

(2) "If someone wants to sue you and take your tunic, let him have your cloak as well" (5:40). Under Mosaic Law, Jews were allowed to sue for the inner garment or tunic. The outer garment, however, was a possession that could not be taken away. Jesus says that when a "supposed" believer sues us for our tunic, we should even give the one who is suing us what he cannot legally take away—and give it to him freely. Yet, if someone asks us for our clothes, we need not give him everything until we have nothing left. This would be "enabling" him instead of helping him.

(3) The third illustration describes the practice of Roman soldiers who could command any non-Roman to carry their bags for one mile. Many would grudgingly carry the bag for the mile and not go one foot beyond a mile. Jesus tells his community that their attitude must be different. They must be a light and carry the bag two miles. We need to imagine the reaction of a Roman soldier as a disciple of Jesus picked up his bags with a smile on his face and kept walking past the one-mile marker, perhaps chatting amiably with him along the way. We are to perform even the most menial tasks of service to the best of our ability and with a good attitude in our hearts.

(4) "Give to the one who asks you, and do not turn away from the one who wants to borrow from you" (5:42). Does this mean that

we should give to anyone anything they ask? No, Jesus is fighting against a legalistic interpretation of the OT teaching on giving. Yet, the apostle Paul said in 2 Thessalonians 3:10, "If a man will not work, he shall not eat." Paul did not expect us to give anything to a person who is lazy.

Love for Enemies (5:43–48)

⁴³*"You have heard it said, 'Love your neighbor and hate your enemy.' ⁴⁴I tell you, Love your enemies and pray for those who persecute you. ⁴⁵Thus you will become children of your Father in heaven. He makes the sun rise on the evil and sends rain on the righteous and unrighteous. ⁴⁶"If you love those who love you, what reward do you have? Do not the tax collectors do the same? ⁴⁷If you greet only your brother, what are you doing more than others? Don't even the pagans do that? ⁴⁸Be true, therefore, as your Father in heaven is true."*

43-47 The Old Testament does not contain any commands of God to "hate their enemies." But this had become the practice of many in first century Judaism. The Zealots taught that the Romans should be hated. The Qumran community also taught the principle of hating enemies. Yet, Jesus taught the opposite: "Love your enemies." His community was to be different. They were to do good to people who hated them. In this way they would be a spiritual light.

48 Jesus raises the standard for those in his community to a height that seems unattainable: "Be perfect, therefore, as your heavenly Father is perfect." The word, "perfect" (*teleios*) can also be translated, "complete, mature or full-grown." It can also mean "true, sincere or genuine," which is the meaning that I use in my translation.

Jesus is not teaching the doctrine of Christian perfectionism — that after we become Christians, we must live an absolutely perfect life. Moral perfectionism is unattainable for us so we must consider the context here of relationships with those outside Jesus' community. He expects his disciples to be genuine or sincere toward them. We must become "perfect" in the way we treat people and the way we respond when we are mistreated. We must imitate God who loves the unlovely and continues to love when people reject him. We must strive toward this high standard.

The Heart of the Matter (6:1–18)

One of the aspects of the Sermon on the Mount that I appreciate the most is how Jesus centers in on the heart of discipleship in his teaching. In this section on giving, praying and fasting—the three most prominent acts of piety for the Jew—Jesus teaches that our motivation behind our actions must be right. In other words, we should not give to be seen by men, but because God sees us give. And we want to please God in all that we do. God will not reward our "acts of righteousness" if we do them for show (6:1). We must check our hearts when we give, pray or fast to make sure that they are in the right place. D. A. Carson outlines the structure that Jesus uses in discussing each action. He lists the following:

1. a warning not to do the act to be praised by men
2. a guarantee that those who ignore this warning will get what they want but not more
3. instruction on how to perform the act of piety secretly
4. the assurance that the Father who sees in secret will reward openly[6]

Incidentally, Jesus says, "When your give...when you pray... when you fast...." He assumes that as his disciples we will be doing all these things. He does not teach against any of these acts when they are properly done, but he teaches against acting ostentatiously while we do them.

Giving (6:1–4)

> [6:1]*"Be careful of doing your righteous actions before men to be seen by them. If you do, you will have no reward from your Father in heaven.*
>
> [2]*"When you give to those in need, do not sound a trumpet before you, as the hypocrites do in the synagogues and in the streets, so they can receive glory from men. I speak the truth, they have received their reward.* [3]*But when you give to those in need, do not let your left hand know what your right is doing,* [4]*thus your giving will be in secret. Your Father who sees in secret will reward you."*

1 Jesus begins this section by talking about almsgiving. Giving to the needy was an important part of first century Judaism. The apocryphal book of Tobit mentions, "It is better to give alms than to treasure up gold. For almsgiving delivers from death, and it will purge away every sin" (Tobit 12:8–9).

2 Scholars are unsure what the reference to sounding trumpets means. At times a trumpet would sound to notify the people of a special need. In the temple, alms were placed in receptacles that resembled the bell of a trumpet. However, Jesus is probably just using a metaphor for calling attention to our actions when giving alms.

We are not to be like the hypocrites. The word "hypocrite" means "actor" or "player" and is derived from a compound word meaning "a double face or a false face." On the Greek stage, actors portrayed different characters by holding masks in front of their faces. This way, one actor could play several parts. "Hypocrite" is taken from this practice of an actor using a mask. Jesus wants his disciples to be genuine—we are not to perform our acts of righteousness for show. A rabbi in the second century wrote that nine-tenths of all the hypocrisy in the world was found in the city of Jerusalem.

Albright and Mann suggest another definition for "hypocrite."[7] They state that the Greek definition above came later than NT times and should not be considered when defining the word. Instead, we must go to an earlier origin of the Greek word. In Homer, the verb *krinesthai*, from which the word "hypocrite" is derived, meant "to interpret (dreams)." This definition stresses a sense or capacity of discernment. It began by implying that someone had a critical, discerning mind. Later it developed the negative connotation of being hypercritical. Albright and Mann write:

> The Greek, *Kritikos*, is similarly neutral, implying a capacity for discernment. We may even carry the sense a step further and speak of someone as "hypercritical," intending to convey the idea that a person is given to fine, hairsplitting distinctions, but we do not at the same time accuse such a person of "being a hypocrite" in our modern sense.[8]

Albright and Mann go on to suggest that "hypocrite" should be translated as "over scrupulous" or "you casuists."[9] The hypocrite was then the person who was overly critical. He would use hairsplitting legalism against other people, put himself on a pedestal, and look down on others who were different from him.

The truth about the word "hypocrite" lies somewhere between these earlier and later Greek definitions. Whichever way we view the definition, as a hypercritical person or as a two-faced one, we do not want the label applied to us!

3-4 When we give, we are to give in secret. This way, God who sees us in secret will reward us. It is the only way he will reward us. We have to ask ourselves which do we desire more—the reward of men or the reward of God? The fact that God sees what we are giving should be our only reward.

Prayer (6:5-17)

⁵*"When you pray, do not be like the hypocrites, who love to pray standing in the synagogues and street corners to be seen by men. I speak the truth, they have received their reward. ⁶When you pray, enter your room and*

close the door and pray to your Father, who is in secret. Then your Father, who sees in secret, will reward you.

⁷When you pray, do not act as the pagans who babble on and on, for they think they will be heard for their verbosity. ⁸Do not be like them, for your Father knows what needs you have before you ask him.

⁹You should pray like this:
Our Father who is in heaven,
Holy is your name,
¹⁰Let your kingdom come,
Let your will be done,
On the earth as it is in heaven.
¹¹Give us today our daily food.
¹²Forgive us our debts,

Practically Speaking ↔

Acts of Righteousness

What does righteousness *(dikaiosune)* mean? The word occurs in Matthew more than in any other book of the New Testament (seventeen times) and is central to his message. Righteousness means "what God requires" or "what is right." Sometimes it is thought of as religious duties or acts of charity. But it means this and more. I usually think of righteousness as "doing the right thing." Another way of thinking of it is "right living." When we are righteous, we are striving to please God by making right choices in our lives. When we say "no" to sin, we are being righteous. When we say, "yes" to God, we are being righteous.

"Righteousness" is a covenant word used between God and his people. It implies "right relationship." In the Sermon on the Mount, Jesus is speaking to his community of followers. He expects them to act righteously because they have a right relationship with him. We need to realize that on our own we are powerless to make righteous choices all the time. But God can give us the power. The more we make righteous choices, the easier it is to continue along that path. This is why it is important that our acts of righteousness come from the heart and not out of tradition. If we perform acts of righteousness without the heart being involved, then we will not grow. If we do them with the right heart, they keep us centered on the path to God and he is pleased by our actions. It is also important to recognize that our acts of righteousness are based on a right relationship with Jesus. Without the right relationship, acts of righteousness become a checklist in which we attempt to earn the love of God. God's love is freely given to us. We are living in right relationship with God because of his love. Because we have a right relationship with God (righteousness), we live a righteous life before him (righteousness).

As we also have forgiven our debtors.
¹³Lead us not into temptation,
But deliver us from the evil one.
    ¹⁴For if you forgive men their trespasses, your Father in heaven will
forgive you. ¹⁵But if you do not forgive men their trespasses your Father will
not forgive your trespasses."

Jesus moves on to the second righteous act: prayer. He was
not against public prayer—he prayed in front of his disciples—but he
was against prayer for show. This must have been a problem in first
century Judaism. We know that the Jews were devoted to prayer. They
prayed the "*Shema* Israel" in the morning and the evening (Deuteronomy 6:4–5). In the morning, noon and afternoon, they would pray
another prayer also. The devout Jew would pray five times a day.
Therefore, the attention seeking Jew could time his prayers so that
he would be in public (in a synagogue or on a street corner) when the
time to pray arrived.

Jesus expected his disciples to pray in secret. He tells them to
enter a room and close the door, but not literally. He is teaching the
principle that prayer is between you and God, therefore we should
find a private place and pray. This way, God sees what we do in secret
and will reward us.

Jesus specifically mentions that we are not to pray like the
pagans or Gentiles. They prayed lengthy prayers, believing their
many words would gain the favor of their gods. The Greek word
translated as "babbling" is *battalogein*. It was used for constant repetition or stammering of words. The Gentiles also believed that if they
said the name of their gods over and over, this would win the god to
their cause. However, our God already wants to answer us—we do
not have to impress him with flowery words or lengthy prayers. We
must simply give God our hearts in prayer and state our needs.

Praying the Lord's Prayer

"The Lord's Prayer," as Matthew 6:9–13 and Luke 11:2–4 are
known, is a good model to follow when we pray. Jesus bids us to pray
like this, but he does not expect us to quote the prayer word-for-word.
We are to use the prayer as a model of topics to cover in prayer. If
we quote the prayer without thinking about its meaning, then we are
doing the very opposite of what he wants us to do.

When we pray, we are usually quick to get to our requests,
skipping over Jesus' example of addressing God with respect, praising
him and having a kingdom focus. But these other parts of prayer help
us to line up our requests within the will of God. We need to not only

include each part of the Lord's prayer when we pray, but we should consider keeping the order of the prayer as well. Let's break it down into sections to see how we can follow this model.

Address: "Our Father in heaven." At the beginning of the prayer, it is good to remember that we are praying to God in heaven. We often get caught up in the concerns of this world, but God is outside this world. When we speak to God, we are tapping into a power completely beyond us, an otherworldly power. In 2 Corinthians 4:7, Paul refers to it as the "all-surpassing power" of God. As we begin our prayers, we need to pause for a moment and realize whom we are addressing: the Creator of the world, who lives in realms above and beyond us. Because of Jesus, we can approach his throne with confidence—but we cannot forget the power and the majesty of the One who occupies the throne.

Jesus uses the term *Abba* for father. This is the same term that a Jewish child would have used for his or her earthly father. There is no evidence in the Old Testament or Rabbinic literature for anyone using this word to apply to God before Jesus. As far as we know, Jesus was the first person to use it, showing the totally unique relationship Jesus had with God.

However, it also shows that Jesus was teaching his disciples a new way to view God: God as Father. He instructs them to say "*our* Father in heaven" (Matthew 6:9, emphasis added). God is not just Jesus' Father, but he is the Father and *Abba* of the disciples as well. Additionally, "our" indicates that this prayer was to be prayed in fellowship with other disciples.

Interestingly, any time Jesus discusses the forgiveness of sin, he uses the term "your Father," but whenever he speaks of his Sonship or authority, he uses the term "my Father." Since he is here teaching his disciples to pray, he teaches them to say "our Father."

Praise: "Hallowed (holy) be your name." In the ancient mind, to know someone's name was to know his character, which is why names were so important. Therefore, to know the name of God would be to know God. And in their minds, by changing a name, someone's character could be changed. "Knowing the name of God was equivalent to fulfilling the terms of Covenant obligation, because ancient Israelite covenants were solemnly sworn by invoking the name of God."[10]

In the opening of our prayers, we should begin by extolling the greatness of God. His name is holy, and he deserves our praise. We are not very good at praise. See how many ways you can praise the name of God—the psalmists were very adept at this. By studying the Psalms, we can learn wonderful ways of praising God. When we praise God, we see where we stand in relationship to him: he is the

Creator and we are his creation. We must keep this distinction always before us.

Kingdom focus: "Your kingdom come, your will be done, on earth as it is in heaven." It is important to have a kingdom focus in our prayers. Do we pray for the kingdom of God to reign in our lives? Are our prayers focused beyond the here and now of our everyday lives? Do our prayers have an eternal focus? Do we pray for God's kingdom to grow and be manifest among humanity as it is in heaven? Do we pray selfish prayers, or do we take time in prayer to focus on the needs of others? Our prayers need to lift others before the throne of God. Now is the time to remember our evangelist and women's ministries leaders, our elders, our small-group leaders, our close Christian friends, and anyone who requested prayers during the week. It is also the time to remember the churches across the world. We should pray for government leaders and ask for peace so that the gospel can be advanced effectively throughout the world. Do our prayers have an otherworldly focus?

Requests: "Give us today our daily bread." Now is the time for us to lay our requests before God. There is nothing wrong with asking God for the desires of our heart. The apostle James wrote, "You do not have, because you do not ask God" (James 4:2). But we must be sure that we ask for what is within God's will and that we ask faithfully, without doubting. If we ask with doubt, then God promises to answer our request with a "no."

But again, let's not be selfish in our requests. The phrase "daily bread" implies that we are asking for necessities—for things that will sustain us in life. If we need a car, we should pray for a car. But perhaps we should refrain from praying that that car be a brand new, bright yellow Mercedes convertible.

Asking for forgiveness: "And forgive us our debts." Whenever we stand before the throne of God, we should remember that we are sinners. When Isaiah received his call in the presence of God, he protested that he was a man of unclean lips. This is to say that he saw his sins clearly. When we pray, we should remember that is by God's grace that we have forgiveness of our sins, and it is not a gift to be taken lightly. When we lose appreciation for the lengths that God went to in order to offer us forgiveness, we are in a terrible place. By talking about our sinfulness whenever we pray, it keeps this idea in the forefront of our minds.

To be forgiven, we must forgive. How overwhelmingly painful it is to hold bitterness, pain and bad attitudes inside. In Charles Dickens' *Great Expectations,* Miss Haversham spins a web of deception, trying to harm a young man in an attempt to avenge a hurt that she had experienced years earlier. She had been left at the altar by her fiancée, and Miss Haversham wanted this young man to fall in love with her niece, so her niece could break his heart. Her bitterness made her a dark, lonely, depressed old woman whom no one loved. She could not let go of her pain. If we are to get on with life and experience forgiveness ourselves, then we must let go of our pain. Jesus tells us to give it to him because he will bear it for us. Life is too short and precious to weigh it down with needless baggage. Who do you need to forgive in your life? Go ahead and forgive them and close that unresolved chapter in your life.

I have great respect for my father, Glen Kinnard. One characteristic of my dad is that whenever I have heard him pray (and I have been listening to him pray all my life), he always thanks God for forgiveness. He actively applies this part of the Lord's Prayer to his life. How are we doing in this regard?

Forgiving others: "…as we also have forgiven our debtors." As God has forgiven us, we should also forgive those who have wronged us. We need to think through and pray about these potentially difficult relationships.

Also, this is a good time to remember anyone who has trespassed against God and who has not yet been forgiven. We need to pray for those we know who are still living in their trespasses. They might be our friends, our family, our coworkers, our fellow students or recent acquaintances.

Dealing with temptation: "And lead us not into temptation" could also mean "deliver us or save us from temptation." We need to pray that we will be victorious over temptation, remembering of course that God himself does not tempt us; rather, he tests us so that our character will be strengthened. We should not pray to avoid the tests of God however, because it is through them that our character will change. But we should pray that when Satan tempts us, God will deliver us from that temptation.

By telling us to pray this way, Jesus adds another weapon to our arsenal against Satan: prayer. In Matthew 4, we saw that Jesus defeated Satan by quoting Scripture. Together, Bible study and prayer can defeat Satan.

Closing: "For yours is the kingdom and the power and the glory now and forever. Amen." Many of us learned the Lord's Prayer with this doxology on the end. It is based on a prayer of David in 1 Chronicles 29:10–13 and is not found in the earlier, more reliable Greek NT manuscripts. It seems to have been added to some manuscripts in the fifth century.

If we close with this line, we end the prayer in the same way we began: by focusing on the otherworldly nature of God. And we need to try to keep this view of God with us as we face the world around us.

In Matthew 6:14–15, after the Lord's Prayer is completed, Jesus closes his teaching on prayer by underscoring forgiveness. Since God has forgiven us so much, we should naturally want to forgive people who have offended us.

Fasting (6:16–18)

[16]*"When you fast, do not look dismal, like the hypocrites, for they disfigure their faces to show men they are fasting. I tell you the truth, they have received their reward.* [17]*When you fast, put oil on your head and wash your face;* [18]*thus your fasting will not be seen by men but by your Father who is in secret. For your Father who sees in secret, will reward you."*

Fasting is refraining from food so that we can better focus of spiritual matters. Giving and praying are common spiritual disciplines, but how are we doing with fasting? Can we call fasting, abstaining from other enjoyments of life–like television, music, movies and candy? As long as we understand that the strict use of the term "fasting" in the Bible is abstaining from food, then we are safe in stretching the definition to include other things. The key to fasting is to take time to really focus on God.

Fasting from food can be especially helpful in heightening our spiritual senses. Having gone on several fasts, I find that when I fast, I am more focused on the spiritual realm. For example, I can spend the time that I would have spent preparing food and eating meals in reading my Bible and praying. If you have not fasted recently, then decide to go on a two- to three-day fast. See if you are not challenged to grow in ways that you have not thought about before. (If you have a medical condition, then you should check with your doctor before changing your diet. Remember there are other ways to fast than going without food.)

Historically, the Jews fasted on the Day of Atonement. They also fasted during times of mourning or national calamities. During the first century, Jews fasted twice a week — probably on Mondays and Thursdays. (In later centuries, Christians would fast on Wednesdays and Fridays). When some of the first century Jews fasted, they called attention to themselves by rubbing ashes on their faces — so much so that their face was unrecognizable! This was rather ironic since they were calling attention to themselves by painting themselves with ash, yet at the same time they were concealing their identity with the ash.

Jesus restates his warning against hypocrisy in prayer when he speaks of fasting. The disciple of Jesus was to keep his normal appearance during a fast by putting oil on his head, a common practice for that day, and washing his face. By fasting in secret, God would reward him — and us — openly.

Where is Your Treasure? (6:19-34)

¹⁹*"Do not treasure up for yourselves treasures on earth where moth and rust destroy and where thieves break in and steal.* ²⁰*Treasure up for yourselves treasures in heaven, where neither moth nor rust destroy, and where thieves do not break in and steal.* ²¹*For where your treasure is, there your heart will be.*

²²*"The lamp of the body is the eye. Therefore if your eye is sound, your whole body will be full of light.* ²³*If your eye is evil, your whole body will be full of darkness. If then the light that is in you is darkness, how great is that darkness!*

²⁴*"No one is able to serve two lords; for he will either hate the one and love the other, or he will be devoted to one and despise the other. You cannot serve God and money (mamona).*

²⁵*"Therefore, I say to you, do not worry about your life, what you will eat or what you will drink, or about your body, what you will wear.* ²⁶*Look at the birds of the heavens because they neither sow nor reap nor store in barns, and your heavenly Father feeds them. Are you not more valuable than they?* ²⁷*Which of you by worrying is able to add a single hour to his life?*

²⁸*"And why do you worry about clothes? Watch how the lilies of the field grow. They do not labor or spin,* ²⁹*but I tell you that Solomon in all his glory was not dressed like one of these.* ³⁰*But if God thus clothes the grass of the field, which is alive today and tomorrow is cast into the fire, how much greater will he clothe you — you of little faith?* ³¹*Therefore, do not worry, saying, 'What will we eat?' or 'What will we drink?' or 'What will we wear?'* ³²*For the pagans strive after all these things. For your Father knows that you need these things.* ³³*But seek first of all the kingdom of God and his righteousness, and all these things will be given to you as well.* ³⁴*So do not fret about tomorrow, for tomorrow frets on its own. Each day has its own troubles."*

Jesus makes it clear that where our treasure is, our heart will be there also. So find your treasure, and you will find your heart. Or, find where your heart is, and you will find your treasure: they go hand in glove. What is your passion? What do you dream about? Where does most of your time and energy go? If you asked your closest friends, what would they say makes you really happy? If you asked your acquaintances at school or work, what would they say describes you best? The answer to these questions is your treasure or your heart.

19-21 It is very easy for us to think of the "here and now" and difficult for us to think about the hereafter. We have the here and now in our faces all day long. "Buy this! See this! Read this! Wear this!" We need to get away from all that to think of the hereafter.

Jesus shows us the temporal nature of treasures on earth by pointing out that moth and rust can consume them and thieves can steal them. During Jesus' day, elaborate clothing was often used as currency, but moths could easily destroy this treasure. Precious metal was also used as currency, but rust could tarnish this metal, causing it to lose its value. Houses were made of mud brick, and thieves could easily break through these walls and steal a person's valuables.

In our day and time, earthly treasure is just as temporary. Styles change overnight. We hide our money behind bank safes and watch inflation eat away at it. The stock market is terribly fickle. The only really safe place to store our treasure is in heaven. In heaven nothing can get at our treasure—not moth, rust, thieves, inflation, stock market scams or even the taxman. Heaven is the only secure place to store our treasure.

Jesus is not against having a savings account or saving for your child's college education. He warns not to store up treasure "for yourselves," implying storing selfishly. He also warns against storing up for self and leaving God out of the picture. The disciple gives to God first and uses what he has left in a wise way.

22-23 Jesus now draws a contrast between the good eye and the evil eye. In the first century mind, the eye was the window to the soul. What we allow into our eyes will influence the way we live our lives. Jesus is using Hebrew antithetical parallelism here by stating opposites. He defines what the evil eye is: selfishness and greed. The sound eye would be the opposite of that: generosity, giving and selflessness. Greed brings darkness, while generosity brings the light of God into our lives. In the context of treasures, Jesus is teaching us that we need to have a generous spirit with what God has given us.

24-34 Jesus introduces a principle that he repeats throughout his ministry: We cannot serve two lords. In this context, one lord is the Lord God and the other lord is money. The Aramaic word *mammon* means "money, wealth or possessions." The word "serve" can also be translated "slavery." "To serve or be a slave of" implies total devotion. You cannot be totally devoted to two masters. You can serve one or the other, but not both. Jesus is telling us that we must make the choice between serving God or money.

If we serve God, will he take care of us? Jesus answers yes—we are not to worry about what we will eat, drink or wear. To illustrate this, Jesus uses two examples from nature. First, he mentions birds, which do not grow their own food, yet have plenty to eat from his hand. Second, he mentions "the lilies of the field." These are purple flowers similar to the color of the royal robes that King Solomon would have worn. Yet Solomon's regal, elaborate dress paled in beauty next to the lilies. Therefore, Jesus reassures us that God will provide for us, so why should we worry? Worry does not add anything to our lives—in fact, it takes away.

Matthew 6:33 has not changed in the last twenty years (or the last two thousand). It still reads, "But seek first his kingdom and his righteousness, and all these things will be given to you as well." Jesus centers in on what is really important, what our priorities should be.

Personally, I look at "his kingdom" as the relationships that I have with people on this earth, thinking of them as "horizontal" connections. Thus, to seek the kingdom first of all means that I place a priority on relationships with others in the church and also with those outside the church. I look at "his righteousness" as the "vertical" relationship that I have with God, who is my superior. If I take care of the vertical relationship and the horizontal relationships in my life, then God will take care of everything else. This is his promise, but it is also his challenge. Try it and see what happens!

Another way to view kingdom and righteousness is to view them as a synonymous parallelism. In this view kingdom and righteousness would be the same thing. To seek the kingdom and righteous of God is the same as seeking God. In other words, are we God-focused? Are we preoccupied with God? Is God first in our lives?

The conclusion of this section is: Do not worry! Take each day one day at a time.

Judge Not (7:1–6)

⁷:¹ *"Judge not, so you will not be judged. ²For in what judgment you use to judge, you will be judged. In what measure you use to measure, it will be measured to you.*

³"Why do you look for the splinter in your brother's eye and do not notice the log in your own eye? ⁴How can you say to your brother, 'Allow me to take the splinter from your eye,' when you have a log in your own eye? ⁵Hypocrite, first take the log out of your eye. Then when you can see clearly, you can take the splinter from your brother's eye.

⁶"Do not give what is holy to dogs; do not cast pearls before swine. They will trample them under their feet and turn and tear you apart."

7:1-2 "Do not judge." By judging, Jesus does not mean that we cannot discern right from wrong in the actions and teachings of others. If so, he would not tell us a little later to "watch out for false prophets" (7:15). What does he mean? He wants us to guard against a critical, negative, cynical outlook that fails to find the good in people. He also wants us to guard against judging the motives of others. We cannot read hearts and must be very careful when we attempt to discern what is in the heart of another person.

Jesus warns us that when we are critical, that same level of criticism will judge us on the last day—but it is also true in this life. If we are critical of others, then we need to get ready, because they will be critical of us. In whatever ways we judge others, they will use those same measures to judge us. It reminds me of the saying, "Don't dish it out if you can't take it." If you view others cynically, then others will view you the same way. If you pick people apart, then get ready, because you will be picked apart.

3-5 Jesus paints a comical picture of the man who is a hypocritical judge. He is busy trying to take a speck of sawdust out of someone else's eye, while a huge two-by-four is stuck in his own. He can barely approach the other person with this gigantic plank in his own eye, but he does not let this stop him from being a critical judge. How ridiculous we look to God when we behave this way! There is nothing worse than a bitter, critical, judgmental hypocrite who is so busy looking at the minor faults of others that he cannot see the major flaws in his own life. Jesus warns us to not fall into this trap.

6 Jesus also warns us to be discerning when it comes to offering spiritual guidance and advice to people. He uses synonymous parallelism to illustrate this: "Do not give dogs what is sacred; do not throw pearls to pigs." The pearls are being equated with what is holy because holiness is valuable. Yet, dogs and pigs would have no idea of the value of pearls. Therefore, before we give spiritual guidance to people, we need to make sure they want to receive it and understand its value.

This principle especially holds true with family and old friends who are not spiritually minded. I have made this mistake before. I remember years ago when some friends were asking a rhetorical question about what to do in a particular situation. They were not looking for spiritual advice, but I thought I would give it anyway—big mistake on my part! They definitely trampled my choice pearls into the ground.

The Search (7:7–11)

> [7]*"Ask and it will be given to you; seek and you will discover; knock and the door will be opened for you. [8]For everyone who asks receives. He who seeks discovers. And the one knocking on the door — it will be opened for him.*
>
> [9]*"Is there a person among you that if his child asks for bread, will give him a stone? [10]If he asks for a fish, will you give him a snake? [11]If you, being evil, know how to give good gifts to your children, how much more will your Father in heaven give good gifts to those who ask him!"*

7-8 Asking, seeking, and knocking are all metaphors for prayer. That the prayer is persistent is implied in the use of the present tense of the verb. Continual, persistent prayer will be answered.

9-11 Since God is a loving Father, he wants to answer our prayers. If earthly fathers are concerned about meeting the needs of their children, then think how much more our heavenly Father wants to meet our needs. What keeps us in want? Is it our lack of devotion to God? God tells the prophet Jeremiah, "You will seek me and find me when you seek me with all your heart" (Jeremiah 29:13).

But we must not think that the spiritual journey to God is a walk in the park. It is the best life to live, but it is not an easy life. The easy life is the life that leads to destruction — it's a wide road and traveled by many. The way of the few, the way to life, is narrow and difficult. But is there anything worthwhile in life that comes easily? At the end of the difficult path is eternal life, therefore the path is worth taking.

Summary of Jesus' Ethics: The Golden Rule (7:12)

> [12]*"So in everything, whatever you wish for men to do for you, you do for them. This is the Law and the Prophets (the Scripture)."*

12 The sum of Jesus' ethics, as seen in the Sermon on the Mount, is found in the phrase, "Do to others what you would have them do to you." Think of how different the world would be if all humanity lived by this one rule. Supposedly, the Roman Emperor Alexander Severus (222-235 AD) had this rule written in gold on his palace walls — thus, "The Golden Rule." The Golden Rule is unselfish love in action. It is the way that we all want to be treated, and the way Jesus wants us to treat other people. It should be a distinguishing mark of a Christian.

Practically Speaking ∝

Wholehearted Prayer

As a doe longs for running streams,
    so longs my soul for you, my God.

My soul thirsts for God, the God of life;
    when shall I go to see the face of God?
– Psalm 42:1–2, **The Jerusalem Bible**

Prayer is a yearning to see God. The person who prays hungers and thirsts for God.

Only God Satisfies

In the Bible a hunger for God always ends in prayer. Psalm 143:6 says, "I spread out my hands to you; my soul thirsts for you like a parched land." The psalmist obviously strongly desired to be close to God and his desire lead him to prayer. Similarly, Psalm 84 begins,

How lovely is your dwelling place,
    O Lord Almighty!
My soul yearns, even faints
    for the courts of the Lord;
my heart and my flesh cry out
    for the living God. (Psalm 84:1–2)

This psalmist longs to enter the court of God and worship at his dwelling place. He feels an absence from God and cries out to be in God's presence. This urgent feeling of isolation and abandonment leads the psalmist to pray: "Hear my prayer, O Lord God Almighty; listen to me, O God of Jacob" (Psalm 84:8).

The reason we urgently go to God in prayer is because we believe that only he can satisfy our spiritual hunger. We have tried to find satisfaction by other means. We turn to sports, work, pleasure and fame. Yet as the preacher in Ecclesiastes noted, all these pursuits are "a chasing after the wind" (Ecclesiastes 1:14, 17; 2:11, 17, 26; 4:4, 16; 6:9).

God invites us to find satisfaction in him. Isaiah 55:1 reads, "Come, all you who are thirsty, come to the waters; and you who have no money, come, buy and eat! Come, buy wine and milk without money and without cost." He freely offers us the most satisfying elixir of life. Once we taste his potion, nothing else compares. Isaiah 58:11 states, "The Lord will guide you always; he will satisfy your needs in a sun-scorched land and will strengthen your frame. You will be like a well-watered garden, like a spring whose waters never fail."

Desiring to Be Alone with God

Many people fail to have satisfying prayer lives because they are double-minded when they pray. On one hand, they believe God's promises, but on the other, they doubt. The apostle James teaches, "That [doubting] man should not think he will receive anything from the Lord; he is a double-minded man, unstable in all he does" (James 1:7–8). If we are not wholeheartedly devoted to God and believing him, then our prayers will not be effective.

To wholeheartedly pursue God, we must rid ourselves of any distractions, which might keep us from focusing on him. Our prayer times need to be "holy time"—set apart and free from any disturbance. We should find a place that we can call our own, away from the phone or the computer or the door. We need to let our families know that prayer time can only be disturbed by an emergency. Unless we passionately fight for time alone with God, it will not happen.

The Blessings of Persistence

When we pray, it allows God to work powerfully in our lives. The Scriptures say, "You do not have because you do not ask God" (James 4:2). And Jesus said, "Blessed are those who hunger and thirst for righteousness, for they will be filled." When we passionately ask God for his blessings, he richly blesses us. This was also true of the nation of Judah: "All Judah rejoiced about the oath because they had sworn it whole-heartedly. They sought God eagerly, and they found him. So the Lord gave them rest on every side" (2 Chronicles 15:15). When they sought God wholeheartedly and eagerly, then he blessed them.

Sometimes we must wrestle in prayer to receive the blessings of God. If we desire a blessing wholeheartedly, then we will be willing to wrestle for it. Jacob, the son of Isaac, wrestled an angel for a blessing. Genesis 32:26 says, "Then the man said, 'Let me go, for it is daybreak.' But Jacob replied, 'I will not let you go unless you bless me.'" Jacob received his blessing because he wrestled for it. God blesses the persistent heart.

Many religious teachers before Jesus had taught this rule in its negative form: "What you do not want done to you, don't do it to others." But apparently, Jesus is the first one recorded as saying it in the positive form, which makes a huge difference. To obey it in the negative requires us to do nothing, but to obey Jesus' Golden Rule requires action: we must actively treat people the way we want to be treated. This moves us to make the world around us a better place.

The Two Roads (7:13–14)

¹³"Enter through the narrow gate, because the gate is wide and the road is broad that leads to destruction. There are many who take it. ¹⁴But the gate is small and the road is narrow that leads to life, and few find it."

13 There are only two paths in life. One leads to destruction and the other leads to life. The road to destruction is broad and easy. It is easy to navigate and well traveled and is the way of comfort and complacency.

14 The road to life is completely opposite. It is difficult and challenging and traveled by a few. It is the road of discipleship, of placing the mission of Jesus above our own desires. Which road are you on?

The Two Trees (7:15–20)

¹⁵"Beware of false prophets, who come to you in sheep's clothing, but inside they are ravenous wolves. ¹⁶You will know them by their fruit. Do people pick grapes from thorns, or figs from thistles? ¹⁷Thus, every good tree produces good fruit, and the bad tree, evil fruit. ¹⁸A good tree is not able to produce evil fruit, nor is a bad tree able to produce good fruit. ¹⁹Every tree that does not produce good fruit is cut down and cast into the fire. ²⁰Thus, you will know them by their fruits."

15-16 We can know people by their fruit. In this context, Jesus is telling us to be on our guard against "false prophets." False doctrine has flooded our world. We have to be careful to discern between false doctrine and sound doctrine because false doctrine kills. Satan deceives many into believing what is false. Next, Jesus warns that not everyone who says, "'Lord, Lord' will enter the kingdom of heaven" (Matthew 7:21). In fact, many that prophesy in his name, drive out demons, and work miracles will not make it into heaven. But aren't these great works evidence that a person must be right with God? Not according to Jesus. Jesus says *the* discriminating factor is whether or not a person is following the will of God. We cannot trust modern prophecy or miracles to determine God's will today. The only way to know if we are following God's will is to know what the Bible says.

17-20 Just as there are two roads, there are also two types of trees and two types of fruit. One tree produces good fruit, and the other tree produces evil fruit. We cannot have good fruit and bad fruit growing on the same tree. By looking at our fruit, we can determine what type of tree we are. But make no mistake, there are only two types of trees: good and bad.

When I was a boy, I used to listen to an album that my father owned by an old country preacher named Marshall Keeble. I remember Mr. Keeble talking about people telling him to not be judgmental in his preaching. They would say, "Mr. Keeble, the Bible says, 'Do not judge.'" Mr. Keeble would reply, "Soon after Jesus said, 'Do not judge,' he also said, 'By your fruit you will know them.'" Mr. Keeble then added, "I'm not a judge—I'm just a fruit inspector!"

Two Types of Followers (7:21–23)

[21]*"Not everyone who says to me, 'Lord, Lord,' will enter the kingdom of heaven, but only they who obey the will of my Father in heaven.* [22]*Many will say to me on that day, 'Lord, Lord,' we prophesied in your name, in your name expelled demons, and in your name we performed powerful miracles.'* [23]*And then, I will declare to them, 'I never knew you, go away from me you lawless people.'"*

21-22 There are two types of followers. One follower calls Jesus "Lord" and does his will. The other follower calls Jesus "Lord," but does not do his will. To tell what kind of a follower a person is, we must look beyond his works. His works might look fantastic—prophesying, expelling demons and working miracles—but what about the real discerning characteristic: is he doing the will of the Father? This is how we can tell if he is a true follower.

23 To do the will of the Father is to follow the teachings of the Bible. We must do things God's way. We can do many great things, but if we fail to do them God's way, then they are unacceptable to him. In fact, they are more than just unacceptable—Jesus calls them evil. On the judgment day many will protest their innocence, essentially saying, "But we prophesied for you, cast out demons for you and performed amazing miracles for you." Jesus will look at them and calls them evildoers. What they do is evil because it is outside God's will. Their mighty works end up confusing people because they do not draw people to the word of God.

Two Types of Builders (7:24–27)

[24]*"Everyone who hears these words of mine and does them, is similar to a wise man who built his house on the rock.* [25]*And the rains fell, the floods rose, and the winds blew and beat against that house. The house stood because it was built on a rock.*

[26]*"And everyone who hears these words of mine and does not do*

them is similar to a foolish man. He builds his house of the sand. ²⁷The rains fell, the floods rose, and the wind blew and beat against that house; and it fell with a great crash."

24-27 Jesus closes the Sermon on the Mount by emphasizing the need to put his word into practice. It is not enough to just hear the word—we must change. This is illustrated in a masterful way with the Parable of the Wise and Foolish Builders. The difference between them was their choice of foundation. The difference between the foundations is not that one is built on the word and the other on something else, like hedonism, gnosticism or stoicism. The difference in the foundations is that the wise man built by hearing the word and putting it into practice, while the foolish one built by just hearing the word. Hearing is not enough: we must be doers of the word. The proof of our faith is in the way we live our lives.

The Conclusion: Jesus As a Teacher (7:28–29)

²⁸When Jesus finished saying these words, the crowds were amazed at his teaching, ²⁹for he taught them as one with authority and not as their scribes.

28-29 What did the people notice the most about Jesus as a teacher? Was it his beautiful ways of illustrating his points? Was it the flawless logic he used to reach his conclusion? Was it the immense vocabulary he showered upon them as he spoke? The one thing that impressed them the most was his authority—"He taught as one who had authority, and not as their scribes." Authority and confidence are closely linked. Jesus knew who he was and he knew that his message came from God. For this reason, he spoke confidently about God, about the meaning of life and about the nature of true spirituality—and people were impressed with his confidence.

Do we know who we are? Do people take note of something different in our lives? Do we live confident lives? Do we say things with authority because we know we are living out what we are talking about? What impresses people is the life that backs up the words. Jesus had both the life and the words; therefore, people were impressed with him.

Endnotes

[1] Albright and Mann, p. 43

[2] Carson, p. 132.

[3] Dietrich Bonhoeffer, *The Cost of Discipleship*, 6th ed. (London: SCM, 1959), p. 119.

[4] Ibid.

[5] For a more detailed discussion on marriage and divorce, see the material in Section 6.

[6] Carson, p. 162.

[7] Albright and Mann, p. 76

[8] Ibid.

[9] Ibid.

[10] Ibid, p. 78.

3

Ministry in Galilee
Miracles, Ministry, and
Messianic Activity
Matthew 8:1-12:50

The genuine realist, if he is an unbeliever, will always find strength and ability to disbelieve in the miraculous, and if he is confronted with a miracle as an irrefutable fact he would rather disbelieve his own senses than admit the fact. Faith does not spring from the miracle, but the miracle from faith.
– Fyodor Dostoevsky, Russian novelist

Why should we follow Jesus? Matthew has just demonstrated that Jesus is a powerful teacher, different from the scribes because he taught with great authority. Matthew lists other reasons: we should follow Jesus because he has the power to heal various sicknesses, he has power over nature and over demonic forces, he causes the blind to see and the mute to talk. As if this were not enough, Jesus raises the dead. Intermingled with these stories of the power of Jesus are lessons on discipleship. Jesus is King. To follow him, we must follow as he directs.

The Power to Heal Various Sicknesses (8:1-17)

Jesus came to make people whole. He ministered to people through healing. Jesus cleansed the leper, made the lame to walk again, and caused the blind to see. He healed the outer person and the inner person. Jesus also reached out to those outside the circle of Israel. He wanted everyone to be whole.

Jesus heals a leper (8:1-4)

8:1When Jesus came down from the mountain, large crowds followed him. 2A leper came bowing before him and said, "Lord, if you wish you have the power to cure me."

3Jesus reached out his hand and touched him, saying, "I wish. Be clean." And immediately his leprosy was cured. 4Jesus said to him, "See that you tell no one, but go and show yourself to the priest and offer the gift which Moses commanded as a testimony to them."

Jesus begins by healing a leper. The word for leprosy (*lepra*) could mean any of several types of dreaded skin disease, such as psoriasis, elephantiasis, or vitiligo. Known as Hansen's disease and treatable today, in the first century, leprosy was one of the most feared diseases. Lepers were outcasts, ostracized and shunned by society. They were called "the walking dead." Along came Jesus with the power to heal them.

When this leper approached Jesus, he asked for cleansing. This was forbidden. The leper was supposed to stay in the leper community. If he did have to venture out, he was to shout "Unclean! Unclean!" as he approached people. When priests and rabbis heard a leper shouting this, they would run and hide to keep from becoming unclean.

Jesus did not hide. Even so, I imagine the last thing the leper expected was for Jesus to reach out and touch him (Leviticus 13-14). How long had it been since this leper was touched in this way? And why would Jesus reach out and touch the leper, knowing this would make him unclean? Because as soon as he touched the leper, the leper became clean. Nothing that Jesus touches is unclean; whatever he touches becomes clean. Therefore he did not break a law by touching an unclean leper, he superceded it by cleansing the leper.

Jesus tells the leper to tell no one and to offer the cleansing sacrifice at the temple. Why would Jesus tell the man not to tell anyone what he had done for him? After all, Jesus' mission was to preach the good news. Shouldn't he expect the man to testify to what Jesus had done for him? This action of Jesus is often described as the Messianic secret. Jesus wanted to have the freedom to travel from village to village and preach the scriptures to people. Too much exposure too early in his ministry would hinder that. Instead of being able to preach the Scriptures, he would have to spend all his time healing. In addition, if the Roman authorities were alerted to his miraculous works, they might come and seize him, which would hinder his preaching. Jesus performed miracles to help people, and Jesus loved to help people. But he did not want to be known as a miracle worker. He was a rabbi and he wanted to teach people the good news of the kingdom of God.

Interestingly, many times when Jesus told people not to mention their healing, they went out and told everyone. Jesus cures them, and he makes one request (or command): Don't tell anyone. The first thing they do is they tell everyone. Why? Their intent was not disobedience; they simply demonstrated uncontrollable gratitude. When Jesus cures you from the walking death, you have to tell someone. In fact, you have to tell everyone! The message burns inside you until you have to share it. Is this how we feel about what Jesus has done for us in our lives? Do we feel that we have to tell everyone what Jesus has done?

Jesus heals the Centurion's servant (8:5-13)

⁵When Jesus entered Capernaum, a centurion came to him, asking for help. ⁶"Lord," he said, "My servant lies at home paralyzed and in terrible pain."

⁷Jesus said, "I will come and heal him."

⁸The centurion answered, "Lord, I am not worthy to have you come under my roof. Only speak the word, and my servant will be healed ⁹For I am a man under authority, having soldiers under me. I tell one, 'Go,' and he goes. I tell another, 'Come,' and he comes. And to my slave, 'Do this,' and he does it."

¹⁰When Jesus heard him, he marveled and said to those following him, "I tell you the truth. I have found no one in Israel with such faith. ¹¹I say to you, many will come from the east and the west and will eat with Abraham, Isaac, and Jacob in the kingdom of heaven. ¹²But the children of the kingdom will be thrown out into the darkness where there will be weeping and grinding of teeth."

¹³Then Jesus said to the centurion, "Go, it will be done just as you have believed. His servant was healed at that hour."

What would it take to astonish Jesus? This is an interesting question. Matthew 8 gives an answer. Normally the local Jewish population hated centurions, Roman army officers with 100 soldiers at their command. The centurion who lived in Capernaum had helped build the synagogue there and had garnered respect from the local population. He came to Jesus requesting that his servant be healed. He felt he did not deserve for Jesus to come into his home since he was a Gentile and a man of authority. Because of this man's faith, the text says that Jesus "was astonished." He declared that he had not found such faith in all of Israel. Have you ever thought that you could astonish Jesus? With great faith, we can astonish the King.

The centurion was a Gentile. Jesus' statement "I have not found anyone in Israel with such great faith (*pistis*)," opens the door to the Gentile mission. Faith in the God's word is often synonymous with confidence and trust. The centurion had faith that if Jesus would just speak a word then his servant would be healed. His faith stood in contrast to the Jewish authorities that asked Jesus for a sign. Although in his lifetime he was committed to go to the lost sheep of Israel, he did not intend to exclude the Gentiles from his kingdom. Encounters like this one demonstrate that it was always in his plan to offer salvation to the Gentiles. After his resurrection, this part of his mission would become clear to his disciples.

In Luke's account, the centurion sends a delegation to ask Jesus to heal the servant. Matthew describes the centurion going out to meet Jesus. Many see a discrepancy here, but just because Luke does not mention the centurion meeting Jesus, does not mean that he never did. Both accounts can be reconciled if the centurion sent a delegation to prepare the way, and then went to meet Jesus himself.

Jesus heals many at Peter's house (8:14-17)

[14]When Jesus came into Peter's house, he saw Peter's mother-in-law lying in bed with a fever. [15]He touched her and the fever left and she got up and served him.

[16]That evening they brought to him many demoniacs and he cast out their spirits with a word and healed all the sick. This was to fulfill the word of the prophet Isaiah, saying:

[17]"He took our weaknesses
And carried our diseases."

Peter was born in the village of Bethsaida; he moved to Capernaum and lived with his mother-in-law there. Jesus is thought to have used Peter's house as his central headquarters in Galilee. In Capernaum, archaeologists have uncovered houses that date to the first century. One of these houses was venerated in antiquity as the house of Simon Peter. It is possible that this is the very house where Jesus stayed when he was in Capernaum.

Jesus healed Peter's mother-in-law. We do not know the type of fever she had, but we do know that when Jesus touched her hand, the fever left her. How did she respond? She immediately got up and began to serve Jesus and the disciples. That is a great response to Jesus' gift.

That evening many sick and demon-possessed people came to Jesus, and he healed them "with a word." This demonstrates the power of the word of Jesus. The Greek for word is *logos*. From John 1:1 and John 1:14, you learn that Jesus is the *logos*. Jesus lived out the word in his life and his words were powerful. What was the purpose of "the Word"? The Bible gives several goals of the *logos*:

1. The Word will judge us on the last day.
   The Bible teaches that there will be a judgment day.
   On that day Jesus' Word will judge us (John 12:17-50).
2. The Word cleanses us (John 15:1-4).
3. The Word produces faith (Acts 4:1-4).
4. The Word gets us ready for baptism (1 Peter 1:22-25).

Again, Matthew uses the fulfillment formula to demonstrate that Jesus is the fulfillment of Old Testament prophecy, his healing ministry proves that Jesus is the Messiah. He quotes Isaiah 53:4, "He took up our infirmities and healed our diseases." Isaiah 53 is one of the four "suffering servant" songs in Isaiah. Jesus is the suffering servant who heals the suffering of people, coming to the earth to suffer for humanity.

The Cost of Discipleship (8:18-22)

¹⁸When Jesus saw the great crowds around him, he gave orders to go to the other side of the lake. ¹⁹A scribe came to him saying, "Teacher, I will follow you wherever you go."

²⁰Jesus answered, "Foxes have holes, and birds of the air have nests, but the Son of Man has nowhere to lay his head."

²¹Another disciple said to him, "Lord, permit me first to go and bury my Father."

²²Jesus answered, "Follow me and let the dying bury the dead."

His healing ministry was becoming a hindrance to Jesus' mission of preaching the good news. There was such a throng of people coming to Capernaum that Jesus gave orders to go to the eastern side of the lake.

After establishing his authority to heal the sick, Jesus encounters two individuals who ask questions about discipleship. The first is a scribe, a teacher of the law, he is ready to follow Jesus wherever he goes. Jesus answers him that his journey will not be easy. Eduard Schweizer makes a great point here:

> Thus to follow Jesus is in fact to step forth into insecurity, because the one in whom God comes to men has no home among men; they fail to recognize him. Therefore the follower of Jesus is promised nothing more than the opportunity to join the Son of Man in his insecurity and share his fate.[1]

Jesus had no place to lay his head. To follow him means to accept his fate.

This is the first time in Matthew's gospel that we see the term "Son of Man" used to describe Jesus. This title, the one Jesus uses most often to refer to himself, is another Messianic reference. It occurs in Daniel 7 as an apocalyptic figure who comes in the clouds. "Son of Man" in the Hebrew, *bar nasa*, is the term that means "man." It emphasizes the humanity of Jesus, but is very ambiguous. It reveals and conceals. Of all the titles that Jesus could have used to describe himself, he chose the one that underscores his humanity.

Another disciple asks Jesus for permission to bury his father before continuing on the path of discipleship. Jesus responds, "Let the dead bury the dead." In Hebrew and Aramaic, "dead" can also mean "dying." In that case this could be translated, "Let those who are dying bury the dead." Jesus tells the man to let the spiritually dead bury those who are physically dead. This strikes us as a harsh answer, which only makes sense if the man were offering Jesus an excuse for not following him. Jesus wants us to love our families and be there for them in times of trouble and distress, but he is unwilling to accept any excuse for not being his disciple. Jesus establishes that following him must be our number one priority.

Power Over the Forces of Nature, Calming the Storm (8:23-27)

²³When Jesus got into a boat, his disciples followed him. ²⁴There was a great storm on the sea, so the boat was being swamped by the waves, but Jesus slept. ²⁵They went, and woke him, saying, "Lord, save us! We're going to die!"

²⁶Jesus said, "Why are you afraid? You of little faith!" Then he got up and rebuked the winds and the seas and there came a great calm.

²⁷The men were amazed, saying, "What type of man is this that the winds and the sea obey him?"

Having taken a brief interlude to share some challenging points on discipleship, Matthew returns to proving the kingship of Jesus. Why should we follow Jesus? Because he has power over the forces of nature, power over the demons, and the authority to forgive sin. As the disciples are crossing the Sea of Galilee, a storm overtakes them, a common occurrence on the Sea of Galilee. Located in the bottom of a basin, the Sea of Galilee is 650 feet below sea level and is surrounded by hills. Winds can quickly build into storms in this environment. The word used for storm here can be translated "earthquake." This was a severe storm that threatened the lives of everyone on the lake.

Where was Jesus while this storm was raging? He was asleep in the back of the boat. When the need arose, he woke up to respond to it. As Lord over nature, Jesus was not worried about the storm, but his disciples were. They woke him, fearing for their lives. Jesus was more concerned with their faith. He rebuked the wind and the waves, and all was completely quiet. The disciples marveled at this asking, "What kind of man is this that even the winds and the waves obey him?" What kind of man is this? This is the King of Kings.

Interestingly, several years ago when there was a drought in Israel, the Sea of Galilee dropped to a level that enabled people to see a boat that had been on the bottom since the first century. With painstaking care, archaeologists recovered the boat, and it can be viewed in a kibbutz on the western side of the Sea of Galilee today. The boat is called "the Jesus boat" because it is similar to the kind of boat that Jesus and his disciples would have sailed on the Sea of Galilee. There is room for a man to curl up and take a nap. Could this be the boat that Jesus rested in? If it is, it sank on a subsequent trip, since the disciples' boat did not capsize, as they had feared!

Jesus heals the Gadarene Demoniacs (8:28-34)

28When he went to the other side into the region of the Gadarenes, two demoniacs came to him from the tombs. They were so violent that no one could pass that way. And suddenly they cried out, saying, 29"What do you have to do with us, Son of God. Have you come here to torment us before the time?"

30Some distance from them a large herd of pigs was feeding. 31The demons begged Jesus, "If you cast us out, then send us into the herd of pigs."

32He replied, "Go." So they came out and went into the pigs. And the entire herd rushed down the steep bank into the sea and drowned in the water.

33Those who saw this ran away, and went into the city reporting everything that happened to the demoniacs. 34Suddenly, the entire city came to meet Jesus and seeing him they begged him to leave their region.

After Jesus calms the storm, the boat lands on the eastern shore of the Sea of Galilee in the land of the Gadarenes. This was part of the Gentile Decapolis, a ten-city region controlled and populated by the Romans. Upon arriving, two demon-possessed men run from the tombs encountering Jesus. In Mark's gospel only one man runs out to meet Jesus. Were these two events or one event told in two different ways? I believe that it is the same event told from two different perspectives. Mark uses the telescopic lens and zooms in on the one man while Matthew uses the wide-angle lens and writes about both men. Matthew also might have included the second man in his depiction because the Jews demanded two witnesses to verify an event.

Nevertheless, Jesus casts the demons out of the men and into a heard of swine. Some wonder why there were pigs, an unclean animal, in this area. Archaeologists have dug on both side of the Sea of Galilee. On the western side of the sea, the Jewish side, mostly lamb bones and very few pig bones have been excavated. On the eastern side, the Roman side, they have found huge mounds of pig's bones. There were many Romans in this area, and Romans loved pork.

After Jesus sent the unclean spirits into the pigs, they rushed down the hillside and drowned in the lake. The whole town was upset by the event, and they asked Jesus to leave their area. Not everyone is going to understand Jesus and receive him with open arms. This rejection foreshadows the way Jesus will later be rejected by the multitudes and eventually crucified.

Some people invariably get upset about the fate of the pigs, just as the townspeople did back then. Why would Jesus allow all these pigs to die? This question might seem silly, but when taken seriously, the answer further illuminates the point of the story. Some believe that Jesus allowed the death of the pigs to demonstrate how evil the demons were. The dumb beasts had no free will to resist the demons, and rushed headlong to their death. The men who had been tortured by these demons could resist them to the point of harming themselves and stop short of the point of death. Yet they were powerless to cast the demons out. Jesus had the power to heal them, and he did, in a way that leaves us no doubt as to the evil intent of these demons that were bent on death and destruction. It is ironic that in the presence of this evil, the townspeople's fear was focused not on the demons, but was misdirected towards the one who could save them (Luke 8:37).

The healing of the paralytic (9:1-8)

¹Jesus got into a boat and crossing the sea came into his own town.

²Some people brought to him a paralytic, lying on a mat. Jesus, seeing their faith, said to the paralytic, "Take heart, son; your sins are forgiven."

³Certain scribes said to each other, "This man blasphemes!"

⁴But Jesus, knowing their thoughts, said, "Why do you think evil in your hearts? ⁵Which is easier to say, 'your sins are forgiven, or rise and walk.' ⁶But so that you will know that the Son of Man has authority on earth to forgive sin"–he then said to the paralytic, "Rise, take your mat and go home." ⁷He got up and went to his home. ⁸When the crowds saw this, they were filled with awe and glorified God who had given such authority to men.

After Jesus goes back to the other side of the lake, to his "own town," Capernaum, a paralytic is brought to him to be healed. The man was lying on a mat, which could be lifted and used as a stretcher for the man. The fact that friends had to bring the man to Jesus shows how helpless he was, unable even to bring himself to Jesus. But Jesus can provide help in seemingly helpless situations.

Jesus sees their faith. This could be the faith of the men carrying the paralytic and the faith of the paralytic himself. Faith is a central ingredient to the healing stories. Jesus heals people who demonstrate their faith in him. To be healed, they must put their trust and confidence in him.

Jewish rabbis taught that sickness was a result of sin. In John 9, Jesus' disciples ask, "Who sinned, this man or his parents, that he was born blind?" Jesus does not draw a connection between sickness and sin. In this story, as in all the healing stories, Jesus is concerned about healing the spiritual sickness of the person as much as the physical sickness. Seeing this man's faith he says, "Your sins are forgiven."

The scribes consider this blasphemy. They know that only God has the power to forgive sin. Jesus does not back down, and proves he has the power to forgive sin by healing the man. Jesus claims to have the authority that only God had. In doing this, Jesus demonstrates his divinity and his kingship.

The Call of Matthew (9:9-13)

⁹*Walking along Jesus saw a man sitting at the tax booth, named Matthew. Jesus said to him, "Follow me." Matthew got up and followed him*

¹⁰*Jesus sat down to dinner in the house, and many tax collectors and sinners came and sat with Jesus and his disciples.* ¹¹*The Pharisees saw this and said to his disciples, "Why does your teacher eat with tax collectors and sinners?"*

¹²*When he heard this, he said, "The healthy have no need for a doctor, but the sick do.* ¹³*Go and learn what this means–I want mercy and not sacrifice. For I did not come to call the righteous but sinners."*

Proof of the kingship of Jesus is interrupted again to give another lesson on discipleship. The lesson comes in the call of Matthew, a tax collector, to be an apostle. Matthew means "gift of God." He worked at a tax booth that was most likely located just north of Capernaum on the border between the territory of Herod Antipas and Herod Philip. Anyone crossing this border was expected to pay a tax. Jewish society looked upon tax collectors as thieves and Roman collaborators. Jesus steps across the social morass of his time and calls Matthew to be one of his disciples. Matthew leaves everything behind and follows Jesus.

Time and again Jesus shows that he has little regard for social conventions. Here he eats with tax collectors and sinners. The tax collector was looked upon as a thief because they padded their income by overcharging for taxes. They were looked upon as ceremonially unclean because they handled currency that had graven imagery on it. This party presumably occurs in Matthew's house, demonstrating that he made a good living from collecting taxes. The house must have been large to accommodate "many people," probably thirty or forty.

People begin to talk about Jesus, but he does not care. He quotes from Hosea 6:6, "I want mercy and not sacrifice." This is introduced by another rabbinic formula, "Go and learn." often used by rabbis to challenge their students. "Mercy" is close to the concept of covenant love. God loved Israel in spite of how Israel acted. Despite her rebellion, God loved her. The Hebrew word is *hesed*. My Hebrew professor, Dr. Emil Scoggins, translated this word "the mercy, love and grace of God."[2] God desires this more than sacrifice. He wants us to demonstrate to others mercy, love and grace. This is exactly what Jesus was doing when he ate with the tax collectors and sinners, demonstrating God's mercy, love and grace for them. Jesus lived out the concept of *hesed* throughout his life. He let it be known that he came to call sinners, and not the righteous, to repentance.

A Question about Fasting (9:14-17)

[14]Then the disciples of John came to him saying, "Why do we and the Pharisees fast often, but your disciples do not fast?"

[15]Jesus answered, "The guests of the bridegroom do not mourn when the bridegroom is with them. The day will come when the bridegroom will be taken from them, then they will fast."

[16]"No one sews a piece of unshrunk garment on a new garment. For the patch will pull away from the garment making the tear worse. [17]Neither do men put new wine into old wineskins. If they do the skin will burst, and the wine will spill out and the skin will be destroyed. Put new wine in new skins, and so both can be saved."

John's disciples, who at this point should be following Jesus, come to Jesus with a question about fasting. They ask why Jesus' disciples do not fast. John's disciples practiced fasting. The Pharisees fasted twice a week. Isn't fasting a sign of spirituality, something that distinguishes the committed from the uncommitted? Jesus never taught that we should perform religious acts as an end in themselves. Fasting is a spiritual practice you only use it to draw closer to God.

There was no need to draw closer to God as long as Jesus walked with his disciples. He was right there with them, bringing joy into the lives of those he touched, bringing something new and fresh into a stale "works-oriented" religion, bringing grace to people's lives. Why should they fast while he was there? We should enjoy our relationship with God. Discipleship should be a joy and not a burden. Worship should be uplifting. If we cannot laugh and enjoy life as disciples, then something is wrong.

Practically Speaking ∞

Discipling From the First Word

Have you ever felt at a loss for words to open a conversation with someone? This can be especially difficult when you intend to share with people about the church. "Would it be best to be subtle or blunt?" "I could start with the weather and then bring the conversation around to the real target." "Maybe I could just write a letter?" Words often elude us.

How would you feel if a complete stranger walked up to you, opened his mouth, and the first words out of his mouth were, "Follow me." You realize he is not saying, "Please, come follow me." Neither is it, "Would you please follow me?" This is not a request; it is a command: "Follow me!" I imagine we would be caught off guard.

Maybe Matthew felt surprised when Jesus walked up to him and demanded, "Follow me!" Matthew had his job to think about. He was a federal worker. Surely the Roman government would expect some type of notice before he quit. What would his family and friends think? They might not have been too happy with him being a tax collector, but surely it was better than giving up his job to follow a Rabbi. Where was Jesus leading him? How much should he pack? How long would he be away? Matthew might have been asking himself questions like this.

Jesus discipled people from the first word. Never did he have a conversation without challenging or encouraging people to think about their relationship with God. Unabashedly and unapologetically he called people to an immediate response of discipleship. Jesus never pleaded or begged for people to follow him. He was looking for immediate obedience. Whether from Peter and Andrew leaving their fishing nets behind or James and John leaving their father Zebedee in the boat, Jesus called for and received an immediate response. He never flinched when he asked people to give up everything to follow him.

Jesus knew that people were not doing him a favor by following him; he was doing them the greatest favor of all by calling them to discipleship. He asked his followers to give up sin, the world, darkness and hell, in order to receive forgiveness, the church, light and heaven. Jesus knew his words were truth and his way righteous.

We can feel differently however. We look at the things that people must give up to be disciples and wonder if they can do it or not. We think, "He is so tight with his family, how can he become a Christian?" We ask, "How can she give up that man she's been with for five years?" We wonder, "How can he ever change that temper? Surely, he'll never change."

It is our point of view that must change. We must view everyone outside of Jesus as if they were in a house on fire. They have no comfort or security where they are. We need to warn them to flee the house and come to the security that only God can offer.

Once a person leaves a burning house, no one congratulates them for what they gave up. "Wow, what a great burning house you gave up." "How could you leave a house like that?" "Hey, I'm really proud of you for getting out of that burning house." How ridiculous does that sound? Yet, that is often how we respond to people when they become Christians. We act like they are doing God a favor.

When people simply make the right choice, no praise is deserved. When they make the decision to become disciples, they are leaving the dung heap of the world to come to a banquet. They are just making a wise, solid, and righteous decision. As we approach non-Christians, we need to have the same confidence Jesus had. We need to influence them from the first conversation, giving them much to think about. Jesus exerted this kind of influence on people.

If Jesus were here today, he would still challenge people to follow him from his first word. He would unapologetically call people out of their burning houses into safety. His confidence would impact people. Why should it be any different for us?

First Century Insights ∾

Zealots

The Zealots became organized in AD 6 under Judas the Galilean who refused to pay taxes and started a small-scale revolt against Rome. The Zealots were extremists who fought against Rome. They sought to overthrow the Romans, believing that success would usher in a Messianic community. They were one of the major causes of the Jewish-Roman War between AD 66-70.

Sicarii

The word, *sicarri,* means "a dagger" or "short sword." The *Sicarri* was a secretive, extremely radical group whose members came to be known as the dagger men. An assassination club who vowed to kill Romans at every opportunity, they were very active during the Jewish uprising of 66 to 70 AD.

Jesus does forecast that a time of fasting is coming, when he will be "taken from them." This is an allusion to his death. He only broaches the idea to his disciples here. Later on he will begin to clearly teach about his death and his resurrection. But this was not the time.

Jesus uses two examples to clarify the difference between the Pharisee's approach to worship verses his approach. The Pharisees are weighed down by legalism. They miss the joy of worship. They keep ceremony, but fail to celebrate. To try and graft the approach of Jesus onto this Pharisaical approach would be like sewing an unshrunken patch of new cloth onto an old garment or putting new wine into old wineskins. This is a recipe for disaster. The new is not compatible with the old, and will eventually destroy it. Jesus did not spend much time explaining his actions to the Pharisees, knowing that their hearts were not prepared to accept him. He went to find the hearts that would accept him.

A Dead Girl and a Sick Woman–Power over Death and Incurable Disease (9:18-26)

[18]While he was saying these things to them, a ruler came in and bowed before him saying, "My daughter has just died. Come and lay your hand on her and she will live." [19]Jesus rose and went with him and his disciples followed along.

[20]Suddenly a woman who had suffered from a hemorrhage for twelve years came up behind Jesus and touched the fringe of his cloak. [21]She said to herself, "If only I can touch his cloak, I will be healed."

[22]Jesus turned and said to her, "Take heart, daughter, your faith has healed you." And the woman was healed from that hour.

[23]When Jesus entered the ruler's house, he saw the flute players and the noisy crowd and [24]he said, "Go away, for the girl is not dead, but asleep." But they laughed at him. [25]After the crowd had been put outside, he went in and took the girl's hand, and she got up. [26]The report of this went throughout the region.

Even as Jesus demonstrates his power over death and incurable disease, he shows how deeply he cares for each individual and their circumstances in life. A synagogue ruler, Jairus, asks Jesus to heal his dying daughter. On his way to Jairus' house, a woman with an incurable hemorrhage approached Jesus. She approached Jesus believing that if she could just touch his garment, then she would be healed. She reached out and touched his garment.

Jesus felt her touch. What would he do now? Would he continue on his way to heal the girl on her deathbed, like a modern-day ambulance driver, in great haste, lights flashing and siren blasting? Jesus did not only want to heal people's physical pain, he wanted to heal their spiritual pain as well. He wanted people to be whole. So he stopped and took time to talk to the woman. He healed her disease and touched her heart at the same time.

What can we learn from this? We can get caught up, living our lives at top speed in the hustle and bustle of a frantic world, feeling that there is no time for distractions or interruptions. The things we do are important: raising kids, working jobs, going to school, studying the Bible with people. Are we willing to drop what we are doing to meet the needs of people around us? Jesus was on an important mission! He was going to heal a dying pre-teen. But he stopped the ambulance and took the time to meet the needs of a woman who had felt helpless for years. He was aware of her when she reached out and touched his garment. Are we aware when people are reaching out for help? Do we stop to meet the needs of others? Sometimes it is difficult to determine what is really important. Setting godly priorities takes wisdom, which comes from prayer, experience, and wise counsel. Before we can set priorities, we need to see the needs around us. Let's be sure to have our eyes open for opportunities to help other people.

Jesus arrived at Jarius' house to find that the girl has just died. A crowd of hired mourners and flute players had gathered. Was it a mistake to stop and help the woman? No. Jesus had the power to bring the girl back from the dead. In fact, he did not even consider her dead, only sleeping. Jesus told the mourners to go away, that they are not needed. The mourners laughed, but Jesus was not joking. He went inside the house and brought the girl back from the dead, demonstrating his power over death.

Healing the Blind (9:27-31)

[27]*As Jesus went on from there two blind men followed him crying out, "Son of David have mercy on us!"*

[28]*When Jesus entered the house, the blind men followed him and Jesus said to them, "Do you believe I have the power to do this?"*

They answered, "Yes, Lord."

[29]*Then he touched their eyes and said, "It shall be done according to your faith."* [30]*And their eyes were opened. Jesus sternly ordered them, "See that no one knows of this."* [31]*But they went out and spread the news over the entire region.*

Two blind men approached Jesus, calling out, "Have mercy on us, Son of David." For the first time, people call Jesus "Son of David." Most visually unimpaired people have not recognized Jesus as king, yet these two blind men see him clearly. They desire for him to make them whole. Jesus replies with words that would become familiar ones, "According to your faith it will be done."

How much faith do we have? Do we believe that God has the power to do great things in our lives? Remember the words of Jesus, "According to your faith it will be done."

Jesus tells the blind men not to tell anyone about their cure, asking them to respect the "Messianic secret" as discussed earlier. Notwithstanding Jesus' stern order to remain quiet, the two men spread the news of what Jesus did for them over the region. They had to speak. How could they keep to themselves what Jesus had done for them? They couldn't help but share what had happened to them.

Healing the Mute (9:32-34)

³²*After they went away, a demoniac who was mute was brought to him.* ³³*When the demon was cast out, the mute man spoke. The crowds were amazed saying, "Never has anything like this been seen in Israel."*

³⁴*But the Pharisees said, "By the ruler of demons, he casts out demons."*

Demon possession had many manifestations in the Gospels. It made people crazy, caused them to hurt themselves, and caused physical disabilities. In this story, a demon caused a man to be mute. The Greek word is *kophos*, and can mean "deaf," "mute," or "deaf mute." He was brought to Jesus, even needing help to get there.

Jesus cast out the demon out of the man, a miracle that amazed the crowds. Nothing like that had ever occurred in Israel.

The Sending of the Twelve (9:35-10:42)

Jesus chooses men of all grades and from all classes. No man in the group is like any of his comrades, and no one of them is like Jesus. There is a mercurial man, Peter; and there is a lymphatic man, Thomas. There is a fire-eater, Simon Zelotes, a member of the fieriest political party in Palestine; and there is the prosaic and slow-going Philip. There is a man of good family and spotless reputation, John; and by his side is a man with a tarnished name, Matthew, the publican. All temperaments are here and all combinations of mental faculties; and here are representatives from various classes and differing social strata. In doing a wide work you must have a broad instrument, and the Christian church, as it left the hands of Jesus, embraced in its membership the types of men which would be able to open all the doors.

–Charles Edward Jefferson, **Jesus the Same**

Here is Matthew's second long discourse of Jesus; the first was the Sermon on the Mount. This one centers on the ministry of Jesus. Jesus sends his twelve disciples throughout the region of Galilee to carry on his ministry. As we study this section, we can gain great insight into how we should carry on the ministry of Jesus today. I especially want to share some insights that I gained during my year on a mission team in Israel.

The need for workers (9:35-38)

35Jesus went about all the cities and villages teaching in their synagogues and proclaiming the good news of the kingdom and healing every disease and every sickness. 36When he saw the crowds he had compassion on them because they were harassed and helpless as sheep without a shepherd. 37Then he said to his disciples, "The harvest is plentiful, but the workers are few. 38Therefore ask the Lord of the harvest to send workers into his harvest."

What moved Jesus to go from city to city and from village to village, teaching, preaching, and healing? Compassion. What should motivate us to go from neighborhood to neighborhood and from house to house, teaching, preaching, and healing? Compassion. Jesus saw the people as sheep without a shepherd, harassed and helpless. The word for "harassed" comes from the Greek, *eskulmenoi*, and means "to flay or to skin." It is often translated as "distressed, worried, trouble, or harassed."[3]

The word for "helpless" is *eppimmeno*, and it means, "to be cast down either from drunkenness or from a mortal wound."[4] This is the condition of sheep without a shepherd. Without guidance, they could easily wander from their green pastures or get eaten by predators. Their future is full of danger. The same can be said about people without Jesus. They are helpless, without guidance. Their future is a scary prospect.

Unlike sheep, people can mask their helplessness with fine clothes, money, a successful career, a smile, and look like they have it all together. But Jesus says that on the inside, they are like sheep without a shepherd. Many look successful at first glance. But when you start digging through the veneer, there is bitterness, sadness, and hurt. People don't want to look like helpless sheep. So they find dozens of way to whitewash their helplessness.

We have to be able to see that without Jesus everyone is helpless, without guidance, and without a future. We must be moved by compassion.

Jesus readies his followers for a mission to let the nearby towns and villages know the good news of the kingdom. The directives that he gives them are found in the next section. Since every disciple is a missionary, we should all pay close attention to what Jesus teaches here. As I discuss this material, I will share some of the lessons that my wife, Leigh, and I learned as we led a mission team in Jerusalem.

When we landed in Israel we knew only a few people there, and those not very well. We had to quickly get to know the disciples there so that we could go out two-by-two as partners.

How do you get close to disciples? How do you forge unity? Unity comes from working together. We had to learn about the culture in Israel. The disciples taught us about the culture. We also had to lead the disciples. So we started teaching them what we knew about ministry. There was so much to learn and to teach, on both sides. We had to learn about the languages, Hebrew and Arabic. We had to learn about different foods, gefelte fish and *maklubah*. We had to learn how to approach people. Should we be direct or indirect? These things could be very confusing. After months of walking a tightrope between the Jews and the Arabs, I came to a startling discovery.

The discovery happened in a restaurant on *Ben Yahuda Rehov* in Jerusalem, where I had teamed up with a good friend to reach out to people in Israel. We were at a table trying to enjoy and meal and have a conversation. At the table next to us were six young Americans who were having a very loud conversation. They were not only loud, they were rude and obnoxious, the stereotypical expatriate Americans, talking about sports, soap operas on television, and even about the endings of movies that I had not had the opportunity to see.

Seeing these Americans act rude, crude and offensive made a light go on in my head. I suddenly saw that I had been walking this tightrope between the Jewish and the Arab cultures, all the while being an American who would never be looked on as anything other than an American. Americans are infamous for trampling conventions. I should just relax, be myself, and share the good news with people. It was liberating to realize that I should just be myself. People didn't expect me to become Israeli or Arab. I could not do that anyway. I should just show them love. Love was the key. People weren't looking for me to adopt their culture; they were looking for love. I stopped trying to be what I thought everyone wanted me to be, and I began to just be myself. This was a valuable lesson.

My friend and I learned this lesson, then we went out to apply it. It is great having someone to work with. We went out two-by-two to share with people, the way Jesus planned for missionaries to go. If one person gets down, the other person lifts their spirits. If one is having a bad day, the other picks them up. Who is your partner in evangelism? If you don't have one, get one. This is a key to doing great things on Jesus' mission team.

The Twelve (10:1-4)

[1]Jesus called his twelve disciples to him and he gave them authority over unclean spirits to cast them out and to heal all disease and every sickness.

[2]The twelve apostles names are these: first, Simon called Peter, Andrew his brother and James the son of Zebedee and John his brother. [3]Philip and Bartholomew, Thomas and Matthew the tax collector, James, the son of Alphaeus and Thaddaeus. [4]Simon the Zealot and Judas Iscariot who betrayed him.

This is the first and only time Matthew refers to the twelve as "apostles." The word *apostolos* means, "one sent on a mission." The term apostle is used in at least two ways in the scriptures. It is used as a technical term for the twelve whom Jesus called into his inner circle at the beginning of his ministry in Galilee. After Judas' death reduced their number to eleven, Matthias was chosen from among those who had followed Jesus and witnessed his ministry from the beginning, to bring the number back to twelve. The term was also used in an unofficial way of anyone who is sent on a mission; others who were not a part of the twelve were sometimes referred to as apostles because they had accepted the mission of Jesus.

The list of the twelve is found in all four gospels. When you compare the different lists of apostles, certain facts begin to emerge. (1) Peter always begins the list of the apostles. Matthew begins his list by saying "first, Simon called Peter." Peter seems to have been the natural leader of the apostles, but "first" here probably means first among equals.[4] (2) The first four names in each list are always the two pairs of brothers: Peter and Andrew, James and John. (3) Judas Iscariot is always the last person named in each list. (4) Simon the Zealot is the same person as Simon the Canaanite. (5) Judas the son of James is the same person as Thaddaeus. (6) Bartholomew is often identified with Nathaniel of John 1:46. (7) Thomas is also known as Didymus, which means "twin."

D.A. Carson has made an interesting observation after comparing the lists of the apostles in the four gospels. He writes:

> In each list there are three groups of four, each group headed by Peter, Philip (not to be confused with the evangelist), and James the son of Alphaeus respectively. But within each group the order varies even from Luke to Acts!), except that Judas is always last. This

suggests, if it does not prove, that the Twelve were organizationally divided into smaller groups, each with a leader.[5]

This suggests that Jesus began his ministry with a practical structure–the twelve divided into three groups of four with a leader over each group.

On a mission, you have to know your team. We can't all be Peter, but someone needs to take charge. If you look in the group that Jesus selected, you see people from all kinds of backgrounds, twelve individuals with different personalities. When you read through the gospels, you can see how much bickering went on in the circle of the apostles. Jesus had to take these individuals and form them into a team. This comes by working together.

The Mission: Ambassadors of Peace (10: 5-15)

[5]Jesus sent out the twelve on a mission, instructing them, "Do not go the way of the Gentiles and do not enter the town of the Samaritans. [6]Go rather to the lost sheep of the house of Israel. [7]Go and preach saying–the kingdom of heaven is near. [8]Heal the sick, raise the dead, and cast out demons. You received freely; freely give. [9]Do not take any gold or silver or cooper in your belts, [10]no bag for your journey and don't take two tunics, or sandals, or a staff. For the worker is worthy of his keep.

[11]Whatever town or village you enter, search for some worthy person in it and stay there until you leave. [12]As you enter the house, greet it. [13]If the house is worthy, let your peace remain on it. If it is not worthy, let your peace return to you. [14]Whoever does not welcome you or listen to your words, shake the dust off your feet when you leave that house or town. [15]I tell you the truth – it will be more tolerable for Sodom and Gomorrah on the day of judgment than for that town."

The apostles were directed not to the area of the Gentiles or the Samaritans, but exclusively to the lost sheep of the house of Israel. This was not the time for the mission to the Gentiles. That would come, but for now the mission was to the Jews.

The message was simple: the kingdom of heaven is near. The Jews were expecting the arrival of the Messianic kingdom, and the apostles were to get them ready for it. This is the same message of John's ministry, the same message of Jesus' ministry. As they go, they are to perform good works to demonstrate the power of God: healing the sick, raising the dead, and casting out demons. Jesus tells them, "You have received freely, now freely give." This could be a practical admonition not to take money for their miraculous signs, (although they could accept hospitality), or it could be an admonition to have a certain attitude: we have been given so much, and we are to give to the people around us.

Jesus then gives specific instructions not to take gold, silver, or copper, but to trust that God would take care of them on their journey. They were not to take two tunics, sandals or a staff. The adjective "two" applies not only to tunic, but also to sandals and staffs. Jesus did not expect them to walk barefoot without a walking stick. They could take what they needed, but not extra. They were to rely on God. This interpretation allows Matthew's and Mark's accounts to be harmonized. In Mark, Jesus allows them to take nothing but a staff, sandals, and one tunic, and in Matthew, Jesus allows the same.

Then Jesus directs the seventy-two that if they are received into a home, they bring their peace to that home. If they are turned away, they leave in peace, but they do not leave their peace behind.

Peace is a wonderful thing. The Old Testament concept of peace (*shalom*) means "wholeness in life." It is contentment, security, and confidence. In the land of *Shalom* today, Israel, there is little peace. It is a very tense place. Every time a car backfires people jump. If you see a bag on the sidewalk you fear it's a bomb. Jews do not get along with Arabs. Arab Muslims do not get along with Arab Christians. The denominational Jewish Christians (Messianics) do not get along with the denominational Arab Christians. The different churches are always quarrelling over something. It is a country full of division, disunity, hatred and fighting.

The Church of the Holy Sepulcher, which is considered to be the holiest site in Christianity, exemplifies this atmosphere of disunity. Five religious groups share the space of the Holy Sepulcher. Each group believes that Jesus was crucified and buried there. The Greek Orthodox, the Syrian Orthodox, the Roman Catholic, the Coptic and the Armenian churches cannot agree over the use of the building. They cannot agree when to open and close the door. Therefore a Muslim family has held the key to the building for hundreds of years. These churches cannot agree on repairing parts of the building. So the building fell into such a state of disrepair that the Israeli government had to step in and repair it. Not many years ago, on the "Festival of Joy," fistfights broke out between the Greek Orthodox and the Armenians over who should stand where. This is not an unusual occurrence. There is no peace in this shrine.

The Jews and the Arabs have been fighting for centuries. One afternoon my son Daniel and I were enjoying an American hamburger at Burger King on Ben Yahuda Street in downtown Jerusalem. We left to pick up my daughter Chelsea from school. As we neared the school, we noticed dozens of official vehicles speeding by us with sirens blaring out. Police cars, army jeeps, ambulances, and emergency vehicles were headed toward Ben Yahuda Street. We discovered that not fifteen minutes after we had left; a bomb had exploded right outside the Burger King where we had lunch. Several people died in the explosion. We had missed the bomb by fifteen minutes.

A month later we traveled with our good friends, the Lawrence's, to Bethlehem to see the Church of the Nativity where many believe that Jesus was born. We could not enter the church on this day because a funeral was being held for a young Arab man who had been shot by Israeli soldiers. We had supper instead, and afterwards we started to drive our rented van back to Jerusalem.

Suddenly we found that we had driven into the closing scene of a riot. People were carrying clubs and rocks, and stones littered the street. Our van had Hebrew lettering all over it. Often these vans are overturned and burned. I held out my American passport and yelled, "American citizens! American citizens! Can anyone speak English?" A man dressed in a beautiful suit walked up and in perfect English said, "We are finished here; you can drive on through."

I drove to the Israeli checkpoint and saw a barbed-wire fence had been spread across the road, and the checkpoint was closed. An Israeli solider pointed a rifle in my face and asked what I was doing there. He was visibly upset. I told him that I was an American citizen with an Israeli visa, and I just wanted to take my children home. He rolled back the wire and let us through. We were fortunate that night.

In a place of unrest, a place without peace, disciples bring peace. The disciples in Palestine are unique. Only when the disciples meet can you hear hymns sung in Hebrew and Arabic. Only the disciples serve communion to Jews and Arabs. One Jewish solider attended a party given by the disciples said; "I've never seen this much color in one room." Disciples reach out to everyone. Disciples show love to everyone. We painted the walls of the Four Houses of Mercy, an Arab hospital in Bethany. We picked up trash in a Jewish neighborhood. We took Jews with us to paint the Arab hospital, and we took Arabs with us to pick up trash in the Jewish neighborhood. What we are doing is different. If you want to find peace, *shalom*, in Israel, you can find it where there are disciples.

Great Motivation and Great Authority (10:16-33)

16"Indeed, I am sending you on a mission as sheep in the midst of wolves. Therefore be wise as serpents and innocent as doves. 17Be on your guard against men. They will hand you over to councils and flog you in their synagogues. 18And you will be brought before governors and kings because of me to testify to them and to the nations.

19When they hand you over, do not worry about how you will speak, for I will give you in that hour what you will say. 20For it is not you who speak, but the spirit of your Father speaking through you.

[21]Brother will betray brother to death and a father his child and children will rebel against their parent and have them killed. [22]And because of my name all will hate you. But he who remains steadfast unto death will be saved. [23]When they persecute you in one town, flee to another, I tell you the truth–you will not have gone through all the towns of Israel before the Son of Man comes.

[24]A student is not above his teacher; nor a servant above his Master. [25]It is enough for the student to be like his teacher and the slave his Lord. If they have called the master of the house, 'Beelzebul,' how much more those in his household."

Jesus warns them that their mission is not without danger. Many will not want to hear their message. As sheep among wolves, they must be wise. They are not agitators. They are not to make people mad just to get a reaction. I've heard people in campus ministries instruct people to "just go in there and shake things up." Jesus teaches against that here. The message itself will "shake things up." We need to get the message across as effectively as we can. If we shut people down before they hear what we are saying, is that effective?

Jesus wants us to be as wise as serpents and as innocent as doves. The word for wise in the Greek is *sophia* and is also translated "shrewd" (NIV), and the word for "innocent" (*akeraios*) also means "pure, unmixed." A common misconception is that "shrewd" and "pure" are opposites. This is not so! The opposite of "shrewd" is not "pure" it is "naive!" We can and we must be shrewd and pure at the same time. The message is that we need to be shrewd in how we present the gospel, and we must be unmixed in our purpose to get the message of Jesus to the nations.

Jesus prepares his apostles for the future: arrests, floggings, facing governors and kings. Their mission was not to be an easy one. But God would be with them. They could take comfort in that, and not worry about what to say, because God would give them the words they needed.

Local magistrates would hand them over, and their own families would turn them in, all because they had embraced the mission and message of Jesus. But no matter who turned against them, they should stand strong. Because if they did, in the end they would be saved

Verse 23 is an interesting verse. Jesus told the apostles that when they were persecuted in one place to flee to another, and this is exactly what the early disciples did. But then Jesus says, "You will not finish going through the cities of Israel before the Son of Man comes." The coming of the Son of Man is a metaphor for judgment. Some say that this refers to Jesus coming after his resurrection, and it could mean that. Others (like Rudolph Bultmann) say that Jesus made a mistake here, that the early church expected Jesus to come back in his lifetime, and when he did not, there was great confusion.

But the early church did not show signs of confusion. Some people, including a group in Thessalonica, did misinterpret what Jesus said and expected a quick second coming of Jesus, but Paul straightened out their misunderstanding. If we take this verse and harmonize it with Matthew 24, we see that Jesus uses the metaphor to refer to the future judgment of Israel in the form of the destruction of the temple in Jerusalem. Thus, the Son of Man did come in judgment of Israel through the Roman army sacking Jerusalem and destroying the temple in AD 70.

Jesus warns the apostles not to be surprised by the harsh treatment they will receive. They are not above their teacher; just as Jesus will receive harsh treatment, so will they. Jesus has already been called Beelzebul, the prince of demons. The apostles can expect the same treatment.

Do not fear men (10:26-33)

26"Do not fear them. There is nothing concealed that will not be revealed or nothing secret that will not become known. 27What I tell you in the dark, speak in the light, and what you hear whispered, proclaim from the rooftops. 28Do not fear those who kill the body, but cannot kill the soul. Fear him who can kill body and soul in Gehenna. 29Are two sparrows not sold for a penny? And not one of them falls to the earth apart from your Father's will. 30Even the hairs of your head are all counted. 31Do not fear. You are of greater value than all the sparrows.

32Everyone who confesses me before men, I will confess before my Father in heaven. Everyone who denied me before men, I will deny before my father in heaven."

Persecution will come. Times will get tough, but we should not fear men, who can kill the body, but cannot kill the soul. The one we should fear is God because he is able to destroy both body and soul. *Gehenna* was the Hinnon Valley south of Jerusalem, site of human sacrifices in Old Testament times and a continually burning garbage dump in the time of Jesus. *Gehenna* became synonymous for hell, the place with unquenchable fire.

The Greek text reads that you are of greater value than "many" sparrows. But this is a Semitism, a figure of speech where "many" means "all." As God cares for the sparrows, he will watch out for us.

After all he keeps count of all the hairs on our head. This shows how much value we have in God's eyes. One of my favorite devotional books is *Shout for Joy* by David Head. In the book, Head places these words in the mouth of an angel:

> 10,467; 10,464; 10,463 (steady, man; anger won't get you anywhere) 10,390; Lord, counting hairs as they fall out is the dullest of occupations. But if doing this helps one of Thy anxious children to know his value in Thy sight, I will not begrudge the labor. By his knowledge that I count, may he know he counts![6]

We do count. And we can count on God's promise that no matter how intense things get around us, he will take care of us.

Therefore we should confess Jesus before men fearlessly. We need not be intimidated. As a disciple of Jesus on the mission field in Israel, it was only too easy to be intimidated. It is a harsh, rude place. I love it, but the people there are tough. The culture is tough. We had to just push back our insecurities and remember we were there to share with people. There are many anti-missionaries in Israel. Their task is to track down people who are trying to convert Jews to Christianity and see that they get kicked out of the country. These men would sometimes show up at our worship services. It was very tempting during those times to water down the message, to speak on an Old Testament verse and not mention Jesus. Some advised us to do that, but we could not. We had to trust that if God wanted us to stay in the country, then he would work it out for us to stay there.

Not peace, but a sword (10:34-39)

[34]"Do not think I have come to bring peace to the earth. I have not come to bring peace, but a sword. [35]For I have come to turn–

A son against his father

A daughter against he mother

A daughter-in-law against her mother-in-law

[36]A man's enemies will be of his own household.

[37]Anyone who loves father or mother more than me is not worthy of me. Whoever loves son or daughter more than me is not worthy of me. [38]Anyone who does not take up his cross and follow me is not worthy of me. [39]Whoever finds his life will lose it, and whoever loses his life for my sake will find it."

Jesus did not come to bring peace, but a sword. Most Jews believed that the Messiah was going to restore past glory to Israel and usher in a time of peace. Jesus says, "Not so." He came bringing spiritual peace, but he never guaranteed physical peace.

The peace that Jesus brought would be disruptive, especially within the family. Jesus knew that in this culture, family ties were tight. Sons were expected to follow the traditions of their fathers. Daughters were to please their mothers. We faced the same culture when we lived in the Middle East. Extended families lived in a single home. When a child got married, an extra room was built onto the house for the new couple. Everyone was expected to be a part of the same religion: Christian, Muslim or Jew. Christians within the family were to go to the same church: Catholic, Anglican, Lutheran, etc. If you changed your religious practice, you left the family. Often a funeral was performed for someone who went against the wishes of the family. It was and is intense. But Jesus said it would be that way. We must realize that the message of Jesus is a disruptive message.

Rewards (10:40-42)

⁴⁰Whoever welcomes you, welcomes me; and whoever welcomes me, welcomes he who sent me. ⁴¹Whoever welcomes a prophet in the name of a prophet will receive a prophet's reward. And whoever received a righteous man in the name of a righteous man will receive a righteous man's reward. ⁴²Whoever gives even a cup of cold water to one of these little ones in the name of a disciple, I tell you the truth, will not lose his reward.

Jesus closes his second discourse with encouraging words about the positive reception that his disciples will receive and the reward they can expect. Although the mission will be tough, some people will welcome them as prophets and will receive a prophet's reward.

The harvest is plentiful and the workers are few. This is a promise of Jesus. But Jesus also taught that there are different types of soils: some hard, some stony, some thorny and some good. In Israel, we studied the Bible with as many people as we could. The Arab Christians valued tradition over the word of God. Their denominational churches often control where people live and even where they are buried. One woman wanted to know where we would bury her when she died, since we did not own a cemetery. I tried to assuage her fear, telling her that we would have her cremated and would take her wherever we went. This didn't satisfy her.

We kept trying. One night I was feeling pretty down. I had studied the Bible with yet another person who decided he did not want to be a disciple. I remember reading Galatians 6:9, "Let us not grow weary in doing good, for at the proper time we will reap a harvest if we do not give up." This verse helped me see that God is in control of the harvest. My job is to not grow weary in doing good deeds. I went out the next day with a renewed sense that it was enough for me to be doing good deeds wherever I went.

A few weeks later we studied the Bible with a couple who did want to become disciples. Some Arab friends of ours stopped up one end of the Pool of Siloam, the same pool where Jesus told the blind man to wash his eyes. After it filled with water, we baptized this couple in the Pool of Siloam. We were able to take part in this glorious event because we decided not to grow weary in doing good. This is a lesson that I will take with me the rest of my life. Do good deeds, keep meeting people, keep sharing, love people, and God will give the increase.

Jesus and John the Baptist (11:1-19)

¹When Jesus had finished instructing his twelve disciples, he went on from there to teach and to preach in their cities.

²When John, who was in prison, heard what Christ was doing, he sent his disciples ³to ask him, "Are you the one coming or are we to wait for another?"

⁴Jesus answered, "Go, repeat to John what you hear and see. ⁵The blind receive sight, the lame walk, lepers are cured, the deaf hear, the dead are raise, and good news is preached to the poor. ⁶Blessed is the one who does not stumble because of me."

⁷As John's disciples went away, Jesus began to speak to the crowds concerning John, "What did you go into the desert to see–a reed shaken by the wind? ⁸What did you come to see–a man dressed in fine clothes? Those dressed in fine clothes live in king's palaces. ⁹What did you come to see? A Prophet? Yes, I tell you, and more than a prophet. ¹⁰This is the one about whom it is written:

Indeed, I send my messenger ahead of you,

Who will prepare your way before you.

¹¹I tell you truthfully, no one born of woman has risen who is greater than John the Baptist. But the least in the kingdom of heaven is greater than he. ¹²From the days of John the Baptist until now, the kingdom of heaven has been enduring violent assault and the violent take it by force. ¹³For all the prophets and the law prophesied until John. ¹⁴If you are willing to accept it–he is Elijah who was to come. ¹⁵Whoever has ears, listen to this.

¹⁶To what can I compare this generation? They are similar to children sitting in the market place calling to teach other, saying:

¹⁷We played the flute for you

And you did not dance.

We mourned

And you did not cry.

[18]For John came neither eating nor drinking and they said – 'he has a demon'. [19]The Son of Man came eating and drinking and they said – 'See, he is a glutton and a drunkard, and a friend of tax collectors and sinners'. But wisdom is justified by her works."

Verse 1 includes the same formula that was used to conclude the Sermon on the Mount: *kai egeneto hote etelesen ho Jesous,* "When Jesus had finished instructing..." Jesus has completed his second discourse, and the mission begins. He leaves to teach and preach in nearby villages and towns. The apostles apparently leave to teach and preach as well.

John the Baptist was now in prison, in a fortress on the eastern side of the Dead Sea. He sends his disciples to Jesus to ask him, "Are you the one who was to come (*ho erchomenos*), or should we expect someone else?" Has John forgotten the time that he baptized Jesus in the Jordan? Does he doubt Jesus now? Perhaps, like the other disciples of Jesus, John was expecting a different type of Messiah, a different type of king. Perhaps he is having trouble believing that the Messiah, coming in the name of the God he had served for so many years, would allow him to suffer in prison. The phrase "someone else" (*heteron*) shows that John does have someone else in mind.[7]

Jesus sends John's disciples back with this report–the blind receive sight, the lame walk, those who have leprosy are cured, the deaf hear, the dead are raised, and the good news is preached to the poor. This is the legacy of Jesus. If they are expecting a modern, apocalyptic Messiah that will kick the Romans out of the land and restore the economic, military and political might of Israel, then they are expecting the wrong person. Jesus is the Messiah that was written about in the Prophets. In Jesus, the Old Testament Messianic prophecies are fulfilled.

The fact that the Bible records the weakness of the great men and women of faith argues strongly for it's being an inspired book. If the early church were promoting a hoax, why include the story where John the Baptist has doubts about the man he had earlier proclaimed to be "the Lamb of God"? Because we see that even a heroic man like John the Baptist had moments of weakness, we can identify with him, and we can more easily believe that we too can do great things for God. This is part of the glory of the Bible, the power of the word of God.

John the Baptist had dark and troubling times in prison. He sent his disciples to Jesus, so that he could reaffirm his faith in Jesus. If a great prophet like John the Baptist can have moments of doubt, what does that say about you and me? We too will be plagued by dark and troubling times. When that happens, we too must return to Jesus to reaffirm our faith. We must read the Gospels, reflect upon the life that Jesus lived and his death and resurrection. This is the way to strengthen our convictions in Jesus and overcome moments of doubt.

Jesus does not hold John's doubts against him. He knows that John is in prison in fear for his life. Instead he holds John up as an example. Jesus asks the crowd what they expected to see when they went out to see John in the wilderness. Did they expect a reed blown about by the wind, someone without conviction? Did they expect to see someone in fine clothes of the king's court? Here Jesus gives a subtle rebuke to King Herod who imprisoned John. John did not wear the rich, purple robes of the king. No, John was tough. He was bold. He lived by his deep convictions. He stood up to religious hypocrites. He stood up to Herod, which is why he was in prison. John was a prophet

11 Jesus says that of everyone born throughout human history, John was the greatest. This must have shocked his audience. Was John greater than Abraham? Was John greater than Moses? Was John greater even than King David? Jesus answers, "Yes." But his next statement was even more shocking: the least member (*ho mikroteros*) of the kingdom of heaven is greater than John. What can this mean? Some believe the phrase "the least" refers to Jesus. But this would be a very awkward way for Jesus to speak of himself. I believe he is referring to anyone who follows him. They are greater than John because they will be privileged to be a part of the kingdom. They will experience what the prophets only anticipated. They get to live out in the present tense what John and the prophets could only talk about in the future tense. The least in the kingdom is greater than John because they have witnessed the fulfillment of prophecy. They no longer have to await the Messiah and the Messianic kingdom. They are a part of the Messianic reign of Jesus.

12 This verse has caused much confusion over the years, and has been interpreted in many ways. Part of the confusion comes from the ways the verse has been translated. The NIV translates this verse, "From the days of John the Baptist until now, the kingdom of heaven has been forcefully advancing, and forceful men lay hold of it." Many people take this to say that the kingdom needs forceful men to advance it. Therefore, if you are not forceful, you will not advance the kingdom. To take it a step further, if you are anything less than forceful, then you are not advancing the kingdom and are not a part of the kingdom. This verse has been used as a club to attack anyone who was weak, insecure, introverted, or otherwise not deemed "forceful." It has made those who have a type A, extroverted personality feel superior. But this interpretation is based on an inferior translation of this verse.

The word translated "forceful" is *biazto*. This word appears twice in this verse once as a verb and once as a noun. The verb *biaztetai* is the middle or passive voice. In the middle voice it means "to apply force or to enter with force." In the passive voice, it means, "to suffer violence, to be treated violently."

The NIV uses the middle voice in their translation. But in the context of the imprisonment of John, the comparison of John with the prophets, and the attacks on Jesus' character it is better to use the passive voice here and translate the verb, "suffering violence."

The noun *biastes* means "violent men, ones who use violence." This noun connotes violence. It is followed by the verb *harpazousin*, which means "to rob, to lay hold of, to take by force, to snatch away." This verb also connotes violence and rapacity. These words are not used to denote positive, energetic, forceful men who are forcefully advancing. They denote violent men who are trying to snatch the kingdom away from Jesus. Using the passive meaning of *biaztetai*, the verse would be translated, "From the days of John the Baptist until now, the kingdom of heaven has been enduring violent assault and the violent take it by force." This is the translation that I prefer. I believe it not only follows the proper definitions of the words, but also fits the context of the passage.

Since the preaching of John, the kingdom has been opposed by violent men. John had to put up with the ridicule and attacks of the Jewish authorities. Now he is in prison at the hand of King Herod. Jesus has had to put up with the attacks of the Jewish authorities. Most recently they have begun calling him "a glutton and a drunkard." These attacks would not go away. In fact, they would intensify, because violent men were trying to rob Jesus of his kingdom. Jesus is foreshadowing what is going to happen. Opposition to his ministry is going to get worse.

13-14 The fact that violent men had seized John and placed him in prison might cause some to doubt that he was the forerunner of the Messiah. Since John now questioned Jesus, some might question John's role. But Jesus affirms that John is the Elijah who was to come and who was to prepare the path for the Messiah.

15-19 People doubt John, and they doubt Jesus. They doubt John because he followed strict ascetic practices. They doubt Jesus because he expressed freedom in his approach and came eating and drinking. To what can Jesus compare this generation? He compares them to little children who cannot be pleased. They don't want to dance, and they don't want to sing mournful songs. You can't make them happy no matter what you do. But wisdom will be proved right by her action. The actions of Jesus will prove who he is. And those who are wise will see him for whom he is.

Woe to Unrepentant Cities (11:20-24)

[20]Then, he began to rebuke the cities in which he performed most of his miracles, because they did not repent. [21]"Woe to you, Chorazin! Woe to you, Bethsaida! If the miracles performed in you had been performed in Tyre and Sidon, they would have repented long ago in sackcloth and ashes. [22]But I tell you; it will be more tolerable for Tyre and Sidon than for you. [23]And you,

> *Capernaum*
> *Will you be exalted to the heaven?*
> *No, you will descend to Hades.*

If the miracles performed in you had been done in Sodom, it would have remained until today. [24]I tell you that it will be more tolerable for the land of Sodom on the Day of Judgment than for you."

See First Century Insights at the top of page 128.

Jesus Gives Rest (11:25-30)

[25]At that time, Jesus said, "Thank you Father, Lord of heaven and earth because you have hidden these things from the wise and intelligent and revealed them to babes. [26]Yes, Father, because this was your good pleasure.

[27]My Father has committed all things to me. No one knows the Son except the Father, and no one knows the Father except the Son and whomever the Son wishes to reveal him.

[28]Come to me, all who are tired and burdened. I will give you rest. [29]Take my yoke on you and learn from me. For I am gentle and humble in heart and you will discover rest for your souls. [30]For my yoke is easy and my burden light."

Having proven his authority through his teaching and his miracles, Jesus now reveals the source of his authority. "All things have been committed to me by my Father." The Father is the source of Jesus' authority. When we submit to his authority, what kind of life do we live? We take on a yoke that is easy and a burden that is light.

Though the life of discipleship is challenging, it is the best life to live. Jesus beckons us to follow him — promising, "My yoke is easy and my burden is light." Jesus came to lighten our load. Life can be hard, but it is harder when you try to live it without God in your life. Jesus came to teach us that the best life is the life lived with him.

First Century Insights ∞

Chorazin and the Evangelical Triangle

As was mentioned earlier, Jesus spent most of his ministry on the northwestern corner of the Sea of Galilee. He traveled between three cities, Chorazin, Bethsaida, and Capernaum in an area scholars call "the evangelical triangle." Jesus cursed all three cities because they failed to believe in him despite the miracles he performed there. Today these cities are the sites of archaeological digs, totally desolate, uninhabited mounds. I have walked on all three of them. As I walked on them, I remembered the curse that Jesus pronounced upon them.

We have already discussed Bethsaida and Capernaum. What do we know about Chorazin? Chorazin or *Khirbet Kerazah,* has been located about two and one-half miles northwest of Capernaum. It is set upon a high ridge overlooking the Sea of Galilee. It was built almost entirely of the black basalt, which is native to that region. The synagogue has the same kind of seats that Jesus mentioned in his rebuke of the Pharisees. Although the Gospels do not record the details of Jesus' ministry in Chorazin, he almost certainly would have spoken in the synagogue.

Jesus compares Chorazin and Bethsaida to Tyre and Sidon. Tyre and Sidon were Phoenician cities. Jesus says these two Gentile cities were more open than the villages of Galilee. He compares Capernaum with Sodom, an Old Testament city notorious for evil. God destroyed both Sodom and Gomorrah for their wickedness, yet Jesus says that Capernaum is more closed than Sodom.

Jesus rebuked Chorazin, Bethsaida and Capernaum. He mentions specifically that Capernaum would descend to *Hades,* the place of the dead. Jesus rebuked all three cities; today all that remains of the three cities are archaeological digs. It is a scary thing to be rebuked by Jesus.

Who is this Jesus of Nazareth? (12:1-50)

Jesus has just declared himself to be the one for whom John the Baptist, the Elijah, was preparing the way. He has denounced those who would not believe in him, and invited those who would believe in him to come to him, and to know the Father through him. He is attracting the notice of many, including the Pharisees. "Who is this Jesus of Nazareth?" they must have been wondering.

Jesus is the Lord of the Sabbath (12:1-8)

¹At that time Jesus went through the grain fields on the Sabbath. His disciples were hungry and began to pick some heads of grain and eat them. ²*The Pharisees saw this and said to him, "Look, your disciples are doing an unlawful act on the Sabbath!"*

³*Jesus replied, "Have you not read what David did when he and his men were hungry? ⁴How they went into the house of God and ate the bread of Presence, which was not lawful for him or his men to eat, but only for the priests to eat? ⁵Or have you not read in the law that in the temple on the Sabbath the priests break the Sabbath, but are innocent? ⁶I say to you--one greater than the temple is here. ⁷But if you had known what this means–I desire mercy and not sacrifice, you would not have condemned the innocent. ⁸For the Son of Man is the Lord of the Sabbath."*

Jesus is not just the Lord of nature and the Lord over sickness and death, but he is also the Lord of the Sabbath. The Sabbath day was holy to the Jews. Not only were the Old Testament regulations strictly enforced on the Sabbath, but many man-made regulations were enforced as well. The Pharisees especially kept stringent laws concerning the Sabbath. They followed not just the written code, do not work on the Sabbath, but they also followed a man made oral code that specified what was to be considered work and what was forbidden on the Sabbath.

Jesus interprets the Sabbath according to the written law of God. He refers back to the time when David and his men were hungry and they ate the consecrated bread, which was meant for the priests. He interprets the law of the Sabbath in light of the scripture, "I desire compassion and not sacrifice." Jesus also makes a bold claim, "For the Son of Man is Lord of the Sabbath." Jesus has called himself "Son of Man" before; he is clearly claiming here that he is Lord of the Sabbath.

Jesus heals on the Sabbath (12:9-14)

⁹*Leaving there he entered their synagogue, ¹⁰and a man with a withered hand was there. Looking for a reason to accuse Jesus, the Pharisees asked him, "Is it lawful to heal on the Sabbath?"*

¹¹*He said, "Which of you, if you have a sheep and it falls into a pit on the Sabbath, will you not seize it and lift it out? ¹²How much more valuable is a human being than a sheep? Therefore it is lawful to do good on the Sabbath."*

¹³*He then said to the man, "Stretch out your hand." And he stretched it out and it was restored, as healthy as the other. ¹⁴But the Pharisees took council about him, how they might kill him.*

The Pharisees were now looking for a way to trap Jesus. They noticed a man with a withered hand and used his handicap to try

First Century Insights CR

The Synagogue

Having originated during the Babylonian exile, the synagogue is never mentioned in the Old Testament. The word refers to a group of people called to an assembly. With the destruction of the temple in 586 BC and the shutting down of the Jewish sacrificial system during the exile, the Jews formed smaller groups, which met together to discuss the Torah.

Worship occurred at the synagogue on Saturday, Monday and Thursday. At least ten men had to gather for worship to start. The synagogue worship consisted of liturgy and instruction. The liturgy was (1) the *Shemah*, Deuteronomy 6:49, which served as a call to worship (2) a prayer with uplifted hands and (3) the chanting of the 18 benedictions. The instruction was comprised of (1) a reading of the law and the prophets (2) a homily on the passage read and (3) a benediction. The synagogue staff was made up of the president who led the synagogue and the *Hazzan* who carried out the orders of the president. The *Hazzan* was the only person who was allowed to handle the scrolls. He also taught the children and administered floggings.

to trap Jesus. They asked a question that was often discussed by the Rabbis, "Is it lawful to heal on the Sabbath?" Most of the rabbis agreed that it was fine to provide medical help on the Sabbath if it were a life-and-death situation, but a withered hand did not fall into that category. So Jesus broadened the finding of the rabbis and argued that medical attention can be given not only in life-and-death situations, but also to do good on the Sabbath.

With impressive logic, Jesus answered the Pharisees' question with a question. This was a typical rabbinical discussion. If a sheep falls into a pit on the Sabbath, will you not lift it out? Yes, we would. Is a human being not more valuable than a sheep? Yes, he is. Therefore, you can do good on the Sabbath.

Interestingly, the Essenes of Qumran wrote that if a sheep or other beast of burden fell in pit, it was unlawful to remove the animal on the Sabbath. This is how seriously some people took the Sabbath. But for Jesus, the Sabbath was created for man and not man for the Sabbath. When legalism clashed with grace, Jesus sided with grace. He healed the man on the Sabbath.

Jesus' actions and his statements upset the Pharisees. They went away and conspired how they might destroy him. By an act of mercy to a crippled man, Jesus enters into the conflict with the Pharisees that will eventually lead to his crucifixion.

The Pharisees did not like the fact that Jesus escaped their trap. They realized that to get Jesus would take planning on their part, and they began to discuss how they could be rid of him once and for all. The tension between Jesus and the religious authorities will continue to mount from this point on.

Jesus is the fulfillment of Prophecy (12:15-21)

15Jesus knew what they were thinking, and left there. Large crowds followed him, and he healed all of them, and he 16ordered them not to tell what he was doing, 17so that the word of the prophet Isaiah might be fulfilled which says:

18Lord, my servant whom I have chosen
My loved one in whom my soul is pleased.
I will put my Spirit on him,
And he will proclaim justice to the nations.
19He will not quarrel or cry out,
Nor will his voice be heard in the streets.
20He will not break a bruised reed
And he will not put out a smoldering wick
21In his name the nations will hope.

Aware of what the Pharisees were thinking, Jesus withdrew to another area. The use of the verb *ginosko* suggests that Jesus heard reports of what the Pharisees were planning. As he left, large crowds followed him. After healing them, he ordered them not to spread the news of his miraculous works. The Pharisees were laying plans to arrest him; and Jesus did not wish his arrest to be hastened because of reports of his miracle working.

Matthew says this happened to fulfill prophecy, and he quotes from the first of four Servant Songs found in Isaiah, from chapter 42. First century Jews knew these songs to be highly Messianic in content. Matthew has used this "fulfillment formula" throughout his gospel to connect Jesus with Old Testament prophecy. This is the longest of the fulfillment prophecies in Matthew.

Isaiah speaks of the Messiah as being the redeemer of Israel, the servant of God. God would place his spirit on his servant, as God had done at Jesus' baptism. The servant would not quarrel. When the Pharisees tried to trap Jesus, he could easily have turned the crowds against the Pharisees and started a rebellion. But Jesus did not stir up the crowds; he was following the path of the Suffering Servant of Isaiah. He would not start protests in the street. He would submit to God's will and suffer any indignity to redeem humanity.

Practically Speaking ❧

Discipleship Means Joy

Life today has become increasingly complicated. Worries permeate our everyday existence. The economy is unpredictable. Politicians speak out of both sides of their mouths until an interpreter is needed to comprehend what they are saying. Crime, drugs and the threat of AIDS alarms us to the point where it is easier to withdraw from society than to venture forth into it. Confusion greets us at every turn.

Even a matter as simple as having a baby has become complicated. Should we have natural childbirth or use anesthesia? Which diapers should we buy? Why do all these magazines seem to say different things? How come every parent you ask has a different opinion on this issue? When Leigh and I had our first child and only daughter, Chelsea, someone gave us organic baby food. I didn't even know they made organic baby food. Must we now feed our child only organic food? Raising a child should not be so complicated. If the baby cries, one of three things is wrong: a dirty diaper, a hungry tummy, or a tired baby. If these three don't explain the crying, then the baby is probably sick. What should be simple has become so complex.

Let's not complicate discipleship. What does it mean to be a disciple? Must a disciple read their Bible an hour a day or will twenty minutes suffice? If I prayed every day this week except Sunday, am I still a disciple? How evangelistic must I be to include myself in the fellowship?

These are the wrong questions to ask. Many people would love to have a checklist that specifies what they must do to be a disciple. Check off prayer, Bible study, evangelism, church attendance, and all is good. This would satisfy a legalistic heart. But Jesus offers us a yoke that is free from legalism. His yoke is different. His yoke is easy.

I love Dietrich Bonhoeffer's definition of discipleship, "Discipleship means joy." Discipleship is not a checklist. Discipleship can never be equated with observance of regulations. Discipleship means a relationship with Jesus who can bring us joy. Jesus makes this offer, "Come to me all you who are weary and burdened and I will give you rest." If you feel burdened by Christianity, then leave Christianity and find Jesus. Following Jesus eases our burdens. He takes away sin, guilt, worry, low self-esteem and other burdens. A fretful, worried countenance is not the true mark of discipleship. A joyful disposition is.

Some ask, "So is discipleship freedom from responsibility?" Absolutely not. Jesus said that we must take on his yoke. He will carry its weight and make it easy and light, but it is still a yoke. To be yoked with Jesus is to share his purpose, his ambition and his desire. We become responsible in the ways he was responsible because we work alongside him.

What burdens you about Christianity? Is it evangelism? Then you are probably sharing your faith to be seen by men; instead of sharing your faith to glorify God. Is it Bible study? Then your study must be just a passing of time staring at pages instead of an inspiring life-changing study. Is it a relationship with someone? Then you should see that relationship as a gift instead of a burden.

Joy is an attitude. The most profound joy we can experience is the joy of our salvation. If we really understood that, deep in our hearts and souls, we would be more joyful. It is so easy to allow our joy to be stolen from us by the distractions and disappointments of this life. At these times, we need a childlike spirit to live in the moment, let go of the past and become joyful. I am not saying that we should stuff our feelings and our grief and just "put on a happy face." Instead, we need to be aware of and allow ourselves to feel what we feel, and take those feelings to Jesus, the only one who can give us rest for our souls. At rest in Jesus is the only place we will find the easy yoke and the light burden that lead to true joy

Jesus is Greater than Satan (12:22-32)

²²Then they brought to him a man who was demon possessed, he was both blind and mute and Jesus healed him so he could speak and see. ²³All the people were amazed and said, "Could this be the Son of David?"

²⁴When the Pharisees heard this, they said, "He casts out this demon only by Beelzebul, the ruler of demons."

²⁵But Jesus knowing their thoughts said to them, "Every kingdom divided against itself will not stand. And every city or house divided against itself will not stand. ²⁶If Satan casts out Satan, he is divided against himself, how will his kingdom stand? ²⁷If I cast out demons by Beelzebul, by whom do your sons cast them out? Therefore they will be your judges. ²⁸But if I cast out demons by the Spirit of God, the kingdom of God has come upon you.

²⁹Or how can anyone enter the house of a strong man without first tying up the strong man? Then he robs the house.

³⁰Whoever is not with me is against me, and whoever does not gather with me scatters. ³¹Therefore I tell you, every sin and blasphemy of men will be forgiven, but blasphemy against the Spirit will not be forgiven. ³²Whoever speaks a word against the Son of Man will be forgiven, but whoever speaks against the Holy Spirit will not be forgiven, neither in this age nor in the coming age."

After Jesus heals the man who was blind and mute, the crowds begin to wonder if he really is the Son of David–the King/the Messiah. The Pharisees claim that Jesus is casting out demons by Beelzebul, the ruler of demons.

Jesus answers their accusations by asking two questions. First, can a kingdom that is divided against itself stand? Why would Satan be divided against himself and destroy his own work? And if Jesus is casting out demons by Beelzebub, by whom do the Pharisees cast them out?

Second, can anyone ransack the house of strong man without first binding him? Jesus had to first bind Satan to be able to cast out his demons. Jesus is stronger than Satan. He is the Son of David. Jesus is King.

Jesus urges the Pharisees to see that the kingdom of God has come upon them and not to speak against the Holy Spirit. He warns them that their own words will either acquit or condemn them.

You can know Jesus by his fruit (12:33-37)

33 "Produce a good tree and its fruit is good, or produce a bad tree and its fruit is bad. For the fruit knows the tree. 34You offspring of vipers, how are you able to speak good when you are evil. For out of the abundance of the heart the mouth speaks. 35A good man brings good things out of the good treasured in him. An evil man brings evil things out of the evil treasured in him. 36I tell you that every careless word that men speak, they will have to give account concerning that word on the Day of Judgment. 37By your words you will be condemned."

In the last section, a question was posed that must be answered–is Jesus Beelzebul or is he the Son of David? How can this question be answered? You can answer it by looking at the works of Jesus. You can know a tree by its fruit. What is the fruit of Jesus' life? He enables the blind to see, the lame to walk, the deaf to hear and the mute to speak. Jesus has produced only good fruit.

The Pharisees are good at talking. But their work is evil, not good. They are the offspring of snakes, out to attack the good things that Jesus is doing. Jesus teaches a principle here that we can all learn from: we produce whatever we have treasured inside of us. Therefore, it is important to watch what we treasure in our hearts. What goes in comes out.

We need to guard our speech. We must answer for every careless word on the day of judgment. The Pharisees were full of careless words directed at Jesus. Jesus lets them know that they will have to pay for all those careless words.

The Ultimate Test of Jesus' Authority–His Resurrection (12:38-42)

³⁸*Then some of the scribes and Pharisees said to him, "Teacher we want to see a sign from you."*

³⁹*He answered them, "A wicked and adulterous generation asks for a sign and it will not be given a sign except for the sign of the prophet Jonah. ⁴⁰For as Jonah was in the belly of the great fish for three days and three nights, so the Son of Man will be in the heart of the earth for three days and three nights. ⁴¹The men of Nineveh will rise up at the judgment with this generation and condemn it. Because they repented at the preaching of Jonah, and behold one greater than Jonah is here. ⁴²The Queen of the South will rise up at the judgment and condemn it because she came from the ends of the earth to listen to the wisdom of Solomon, and behold one greater than Solomon is here."*

Even though Jesus has demonstrated his power through his teaching and his miracles, the scribes and Pharisees were still not convinced that Jesus was king. They asked Jesus for a sign that would demonstrate beyond a doubt that he was the Messiah. The only sign he gave them was the sign of Jonah: "As Jonah was three days and three nights in the belly of the sea monster, so will the Son of Man be three days and three nights in the earth." Jesus foreshadowed his

Practically Speaking ☙

The Unpardonable Sin?

What is "the unpardonable sin?" We must consider the context of this verse to answer the question. Jesus has just healed a blind and mute man by casting out the demon that caused his illness. The Pharisees say that he did this by the power of Satan and not by God's power. Therefore Jesus says, "Whoever speaks a word against the Son of Man, it shall be forgiven him; but whoever speaks against the Holy Spirit, it shall not be forgiven him, either in this age or the age to come." What is this sin against the Holy Spirit? Simply put, it is when you claim that the mighty works of Jesus are a product of Satan and not the Holy Spirit. When you claim that Jesus is working miracles because of Satan's power, then you have blasphemed the Holy Spirit.

Some would say that since Jesus in not here in the flesh working miracles today, you cannot blaspheme the Holy Spirit today. I would not be so quick to rule out the possibility today. I think this verse stands as a warning to us. We had better not get in such a wicked, corrupt place that we claim that the work of Jesus is the work of Satan. When we get in that place, then we are past the point of returning to God; we have committed the unpardonable sin. This should be a word of caution for anyone who wants to attack the works of Jesus in today's world.

resurrection, the ultimate sign of his authority. If he is not who he claims to be, then produce his body. If he is who he claims to be, then he will rise from the dead. The resurrection is the greatest sign that he is who he claimed to be.

Jesus Challenges "This Evil Generation" (12:43-45)

43"When an unclean spirit has been cast out of a man, it goes through dry places seeking a resting place, but does not find it. 44Then it says, 'I will return to my host that I left.' When it comes, it finds it empty, swept and put in order. 45Then it goes and brings with it seven other spirits more wicked than itself, and they enter and live there, and the last condition of the man is worse than the first. Thus it is with this evil generation."

Jesus states what he really thinks of this evil generation. They are like an unclean spirit that has been cast out of a person. The spirit tries to find a resting place in the desert, but is unable to. So he returns to his old host. But this time he goes back with seven other spirits who are worse. The condition of the man is worse than he was at first.

Jesus has been trying to sweep clean this generation. He has taught them, healed them, answered their questions, and walked among them. But after all he has done, they fail to see him as the Son of David. If they will not invite the Spirit of God into their lives, then the spirit of Satan will gladly take residence there. Their condition will be worse than when they began to listen to Jesus.

Who is the family of Jesus? (12:46-50)

46While Jesus was speaking to the crowds, his mother and brothers stood outside, wanting to speak to him. 47Someone said to him, "Look, your mother and your brother are standing outside wanting to speak with you."

48He answered, "Who is my mother and who are my brothers?" 49Pointing to his disciples, he said, "Look, my mother and my brothers. 50For whoever does the will of my Father in heaven is my brother and sister and mother.

Jesus' mother and brothers want an audience with him. Mark tells us the names of Jesus' brothers: James, Joseph, Judas, and Simon. Mark also tells us that the Jesus' family tried to seize him because they thought he was out of his mind (Mark 3:21). But Jesus does not look at family from a physical point of view. His family is made up of those who do the will of the father.

Jesus is not teaching us to be rude to our family. At the cross, Jesus asks one of the disciples to take care of his mother. He cared for his mother and for his family. But in the present context everyone is discussing who Jesus is. His own family does not accept him (John 7:3-5). If they will not accept him, then he will not accept them. His family is made up of whoever sees him for who he is: the Son of David.

Endnotes

[1] Eduard Schweizer, *The Good News According to Matthew* (Atlanta: John Knox Press, 1975), pgs. 219-220.

[2] Dr. Scoggins was my Hebrew professor at Southeastern Baptist Theological Seminary in Wake Forest, North Carolina in 1982. I heard him define *hesed* in this way in several of his lectures.

[3] Rienecker, p.28.

[4] Ibid.

[5] See Carson, p. 237.

[6] David Head, *Shout for Joy* (New York: The Macmillan Company, 1962), p. 19.

[7] Gene Edwards has written an interesting novelized version of this account entitled, *The Prisoner in the Third Cell*.

4
Ministry in Galilee
Parables and People
Matthew 13:1-16:20

The following parables make up the third major discourse section in Matthew. Although the parables are preached before large and small audiences, the real audience for the parable is the close circle of disciples to whom Jesus wants to communicate the secrets of the kingdom of God.

Parables (*parabole*) have been interpreted in many ways throughout the history of the church. The least effective way of interpreting the parables is by allegorizing them. This was the common method of interpretation used by the early church Fathers like Origen. In this method you take each image in the parable and give it a specific meaning. By doing this you can make the parable mean whatever you want it to mean. Most of the time the parable is making one simple point. At times, Jesus interpreted his own parables and made points of each image within the parable. But most often Jesus spoke the parable and left it for his audience to determine its meaning.

Here are some rules that can help with the interpretation of parables:

1. Note that there are different types of parables: true parables, similitudes, metaphors, epigrams, and proverbs.
2. The parables are not allegories.
3. The function of a parable is to call forth a response from the hearer. Jesus was sifting hearts through his parables. He was teaching discipleship.
4. Find the point/points of reference in the parable.
5. Listen to the parable very carefully. Determine how the original hearers would have identified with the story.
6. Once you discover the point of reference in the parable, translate it into your own context.

The Parable of the Sower (13:1-9)

^{13:1}*The same day Jesus went out of the house and sat by the sea.* ²*And large crowds gathered around him, so that he sat in a boat. The crowds stood on the beach.*

³*Then he told them many things in parables, saying, "A sower went
to sow seed.* ⁴*As he was sowing, some fell by the road, and the birds came and
ate it.* ⁵*Other fell on the rocky ground, which did not have much soil, and
immediately it sprang up because it did not have much depth of soil.* ⁶*When
the sun rose, they were scorched, and since they did not have any root, they
withered.* ⁷*Other fell among the thorns, and the thorns grew up and chocked
them.* ⁸*Other fell on the good soil and produced grain some one hundred,
some sixty, and some thirty.* ⁹*He who has ears to hear let him hear."*

The parable of the sower is not really about soils. It is about
hearts. Each soil represents a type of heart. Although some parables
are open to interpretation, the parable of the soils is not. After telling
the parable, Jesus explains it to his disciples. The hard soil or the
pathway soil represents hearts that are not open to the Word of Jesus.
These people do not want to even consider that Jesus' words are true.
Today we might label these people as atheist. They have closed their
mind to the possibility that God does exist.

When Jesus explains the parable below, we will compare each
type of soil with a type of heart.

The Purpose of Parables (13:10-17)

¹⁰*The disciples came to him asking, "Why do you speak to them in
parables?"*

¹¹*He answered them, "Because to you it has been given to know the
secrets of the kingdom of heaven, but to them it has not been given.* ¹²*For
whoever has, he will given more and given in abundance. Whoever does not
have, even what he has will be taken from him.* ¹³*This is why I speak to them
in parables:*

That seeing, they will not see,
And hearing, they will not hear or perceive.
¹⁴*The prophecy of Isaiah is fulfilled in them which says:*

Hearing, you will hear and not understand,
Seeing you will see and not perceive.
¹⁵*For the heart of this people has become calloused,*
And their ears are hard of hearing,
And their eyes are shut.
So they might not see with their eyes,
Or hear with their ears,
Or understand with their heart and repent,
And I would heal them.
¹⁶*But blessed are your eyes because you see and your ears, for they
hear.* ¹⁷*I tell you the truth that many prophets and righteous men wanted to
see what you see and did not see it, and wanted to hear what you hear, but
did not hear it."*

The disciples approach Jesus asking why he speaks to the people in parables. This is the first time Jesus has used parables, and his disciples are curious as to their purpose. Jesus informs them that the purpose of the parable is to conceal the message from the multitudes and to reveal the message to his closest disciples. Jesus has chosen to reveal the secrets of the parables to his closest followers.

I think of the parables as Jesus' love language with his followers. It is "insider language." When you love someone, you begin to develop a vocabulary that you understand but no one else does. You have gestures that mean something to you, but not to anyone else. You develop signals for "it is time to go," or "I need to talk to you in private." Although everyone sees these gestures, they don't know what they mean. Jesus was using insider language to teach his disciples the secrets of the kingdom.

For many years I was confused with the quote from Isaiah 6: 9-10, because I thought that it was saying that Jesus spoke to people to keep them from understanding his message. It seemed to say that he did not want people to repent and be healed or saved. But then I understood that Isaiah is simply reporting the natural outcome of anyone who is faced with the decision to follow God. The message of God will test their hearts. If their hearts are calloused, they will not respond to the message of God. Their hearts do not get calloused by hearing the parable. They bring a calloused heart to the parable and fail to understand the parable because of the condition of their heart.

I realized that even in the parables Jesus was discipling people's hearts. Who would understand the parables? Not those people who just heard them and went away thinking, "That was a nice little story." The people who understood the parables would have to work at understanding them. They would have to search for its meaning. They would have to follow Jesus after he told the story and ask him its meaning. They would have to learn the insider language. Jesus was always challenging people to examine their hearts. Even in the nice, beautiful stories known as the parables, Jesus was discipling people's hearts.

Then Jesus gives one of my favorite sayings in the Bible, "But blessed are your eyes because you see and your ears for they hear. I tell you the truth that many prophets and righteous men wanted to see what you see but did not see it, and wanted to hear what you hear, but did not hear it." I write this verse in the front of each of my study Bibles. I write it to remind me how blessed I am to be a part of God's kingdom. I get to see things that prophets and righteous men of the Old Testament only dreamed about seeing. Luke mentions prophets and kings instead of prophets and righteous men. I get to see things that King David longed to see. I get to see things that the prophet Jeremiah longed to see. They looked forward to the Messiah. I have a relationship with the Messiah. We must always remember how blessed we are to be a part of God's kingdom earth.

The Parable of the Sower Explained (13:18-23)

[18] *"Hear the meaning of the parable of the sower.* [19]*When anyone hears the message of the kingdom and does not understand it, the evil one snatches what was sown from his heart. This is what was sown on the path.* [20]*What was sown on the rocky ground is the one who hears the word and immediately receives it with joy.* [21]*But he has no root, and he endures for a short time. When tribulation or persecution comes because of the word, he immediately falls away.* [22]*What was sown among thorns, this is the one who hears the word, but the worries of life and the deceitfulness of wealth choke the word and it is unfruitful.* [23]*What is the seed sown on the good soil, it is the one who hears the word and understands it. He produces and gives a crop–a hundred, sixty or thirty times what was sown."*

Because the disciples continue to walk with Jesus and desire to learn from him, he gives them the gift of the meaning of the parable of the sower. The meaning is stated very succinctly:

The pathway soil is the person who does not embrace the message of Jesus; therefore, Satan snatches the message from his heart.

The rocky soil is the person who loves the message but doesn't take it deep into his heart and make changes based on the message. When tough times come, he or she abandons the message.

The thorny soil is the person who receives the message and starts living by it. But thorns begin to encircle this person. He is concerned by the worries of life and the deceitfulness of wealth. The message loses its effectiveness in his life. He is unfruitful because of the distractions of life.

The good soil receives the message and lives by it. He produces an abundant crop, some one hundred, some sixty, some thirty times what was sown.

The natural conclusion to the parable is to ask, "What type of soil am I?" Everyone fits into one of these categories. The only soil that is acceptable to God is the good soil.

The Parable of the Weeds Among the Wheat (13:24-30)

[24]*Jesus told them another parable: "The kingdom of heaven is like a man who sowed good seed in his field.* [25]*While everyone was sleeping, an enemy came and sowed weeds among the wheat, and then he left.* [26]*When the wheat came up and bore grain, then the weeds appeared.*

²⁷*Then the slaves of the house owner came and said to him, 'Master, did you not sow good seed in your field? Where, then, did these weeds come from?'*

²⁸*He answered, 'An enemy did this.'*

²⁹*The slaves said, 'Do you want us to go and pull them?'*

³⁰*He replied, 'No, in pulling the weeds you will uproot the wheat with them. Allow them both to grow together until the harvest, and at the harvest time I will tell the person--first collect the weeds and bind them in bundles to be burned, then gather the wheat into my barn.'"*

What do you do with people who act like they are a part of God's kingdom, but really are not? Do you immediately withdraw from them? Jesus speaks to this question in the parable of the weeds growing among the wheat. We will take a look at the meaning of the parable, when he explains it below.

The Parables of the Mustard Seed and the Yeast (13:31-33)

³¹*He told them another parable: "The kingdom of heaven is like a mustard seed that a man took and sowed in his field. *³²*It is the smallest of all the seeds, but when it has grown it is the greatest of shrubs and becomes a tree. So that the birds of the air come and perch in its branches."*

³³*He told them another parable: "The kingdom of heaven is like yeast that a woman took and mixed into three measures of flour until the whole amount was leavened."*

Jesus compares the kingdom to a mustard seed. The mustard seed is a tiny, small seed. In Palestine it was commonly referred to as the smallest of seeds. It is just a little bigger than the period at the end of this sentence. Yet this tiny seed grows up into a bush that can house birds. It was not uncommon for the Palestinian mustard plant to grow ten to twelve feet high. Jesus could have been standing beside a mustard plant with birds resting on its branches as he delivered this parable. Certainly most Jews of Jesus' day could easily picture this story in their heads.

The implication is that the kingdom will experience growth, (and not slow, anemic growth), but dynamic, vibrant growth. Is the kingdom growing your heart? Do you feel closer to God and more excited about being in his kingdom than you ever have? Do you see growth in your maturity as a Christian? What about the church or the ministry that you are a part of? Do you see growth there? How can you help to cause growth within your ministry? The mustard seed has potential for great growth. But unless it is planted, watered, and cared for, it will not grow. All of us can do something to help the kingdom of God grow. What can you do to help the kingdom grow?

Jesus also compares the kingdom to yeast or leaven. Yeast is alive; when it is added to dough, it multiples until it completely permeates the dough. In New Testament times, yeast was not added to the dough as a separate ingredient, but some yeast-containing dough from the previous day's bread was added to the fresh dough. The quality of yeast that Jesus focuses on here is that yeast influences the entire batch of dough. It has an invasive quality. Yeast grows aggressively. It will not stop until all the dough has been leavened. The early church was this way. Each disciple went out making other disciples. This happened to such a degree that people commented about the early church, "They have turned the whole world upside down." As disciples, we must take the influence of Jesus to everything we are a part of. We must turn our part of the world upside down.

The Use of Parables (13:34-35)

34All these things Jesus said to the crowds in parables, and he did not say anything to them without a parable. 35This fulfilled the word of the prophet, saying:

"I will open my mouth to speak in parables,

I will proclaim what has been hidden from the creation of the world."

Jesus has spoken to the multitude in parables. Now he will leave the crowds and go into a house with his disciples. He will explain the parable of the weeds growing with the wheat to them, and then he will tell them more parables.

Matthew notes that Jesus spoke to the people in parables, in fulfillment of prophecy. He quotes Psalm 78:2, a psalm of Asaph. Throughout his Gospel, Matthew is keen at every juncture to demonstrate that Jesus is the fulfillment of Old Testament prophecy.

Jesus Explains the Parable of the Weeds Among the Wheat (13:36-43)

36He then left the crowds and went into the house. His disciples came to him saying, "Explain to us the parable of the weeds in the field."

37He answered, "The one who sowed the good seed is the Son of Man. 38The field is the world. The good seed is the children of the kingdom. 39The weeds are the children of the evil one. The enemy is the one who sows them–the devil. The harvest is the end of the age, and the reapers are angels.

40As the weeds are collected and burned in the fire, so it will be at the end of the age. 41The Son of Man will send his angels, and they will gather out of his kingdom everyone who causes sin and all who do evil. 42They will throw them into the furnace of fire, where there will be weeping and gnashing of

teeth. ⁴³*Then the righteous will shine like the sun in their Father's kingdom.*
Anyone who has ears, let him hear."

Jesus leaves the crowds and enters a house with his disciples.
You see the teachable heart of the disciples here. They ask Jesus the
meaning of the parable of the weeds sown among the wheat. They
don't want to just go into the house, have a bite to eat, and relax. They
want to know the meaning of Jesus' words. So they ask, "Explain the
parable to us."

Jesus breaks down the parable to them in simple terms:
The one who sowed the good seed is the Son of Man.
The field is the world.
The wheat are the children of the kingdom.
The weeds are the children of the evil one.
The enemy is the devil.
The harvest is the end of the age.
The reapers are the angels.

The parable speaks to what will happen at the end of time.
The Son of Man will send his angels into the world to harvest the
world. The weeds will be thrown into the furnace of fire. The wheat
will be invited into God's eternal kingdom.

The Parable of the Hidden Treasure and the Pearl (13:44-46)

⁴⁴*"The kingdom of heaven is like a treasure hidden in a field. When a*
man discovered it, he hid it. Then in his joy he went and sold all that he had
and bought that field.

⁴⁵*The kingdom of heaven is like a merchant searching for fine pearls.*
⁴⁶*When he found one of great value, he went and sold all he had and bought*
it."

How much do you want something? What are you willing to
do to get what you want? These are the questions that the parables of
the hidden treasure and the pearl attempt to answer. Let me tell you a
true story about desire. This is about the desire to live. A certain man
had bought some property in Pennsylvania and was clearing the land
in order to build a house. While clearing the land, a tree fell on his leg
and pinned him to the ground. He knew that deep in the woods, no
one would hear him shouting. He could not move the tree, dig out
from under the tree, or cut the tree to free himself. He was bleeding
and would soon die if he did not do something drastic. So what did
he do? First, he tore his shirt and made a tourniquet. After he had
tightened the tourniquet around his leg, he got out his pocketknife and

began cutting/sawing his leg off above his knee. He cut through the flesh and hit the bone. The most difficult part of cutting himself free was cutting through the bone, but after fifteen minutes he was able to do that. Once he was free, he crawled into his truck and drove to the first house that he could find. He made his way to door and asked the owner to take him to the nearest hospital. He survived. Later, after learning to run with a prosthesic leg, he finished a marathon. When that tree fell on him, he had one thought: survival. He desperately wanted to survive. This desperation led him to a desperate act.

In the parable of the hidden treasure and the pearl the lesson is the same. God is offering you a valuable gift; what are you willing to do to receive that gift? Are you willing to fight through character changes? Are you willing to read, to pray, to meditate? Are you willing to stay up late, get up early, do whatever it takes to get close to God and stay close to him?

Do we appreciate the fellowship that God has given us? I recently asked a number of people of various ages and backgrounds why they loved our fellowship. Here are some of the responses:

"Because my friends and pre-teen leaders care for me and love me and encourage me. They notice when I'm gone, and they want to know that I'm okay. I trust my friends and the pre-teen workers." –a ten-year-old girl.

"Because by being in the church, you get to go to heaven." –an eight-year old boy.

"I like church because it's fun." –a five-year old girl.

"Because of all the bad things going on in the world, the fellowship is a place where you feel safe and you can trust people. You know that people are watching out for you and want what is best for you." –a twelve-year old girl.

"Relationships." –a twenty-eight year old man.

"For the relationships." –A thirty-two year old woman.

"You can always find answers."–a forty-three year old woman.

"It's hot, it's on the edge." –A forty-two year old man.

"I've always wanted to be a part of something great. I've found that in the church." –a forty-five year old man.

The Parable of the Net (13:47-50)

47"Again, the kingdom of heaven is like a net that was thrown into the sea and all kinds of fish were gathered into it. 48After it was full, the fishermen pulled it onto shore. They sat down sorting the fish–keeping the good and throwing away the bad. 49This is how it will be at the end of the age. The angels will come and gather the wicked from the righteous 50casting the wicked into the furnace of fire. Where there will be weeping and grinding of teeth."

In this short parable, Jesus launches into an eschatological topic. The Jews were very confused over what was going to transpire at the end of time. One group, the Saducees, believed there was no resurrection at all. They believed that after you died, you were dead and gone. The Pharisees believed in the resurrection, but there was much discussion among this sect as to what was going to happen at the resurrection. Jesus wanted to take the confusion away, so he speaks often about the end of time.

In this passage Jesus compares the separation of the good from the evil on the last day to a fisherman who catches a net full of fish and then sorts through them, saving the good and tossing away the bad. In this case, God is like the fisherman. At the end of days, he will judge the world, saving the good and giving them an eternity with him. But Jesus is very clear on what will happen to the evil. They will be cast into the fiery furnace. Will they feel anything as they enter this place of torment? Yes, there will much weeping and grinding or gnashing of teeth. The present tense is used here and could imply that the weeping and gnashing will last for eternity.

Do you know what it feels like to go through intense pain? You ball up your fists, tighten your shoulders, and clench your teeth. If your tongue gets in the way, you bite all the way through it. Jesus makes it clear that hell is a place of pain and torment, a place to be avoided at all costs. Although we are not given quite as dramatic a picture of hell as Dante gives us in his *Inferno*, Jesus gives us a clear enough picture to know that we do not want to go there.

Jesus questions their understanding (13:51-53)

⁵¹Jesus asked them, "Have you understood all these things?"
They answered him, "Yes."
⁵²Jesus said to them, "Therefore every scribe (teacher of the law) who has been taught about the kingdom of heaven is like a man who owns a house who brings out his treasures both the new and the old."
⁵³After Jesus finished giving these parables, he left that place.

This section closes the third major discourse of Jesus. He asks them if they have understood his parables. They reply, "Yes." He adds one last parable about teachers who have been taught the kingdom. They are like a man who owns a house and brings out his treasures both old and new. The disciples are the new teachers who have been taught about the kingdom. What should they do with these teachings? Do they keep their treasures hidden, or do they share them with others? They are to share their treasures both new and old with others.

The Rejection of Jesus at Nazareth (13:54-58)

[54]And Jesus came into his hometown. He taught them in their synagogue, so that they were astonished and said, "Where did he get this wisdom and these miraculous powers? [55]Is this not the son of the carpenter? Isn't his mother Mary and his brothers James, Joseph, Simon, and Judas, and [56]aren't all his sisters with us? Where did he get all this?"

[57]And they stumbled (were scandalized) because of him. But Jesus said to them, "A prophet is not without honor except in his hometown and in his own house." [58]And he was not able to perform mighty works there because of their lack of faith.

This account of the rejection of Jesus at his hometown, Nazareth, gives the plain details of Jesus' offense to his own people, and it also presents a more significant meaning from the view of Matthew and his readers in the first century.

Scholars differ as to what they consider the form of this text. Martin Dibelius calls this pericope a "paradigm."[1] He states that the notes on Jesus' family were special materials, which were authentic in the text; but Dibelius goes on to note that the rest of the story was tradition, which Matthew transforms into the end of the paradigm. Dibelius adds that he believes the story, "originally concluded with the saying of Jesus."[2]

Another scholar, Rudolf Bultmann, labels this text an "apothegm."[3] By this term he means, "a saying of Jesus, in which according to the tradition, they were spoken."[4] Bultmann states that it was characteristic with apothegms that the scene narrated should serve only as a framework to give the occasion and situation in which an important saying was found. Bultmann calls this a biographical apothegm, which he defines as a creation of the Christian community. Bultmann writes, "Even the scene in Nazareth may perhaps not reflect a particular historical event, but it is rather a symbolic picture, setting forth the attitude of the people as a whole to the preaching of Jesus."[5] Bultmann's view of this text can be seen clearly in another work of his where he writes, "This seems to me to be a typical example of how an imaginary situation is built up out of an important saying."[6]

Other scholars have still different ideas as to the form of the passage. Edward Schweizer believes that the story was handed down as a genuine oral tradition and states that the church thought of Jesus as far more than a prophet so it would not have applied the saying in verse fifty-seven to him without reason.[7] Schweizer also sees too much historical detail in this passage for it to be fabricated.

Following the same line of thought, Vincent Taylor denies the subjective criticism, which questions the historicity of this pericope by writing:

> In it justice is not done to the realism of the narrative: the naming of the brothers, the mention of the sisters, the reflection in the word 'kin' on those who were subsequently prominent in the Church, the implication that Jesus could not heal in absence of faith, his surprise at unbelief. These feature mark genuine tradition.[8]

Through a form critical examination, we are able to see the text is historical tradition, which was placed in the gospel by Matthew for a particular theological reason.

Shifting our attention to a view of the contents of this passage, we notice the characters mentioned by Matthew in the scene at Nazareth all play different roles. The scene opens with Jesus going, and the disciples following. The mention of the disciples following is seen by some scholars as a redactional touch, but Taylor states that this statement is made to present Jesus as a Rabbi with a following of scholars approaching Nazareth to teach in their synagogue.[9]

"To follow Jesus" can mean, not only to attach oneself to a moral and spiritual teaching, but also to share in his destiny. This is the word used to denote the soldier following his leader, or the slave his master.[10]

In the passage we see the disciples follow, Jesus is rejected, but the disciples still follow. Matthew shows the difference between proper faith and sight faith by contrasting the hearers and the disciples' reactions to Jesus' teaching. In this reference one can also see a foreshadowing of the rejection of the disciples for following the teachings of Jesus.[11]

Jesus' role here is the role of a Rabbi coming to a homecoming service (John 13:13). Jesus' teaching in the synagogue is understood as "ethical instruction, or occasionally apologetics or instruction in the faith."[12]

The Greek word, *didaskein*, calls attention to two aspects, being applied on the one side to the insight of the one who is to be instructed and on the other to the knowledge presupposed in Jesus.[13]

Jesus taught in the form of a Jewish Rabbi of his time. Recognizing these statements, even though the synagogue sermon is not recorded, one can deduce that the whole teaching of Jesus is with a view to the ordering of life with reference to God, and one's neighbor. Since this is true, when the crowd rejected Jesus, they were also choosing to neglect his teaching.

Jesus' astonishment at this rejection shows his humanness. Jesus believed in himself and his mission; therefore, his astonishment is due to the contrast between his belief and the crowd's unbelief. Mark plainly states that Jesus was unable to work miracles because of unbelief, but Matthew and Luke both rework this and leave out the humanness of Jesus. It must be remembered that Jesus worked miracles as a sign to produce faith and out of compassion; he never worked mighty acts to fascinate or entertain people. One writer comments, "It was not as a wonder worker that he desired to be sought after, as his various commands to silence after a cure make abundantly clear."[14]

All his miracles are signs for the eyes of those who can see who Jesus really is. Matthew is not bothered by Jesus inability to work miracles; he realizes that the setting of unbelief is the reason Jesus is incapable of mighty acts. Matthew's record of Jesus' humanness in his response to the crowd and his inability to work miracles demonstrates that Matthew was conscious of making faith the pivotal point of this pericope.

In turning attention to the role of the hearers, it must be remembered that their response was to both the person and teachings of Jesus. Schweizer writes, "The decisive acceptance or rejection is made in response to Jesus' teaching. Their rejection of Jesus occurred because of the difference of how they knew Jesus as one of their own and what they heard from him in the synagogue."[15]

In this case, they were scandalized that a man who came from a background like Jesus should say and do the things he did. Familiarity had bred a mistaken contempt. In this passage, the word "scandalize" or "offense" is taken from a classical root meaning, "the bait-stick on a trap."[16] The people's presuppositions of Jesus were trapping them into unbelief. Jesus' teaching must be approached without prejudice, or offense and rejection will always occur.[17]

What is the historical-critical background of this passage? It was set in Nazareth, the hometown of Jesus. Nazareth was a small village of 100 to 150 people. Why would this village balk at Jesus being a rabbi? Perhaps they knew of his suspect birth. Taylor records, "it is contrary to Jewish custom to describe a man as the son of his mother, even when the father is no longer living."[18]

If the Jews were looking for a kingly Messiah, then another stumbling block would have been Jesus' occupation as a carpenter. The word can mean "stone mason." Very few people in Galilee were well to do in Jesus' day. Lohse writes, "The Jewish population of the country earned their living by farming, handicraft, and small business."[19] This means that Jesus would have been like the majority of people in Galilee: poor. This commonness of Jesus would have been offensive to Jews who longed for a priestly "Son of Man" or a kingly "Son of David" to come and liberate the Israelites from Roman rule.

Another historical study, one of the synagogue and Sabbath worship, will illuminate the meaning of this story even further. It has been suggested that the synagogue came into existence at some point during the destruction of the Jerusalem temple in 587 BC. By Jesus' day the synagogue was the accepted place of worship for the Jewish community. The content of synagogue worship consisted of two parts, namely: a segment with a strong liturgical stamp, which was followed by an instructional worship. During the instructional vein of worship, men were asked to read from the Book of the Law and the Prophets. Lohse comments, "To be sure a homily could be appended to a reading of the scripture; for any male member of the community was permitted to preach."[20] Such a custom allowed Jesus the opportunity to speak in his native synagogue on his visit to Nazareth.

Why did the early church keep alive a tradition of Jesus being denied by his hometown? As Christians took the good news of Jesus to their own families and hometowns, this passage was used in practical ways. As the early church experienced rejection because they taught Jesus' message and had to continually face the lack of Jewish acceptance of Jesus, this story of Jesus' rejection must have grown in their favor. This tradition, which at first glance seems so offensive to the Christian, must have become a great source of encouragement for a chronically rejected people.

Why did the town of Nazareth reject Jesus? The real hindrance to their faith was that God incarnated himself in a common man. They could not imagine the Messiah being Jesus. The disciples did not fully understand who Jesus was, but they were willing to follow him and discover more about him. Faith is not a state of mind, but it is an act of doing and following. The proper response to Jesus is a response to his radical message of discipleship. Discipleship demands that one try to understand Jesus by doing the will of God. Active faith is the only faith Jesus can recognize. Anything less is rejection.

In the original setting, Jesus was offering his hearers the chance to encounter God in his life. Jesus had the power of salvation to offer the faithful, but those lacking faith, would be lost. The early church probably used this story to make sense of how men were treating them. The rejection they suffered was like the rejection of Jesus whom they served. The Evangelist was showing his community the need for a proper faith of action, faith not in a miracle worker, but in one who was much more and much less than a miracle worker. It is their call to active faith, which addresses our religious community today. May we develop the faith to see this Jesus of Nazareth in all his humanness and still respond in active service.

First Century Insights ❧

The Physical Family of Jesus

Jesus' return to his hometown was not a grand reception. Although Jesus had gone throughout the country doing good for many people, his hometown neighbors failed to see his greatness. They questioned whether the son of Joseph, the carpenter, could accomplish any of the mighty works that Jesus was reported to have done. Even after hearing his message and witnessing the works, they still rejected him. I believe Shakespeare said, "Familiarity breeds contempt." In this case, the saying is true.

The story does demonstrate that Jesus had brothers and sisters. The Catholic church does not agree with this translation because it challenges their doctrine of the perpetual virginity of Mary. Understand though that the virginity of Mary is so sacred to them that they not only attest that Mary was always a virgin, but also that she was born of virgin herself. They attempt to get around this verse by saying that the word for brothers and the word for sisters should actually be translated as "cousins." They have no lexicographical basis for such an argument. Since that argument is not convincing, they go on to argue that Joseph was married before Jesus and these brothers and sisters are from that earlier marriage. This is an argument from silence, in other words, a fabrication. The text is clear: Jesus had brothers and sister.

The text is also clear in stating that the brothers and sisters of Jesus went along with the rest of his hometown and failed to believe in him. This is consistent with other material presented in the gospels. This gives us a very convincing argument for the resurrection of Jesus. James the half-brother (half-brother because they share the same mother, but different fathers) later becomes a loyal disciple who leads the church in Jerusalem and writes the letter of James. Jude the half-brother of Jesus also becomes a disciple and writes the epistle of Jude. What turned them around? Paul informs us that Jesus appeared to James after his resurrection. It must have been this resurrection appearance that turned James around. The fact that James and Jude both became believers is a strong argument for the resurrection of Jesus.

To me the most intriguing part of this passage is the last verse, "And he was not able to perform mighty works there because of their lack of faith." According to this verse, the only thing that can limit the power of Jesus is lack of belief. This idea is supported by other verses such as Matthew 17:20, which says that if we say to this mountain, "Be thrown into the sea," and believe, then it will be done. We must understand that belief is the most powerful weapon in the disciple's arsenal. With belief, we can do amazing things for God. We can tap right into the power of God. Without belief, we limit God's ability to do anything through us. How much do you believe?

The Death of John the Baptist (14:1-12)

¹⁴:¹*At that time Herod the tetrarch heard reports about Jesus,* ²*and he said to all his servants, "This is John the Baptist who has risen from the dead. This is why all these powers are at work in him."*

³*For Herod had arrested John, bound him, and thrown him in prison because of Herodias, his brother Philip's wife.* ⁴*Because John said, "It is not lawful for you to marry her."* ⁵*Herod wished to kill John, but he feared the people because they thought he was a prophet.*

⁶*On Herod's birthday, the daughter of Herodias danced for his guests, making Herod very happy. So happy,* ⁷*that he promised to do whatever she asked of him.* ⁸*Guided by her mother, she said, "Give me the head of John the Baptist on a platter."* ⁹*This grieved the King, but because of his promise and his guest, he ordered that her request be granted.* ¹⁰*He sent to have John beheaded in prison.* ¹¹*His head was brought on a platter and given to the girl. She then gave it to her mother.* ¹²*John's disciples came and took his body and buried it. Then they went and reported the event to Jesus.*

John the Baptist was a great prophet. Being a great prophet, he exited life the way many great prophets left: he was murdered, executed by King Herod. This would foreshadow the way that Jesus would die. He would also die at the request of Herod. Herod did not want to kill these men, but he cowered underneath the fear of the people around him.

Feeding the Five Thousand (14:13-21)

¹³*When Jesus heard about this, he went in a boat to a secluded place with his disciples. The crowds heard of this they followed him on foot from their towns.* ¹⁴*When Jesus arrived on shore, he saw a great crowd and had compassion on them and healed their sick.* ¹⁵*When evening arrived, his disciples came to him and said, "This place is secluded, and it is late in the day. You should send the crowds away so they can go to the villages and buy some food for themselves."* ¹⁶*Jesus answered them, "There is no need for them to go away. Just give them something to eat."* ¹⁷*Then they answered Jesus, "We don't have anything except five loaves and two fish." Jesus said,* ¹⁸*"Bring them here to me."*

¹⁹*Jesus ordered the crowd to sit down on the grass. He took the five loaves and two fish. He looked up to heaven, gave thanks, and broke the loaves. He gave these to his disciples who gave them to the crowds.* ²⁰*Everyone ate and was satisfied. The disciples gathered what was left and it filled twelve*

baskets. [21]*Those who ate numbered about five thousand men, along with women and children.*

When Jesus heard about the death of John the Baptist, he went to a secluded place. Most likely he sailed out of the region of Herod Antipas across the Jordan on the northern tip of the Sea of Galilee around Bethsaida. This would have placed him in Herod Philip's district. The fact that he went to a secluded place implies that he wanted some time away from the multitudes perhaps to mourn and to gather his feelings. He had lost a family member and a fellow prophet.

But Jesus did not have much time to mourn. When the crowd discovered where he was, they followed him on foot around the edge of the sea. He could have been selfish and ignored the needs of the crowds. He could have thought, "I have needs too. Why can't they be sensitive to what I'm feeling? Don't they know that I just lost my cousin and my friend?" But Jesus denied his needs to meet the needs of others. This is the constant example of Jesus—he denied himself and helped others. He had compassion on the multitude and healed their sick.

By evening, a problem had arisen. The disciples wondered how such a large crowd was going to be fed in such a secluded place. The disciples suggested that Jesus disperse the crowds so they could go to the nearby villages and get food. Jesus had another suggestion, "You feed them." This must have seemed like a strange request to the disciples. How were they going to provide for this multitude? They answer, "We only have five loaves and two fish." This was the typical meal for the poor of that region–bread and fish. Jesus then took control of the situation.

He ordered the crowd to sit down on the grass. Mark adds that the grass was green, so this occurred in the spring. He also adds that the multitude sat in groups of fifty and one hundred. Some have seen this as military divisions. Jesus is feeding his army the Messianic banquet. But the division could have been based on the easiest way to distribute the food. Jesus gave thanks for the food and began breaking the bread and fish into pieces. The disciples distributed these to the crowd. Everyone who ate was satisfied. The disciples began to collect what was left over. It was enough to fill twelve baskets. The baskets were not large deep baskets used for storage, but small baskets for carrying daily provisions. The twelve baskets probably represent the twelve tribes of Israel. Many scholars attack this miracle as false saying it was a fabrication of the early church. But it is unlikely that the early church would have invented this final detail of the twelve baskets of leftovers. Jesus completely satisfied the crowd (5,000 men plus women and children could have been a crowd of 15 to 20 thousand), and he had leftovers. This is the type of God that we serve. He wants to completely satisfy us. His blessings never end.

Jesus Walks on the Water (and so does Peter for a few steps) (14:22-33)

[22]Immediately he made his disciples get in the boat and go ahead of him to the other side, while he dismissed the crowds. [23]After dismissing the crowd, he went up to the mountain to pray by himself. When the day ended, he was there alone.

[24]Now the boat was already a good distance from the land. It was beaten by the waves for the wind was against it.

[25]Early in the morning (the fourth watch of the night), Jesus came to them walking on the sea. [26]When the disciple saw him walking on the sea, they were terrified and shouted with fear, "It's a ghost!"

[27]Immediately Jesus said to them, "Take heart, it's me, don't fear."

[28]Peter answered him, "Lord, if it is you, command me to come to you on the water."

[29]Jesus said, "Come."

Peter got out of the boat, walked on the water, and went to Jesus. [30]But seeing the strong wind, he feared and began to sink. He cried out, "Lord, save me!" [31]Immediately Jesus reached out his hand and grabbed him. He said, "You of little faith, why did you doubt?"

[32]When they got back in the boat, the wind ceased. [33]Those in the boat fell down to worship him saying, "Truly you are the Son of God."

After the feeding of the multitude, Jesus compels his disciples to go ahead of him to the other side of the sea (to Gennesaret). Jesus did not get much time by himself because of the crowd. Now he is going to make sure that he spends time alone with God. He goes up to a mountain and prays. Jesus makes time to be alone with God. You can see this emphasized in the text with the repetition of "to pray by himself" and "he was there alone." Although most of the ministry of Jesus was spent with his disciples or with the crowds, we do know he had a habit of getting away to be alone with God. This was his time to regroup, to recharge his batteries, and to set his mind on his mission. If Jesus needed that time, how much more do we need it?

After Jesus finished praying, he went to find his disciples. He saw them in the boat struggling against the wind. It was the fourth watch of the night, between 3:00 and 6:00 a.m. It was either very dark or the first light of dawn was breaking over Galilee. Jesus came to them walking on the water, again demonstrating his authority over nature. I'm sure all of us have tried walking on the water for a few steps. Many scholars try to explain away this miracle by saying that Jesus was walking over a flooded beach where the water was shallow. Some say that the reflection on the water made it look as if Jesus were walking on the water, but he was on shore. But there is no explanation for the fact that when Peter got out of the boat he sank. Jesus reached out his hand to save Peter. They were in the same depth of water. Jesus walked on the water. Peter was walking on the water for a moment, but then he sank. This is a real miracle.

When the disciples first saw Jesus walking on the water, they mistook him for a ghost. I imagine they were very tired of rowing against the wind by this time. I can picture them seeing Jesus and thinking he was a ghost. They immediately start rowing with all their might as they cry out in fear. It must have been a comical scene.

When they cry out in fear, what is Jesus' response? He tells them "Take courage; it is I; don't be afraid." Jesus was always trying to dispel fear. God wants us to fear him in the sense of respecting him, but he never wants us to be afraid. Fear is a tool of Satan. Throughout the Gospels, Jesus tries to dispel people's fears. He gives people courage to overcome their fears. What are you afraid of? Jesus can help you overcome your fears.

When Jesus identifies himself to the disciples, he uses an interesting phrase, "It is I." In the Greek, this is "*ego eimi.*" In the Greek Old Testament this is the exact phrase that God uses to identify himself to Moses on Mount Sinai (Exodus 3:14). When Moses asks God, "Who will I say sent me?" God tells Moses to say, "'I am' (*ego eimi*) sent you." Jesus uses these same words to identify himself to the disciples here.

That Peter does what he does is consistent with his character throughout the Gospel. He speaks up first and asks, "Lord if it is you, tell me to come to you on the water." Peter has taken a beating over the years because he sank, but I appreciate his courage. I appreciate that Peter was always the first one to speak. He made mistakes because he tried things. But that is better than making mistakes because you do nothing. I recently read a book entitled, *If You Want to Walk on the Water, You Got to Get Out of the Boat.* I liked the title, and I liked the book. Peter got out of the boat. What about the other eleven disciples? They stayed in the boat. Yes, Peter sank. But Peter is still the only person besides Jesus to walk on the water. Imagine the thrill of walking on water. He was doing it; he was surfing without a board. He got out of the boat.

Peter walked on the water. Then Peter made a mistake. He took his eyes off of Jesus. He began to look at the wind, and he became afraid. When he stopped focusing on Jesus, he made a crucial error. His fear caused him to sink. But even as he sank, Jesus reached out and saved him. Jesus wants us to be adventurous. He wants us to try. The saying goes, "Better to have tried and failed, than to have never tried at all." Jesus wants us to try. When we try and fail, he will be there to pick us up off the ground or out of the water.

Jesus teaches the disciples a lesson here. He lets them know that it is all about faith. The phrase "little faith" is better translated "no faith." With a little faith you can move mountains. With no faith, you can do nothing. Doubt causes us to sink. When Peter was faithful he walked on water. As soon as he gave in to fear and doubt, he began to sink.

When Jesus got into the boat with the disciples, they begin to worship him. They saw his authority over nature and were impressed. They exclaim, "Truly, you are the Son of God!"

Jesus Heals the Sick in Gennesaret (14:34-36)

34When they had crossed over, they came to the land at Gennesaret. 35When the people there recognized him, they reported throughout the region and all who were sick were brought to him. 36They begged him that they might just touch the bottom of his garment. All who touched it were healed.

As they enter the region of Gennesaret, people recognized who Jesus was and brought all their sick to him. Jesus demonstrated his power to heal sickness. He did not need to touch people. He did not need to say anything. If they just touched the hem of his garment they were healed. Jesus had great power and authority.

The Tradition of the Elders (15:1-9)

15:1Then the Pharisees and scribes came from Jerusalem to Jesus saying, 2"Why do your disciples break the traditions of the elders for they do not wash their hands before they eat?"

3Jesus answered, "Why do you break the commands of God for your traditions? 4For God said, 'Honor your Father and Mother,' and 'the one who speaks evil of his father or mother must be put to death.' 5But you say, 'whoever says to his father or mother–the support that I should give to you, I am giving it to God,' 6he does not honor his father. You make void (useless) the word of God for your traditions."

7"Hypocrites," he went on to say, "Isaiah prophesied correctly about you, when he said, 8'these people honor me with their lips
But their hearts are far from me.

⁹They worship me falsely
Their teachings are just human rules.'"

These Pharisees and Scribes, lawyers or legal experts, were highly respected by the Jews. That they came from Jerusalem also underscores their high rank and influence. The sect of the Pharisees was the largest Jewish sect in the first century. They were from the rank and file of the Jews. They believed in the resurrection and in all three divisions of the Old Testament: the Pentateuch, the Prophets and the Writings. They were highly legalistic, believing that the oral tradition of the rabbis was just as binding as the Law of Moses. They taught that these oral laws created a hedge or fence around the law that protected the Jewish people. If you did not break one of the oral laws, then you would never get close to breaking one of the written laws.[21]

The Scribes or teachers of the law were a sect of very educated Jews that specialized in interpretation of the Law of Moses. Since their job was to make sure that the law was followed exactly, it makes sense that they teamed up with the Pharisees to question Jesus on his view of tradition. The Scribes not only interpreted the law, but they also served as translators and letter-writers for the people. Most of the people of the first century could not write. If they needed to correspond with someone, they would hire a scribe. The scribes were very influential in first century Jewish culture.

The Pharisees and scribes are concerned with Jesus' lack of concern for the traditions of the fathers. These traditions of the rabbis were passed along orally in Jesus' day, and it was the job of the rabbi to teach these traditions to the people. To the Pharisees Jesus was not doing his job as a rabbi when he failed to teach his disciples the traditions of the elders.

They question Jesus on the issue of hand washing. This is not a quick washing of the hands before the meal to clean up. This hand washing was ceremonial, highly stylized and dramatic. It was done for show. That the disciples of Jesus did not practice it was very conspicuous.

When the Pharisees and scribes question Jesus, he turns the question back on them. Jesus often used this tactic when attacked. He would not answer their question, but would put the accuser on the defensive by firing a question back at them. Here his question is highly polemic. Their question accuses Jesus' disciples of breaking the unwritten law, the traditions of men. Jesus' question accuses the Pharisees and scribes of breaking the written law, the commands of God.

Jesus did not see the traditions in the same light as the Pharisees and the scribes. Instead of building a hedge around the law to protect the law, these traditions had become a stumbling block to the Jew, keeping him or her from understanding the law. At times the traditions went against the heart of the law. Jesus brings up the tradition of "*korban*" to illustrate his point. The law commanded that a child should take care of his parents in their old age. But the rabbis taught that a child could make a donation to the temple in place of supporting their elderly parents. This tradition was certainly good for the priests and Jewish hierarchy, but it was tragic for the aging parents. Jesus condemns this tradition and declares that it makes the command of God void or useless. "To make void or null" is used in the papyri in the sense of canceling something out, like to void a will. You see the strength of Jesus' words here. He also calls the Pharisees and scribes "hypocrites."

What was important to Jesus? Jesus wanted to make sure that the heart was involved in obedience. He quotes from Isaiah who says, "These people honor me with their lips, but their hearts are far from me." Jesus doesn't want lip service. He wants us to obey from the heart. When we do something for God or for the church we should ask, "Why am I doing this?" Why am I getting up early to go to church service? Why am I staying up late talking to this weak brother or sister? Why am I giving my money to world missions? If we forget the "why," then our actions are just traditions—lip service without the heart. Jesus makes clear that this type of worship is vain, unacceptable to God. We should put our hearts into our acts of service for God.

Things that Defile (15:10-20)

¹⁰Calling the crowd to him, Jesus said, "Listen and comprehend! ¹¹It is not what goes into the mouth of man that makes him unclean, but it is what comes out of his mouth that makes him unclean."

¹²His disciples approached him and said, "Do you know that the Pharisees took offence (were scandalized) by what you said?"

¹³He answered, "Every plant that my heavenly Father has not planted will be uprooted. ¹⁴Don't be concerned about them, they are like the blind leading the blind. If a blind person guides another blind person, both will fall into a pit."

¹⁵Peter asked another question, "Will you explain the parable to us?"

¹⁶Jesus replied, "Even at this crucial juncture, do you still lack understanding? ¹⁷Don't you see that everything that enters the mouth enters the stomach and goes out into the latrine? ¹⁸But whatever comes out of the mouth comes from the heart–this is what defiles man. ¹⁹Out of the heart comes evil intentions, murder, adultery, sexual immorality, theft, false testimony, slander. [20]*This defiles a person. But to eat with unwashed hands does not defile him.*

If it was the purpose of the Pharisees to coerce Jesus into teaching the oral traditions like they did, they could not have gotten a worse response. Instead of teaching the people the traditions, Jesus teaches them the need to understand what they are doing in their relationship with God. He asks them to think before they act, to put their heart into their worship and service to God. It is not what you eat that makes you unclean, but what comes out of your mouth.

Peter approaches Jesus out of a concern that the Pharisees and scribes might have taken offense at what Jesus said. The word "to offend" or "to cause to stumble" has the nuance of a deep religious offense, an offense that would keep the Pharisees from believing in Jesus. Peter's worries are not Jesus' worries. Jesus is more concerned about the people who follow the Pharisees and scribes, than about the leaders themselves. He wants to free the followers from legalistic, tradition-bound religion. He considers the Pharisees blind guides who are leading blind people into a pit. Jesus wants to spare the helpless people from that pit.

Then Peter goes on to ask Jesus to explain what he means when he says it is not what goes into a man but what comes out that makes him unclean. Jesus will explain, but he first tries to get Peter to pay closer attention to what he is saying. He asks him, "At this crucial juncture, are you still without understanding?" This demonstrates how slow Peter and the disciples were in understanding the message and mission of Jesus. It foreshadows what will happen to Peter as he denies Jesus three times after the crucifixion. In the following chapters the dullness of the disciples will be demonstrated time and again. This will stand in stark contrast to the disciples of Acts who boldly venture forth to evangelize the world. This will become one of the most convincing evidences for the resurrection of Jesus.

Jesus breaks it down nice and simple for Peter. In the Greek it is very clear, "Don't you know that what enters the mouth then enters the stomach and goes out into the latrine?" So simple that even a simple person like Peter could understand it. It is what comes out of the heart that is important. For sins like murder, adultery, lying and slander all begin in the heart. Jesus teaches us to guard our hearts.

The Faith of the Canaanite Woman (15:21-28)

[21]*Jesus left there and went into the area of Tyre and Sidon.* [22]*A Canaanite woman from that region came out to him crying, "Have mercy on me, Lord, Son of David. My daughter is tormented by a demon."*

²³*But Jesus did not answer her, not even a single word. His disciples approached him saying, "Send her away. She is constantly crying out after us."*

²⁴*Jesus answered, "I was sent only to the lost sheep of the house of Israel."*

²⁵*The woman came to him and bowed down to him, saying, "Lord, help me."*

²⁶*Jesus replied, "It is not good to take the children's bread and throw it to the dogs."*

²⁷*"Yes, Lord," she said, "but even the dogs eat the crumbs from under their master's table."*

²⁸*"Woman, your faith is great," Jesus answered, "What you wish will be done."*

Her daughter was healed at that hour.

Jesus now leaves the territory of Israel proper to travel north by the Mediterranean Sea into the land of the Canaanites. Tyre and Sidon were coastal cities. They were located in what today is the country of Lebanon. This is the only record of Jesus leaving the territory of Israel and it is as far outside of Israel that he traveled. He left the traveling to his disciples who went to every corner of the world spreading his message.

When Jesus was in the region of the Canaanites, a woman approached him begging for mercy. She had a daughter who was tormented by a demon. Anyone who has children can relate to her desperation. She was willing to do anything to save her daughter. In this case, she approached a rabbi from a region that was historically hostile to the Canaanites. Because of her desperation, she looked for any answer to her child's dilemma.

This is true of us today. If we are desperate, then we will do anything to get help. We will get up early in the morning to study the Bible. We will drive distances that others might think crazy. It is a matter of desire. The Canaanite woman had to demonstrate her desire to Jesus.

The disciples asked Jesus to send her away. Some scholars believe that they were asking Jesus to send her away with her request granted. The request was certainly an important one. But Jesus wanted to press beyond the request to see if the woman really had faith. Perhaps that was also a lesson for his disciples. Discipleship had to be accompanied by faith.

So Jesus responded, "I have come for the lost sheep of the house of Israel." In other words, "She is not a Jew, so I can't help her." But the woman bowed down before him, which in the Greek implies that she worshipped him. She humbly asked, "Lord, help me." Jesus

Practically Speaking ✑

The Heart

In Matthew 23:26, Jesus said, "First clean the inside of the cup and dish, and then the outside also will be clean." Jesus understood our tendency to work and worry about appearances more than the heart. So much today is about appearances and performance. We have to wear the right clothes, drive the right car, listen to the right music, and talk the right talk. If we don't have these together, we might not be accepted, we might be unpopular.

Jesus does not judge us on outward appearances. He judges our hearts. When we think of heart, we think of a muscle that pumps blood. But in the ancient mind, heart meant something else. The Hebrew word for heart is *lav*. It means the "seat of our emotions" or the "center of our life." Heart is our will, our drive, our understanding. Proverbs 4:23 reads, "Above all else, guard your heart, for it is the wellspring of life." What drives you? What do you spend most of your emotional energy doing? This is where your heart is.

Have you ever walked across the Brooklyn Bridge? My wife and I lived in Brooklyn, New York for about six years. We loved it there. I loved riding my bike across the Brooklyn Bridge into Manhattan. I actually got a traffic ticket once for not stopping at a stop sign on my bike. I saw the sign and thought it didn't apply to bikes. A policeman was waiting at the bottom of the bridge and waved for me to stop. He wrote me out a ticket. Next time I stopped at that stop sign. Even with that, it didn't sour my love for riding across the Brooklyn Bridge.

In 1883, most people said a bridge could not and should not be built between Manhattan and Brooklyn. John Roebling and his son Washington believed it could be and should be done. They began to seek financing for the project. Just a few months after the project began, a tragic, on-site accident killed the father, John, and left the son, Washington, paralyzed and unable to walk or to talk. The project stood to be scrapped. Washington Roebling could move only one finger of his body, but with that finger he learned to communicate with his wife by tapping out a code. For the next thirteen years Washington Roebling oversaw the completion of the Brooklyn Bridge by tapping instructions to his wife with his finger. That is heart. Do you have a heart for God?

still did not grant her request. He pressed her a little further, testing her heart. He declared, "It is not good to take the children's bread and give it to the dogs." In this analogy the children are the Jews. So who are the dogs? The Canaanites are the dogs. Jesus is indirectly referring to the woman as a dog. Did Jesus mean to insult her? No, he was testing her heart. How much faith did she really have?

How many of us would have stood the test this far? So often

we wear our hearts on our sleeves. We get hurt over little things. We get upset with people for not greeting us. If someone appears not to be friendly, then we think they have something against us. We leave church mad and bitterness enters our hearts.

This woman endured what many of us would have perceived to be insulting or rude. She agreed with Jesus, "Yes the bread is for the children, but all I'm asking for is a crumb." The word for crumb (*psichion*) refers to a tiny morsel of bread. She would take just a crumb. She had passed the test. She pursued Jesus and he granted her request. At that hour her daughter was healed. This is the type of faith that Jesus admires. Do we have this type of persistent, relentless faith?

Jesus Heals Many People (15:29-31)

29Leaving there, Jesus went to the Sea of Galilee. He went upon a mountain and sat down. 30Great crowds came to him with the blind, crippled, mute, and many others; and placed them at his feet; and he healed them. 31So that the crowd was amazed when they saw the mute speak, the lame walk, and the blind see; and they glorified the God of Israel.

One goal of Matthew is to demonstrate why Jesus was different from other rabbis. Remember that he was writing to a Jewish audience who could appreciate the importance of a great rabbi. But Matthew wanted to demonstrate that Jesus was greater than the other rabbis, in fact, Jesus was greater than all the rabbis. Jesus was actually the Christ, the Messiah and the King.

One way that Matthew accomplished his goal was by showing all the mighty works of Jesus. In this scene, people bring all types of sick people and place them before Jesus. You can picture the crowd that looks like an infirmary of a hospital after a terrible accident. Matthew lists the condition of some of the people: the lame, blind, crippled and mute. But there were many other conditions that he did not list. Jesus healed all these people regardless of their condition.

Because of his mighty works, the people had two reactions. First, they were amazed at his power. This harkens back to the amazement of the Hebrews in the Old Testament to the mighty works of God. Matthew wanted his audience to make that connection. This led to the second reaction: they glorified the God of Israel. Matthew was careful to specify who was glorified through the miracles of Jesus: the God of Israel. This is the point that Matthew made—Jesus' mighty work demonstrates that he is greater than the rabbis. He is greater than the chief priest. He is greater than Abraham, Moses, or David. Jesus is greater because he is the Messiah. Jesus is King.

Jesus Feeds the Four Thousand (15:32-39)

[32]*Jesus called his disciples to him and said, "I have compassion on the crowd because they have been with me for three days and have had nothing to eat. I do not want to send them away hungry for they might faint on the way."*

[33]*His disciples said to him, "Where could we get enough bread in this secluded place to feed a crowd?"*

[34]*Jesus said to them, "How much bread do you have?"*

"Seven loaves, and a few small fish," they answered.

[35]*He told the crowd to sit on the ground.* [36]*He took the seven loaves and the fish and gave thanks, breaking them and giving them to the disciples. The disciples gave them to the crowd.* [37]*All that were hungry ate and were satisfied. They collected the leftovers and they filled seven baskets.* [38]*Those who ate were four thousand men along with women and children.* [39]*He dismissed the crowd and got into a boat and went to the area of Magadan.*

The crowds were enamored with Jesus. They could not get enough of him. They would follow him into a village, through the countryside, up one side of a mountain and down the other. Once, when he took off in a boat to get to the other side of the Sea of Galilee, the crowds followed along the shore, keeping an eye on the boat anticipating where it might dock. When Jesus arrived at his port, he saw the crowds he had just left, waiting in anticipation for him.

The crowds loved Jesus for his teaching. He taught as one with authority and not as the scribes and Pharisees. They loved him for his miracles. Jesus often found himself surrounded by people with various types of diseases waiting for his healing touch. They loved Jesus for his leadership. He recognized that they were helpless sheep without a shepherd, and he came to shepherd them. They loved Jesus for his compassion. In this passage, the crowds follow Jesus for three days without eating. He understood that if he sent them away that some would faint from hunger. So he fed them.

Jesus taught a lesson on compassion here. But what other lessons did Jesus teach? He teaches us to be solution oriented. When Jesus raised the problem for his disciples, "I want to feed these people," what was the disciples' response? "Lord, where can we find bread in this secluded place?" "Lord, how are we to feed this many people?" Even though Jesus had fed a larger crowd early in his ministry (5,000 people in chapter fourteen), the disciples seem to have forgotten that and offer no solution here.

So Jesus solved the problem. He asked them how much food they could find. The disciples responded, "Seven loaves and a few fish." Jesus ordered the crowd to sit down, blessed the food, divided it, and fed the crowd. No problem was too big for Jesus. What others saw as impossible, Jesus knew was possible. Jesus teaches us to look at the possibilities and not at the impossibilities.

Jesus also teaches us a lesson on patience. The disciples should have known what to do in this situation. After all, Jesus had performed this miracle once before. But they were slow. They were dull. Jesus did not get frustrated with them. He did not lose his patience. He walked them through the procedure once again. He performed the miracle exactly as he had done before, hoping they would get it this time.

Here we see the patience of Jesus. He spent time educating the disciples. He told them once, told them twice, and showed them what to do. There is a time to get upset when people aren't learning. But that is a long way down the road, after you have tried to patiently instruct and teach them. Very shortly, we will see Jesus get upset at his disciples for their lack of understanding and their lack of faith. That does not mean that he lost his patience with the disciples.

After Jesus fed the people, he got into a boat and headed to Magadan. I have been to Magadan. It is located on the Sea of Galilee just a little south of the village of Capernaum. In the first century, Magadan was larger than Capernaum. The village was known for its pickled and smoked fish. The fishermen of Capernaum would unload their boats at Magadan, and the villagers would process the fish for exporting across the Roman Empire. This is the village where Mary Magdalene grew up. Today you can visit the first century ruins of this village. There is a public beach at Magadan where you can picnic or swim. My family swam and picnicked there with our friends the Fridleys. When you are there, you can envision Jesus getting out of his boat with his disciples to preach in this small village on the banks of the Sea of Galilee.

The Demand for a Sign (16:1-4)

16:1*The Pharisees and Sadducees came to test Jesus asking him to show them a sign from heaven. ²He answered them, "When it is evening, you say, 'It will be fair weather for the sky is red like fire.' ³And in the early morning, 'It will be stormy for the sky is red and gloomy.' You know how to interpret the sky, but you cannot interpret the signs of the appointed times. ⁴An evil and adulterous generation asks for a sign, no sign will be given it except the sign of Jonah." Then he left and went away.*

The tension between Jesus and the religious authorities begins to intensify. The Pharisees and Sadducees, two sects that often opposed each other and rarely got along, join forces to test or to trap Jesus. They ask for a sign from heaven. The reason for this sign is left unexplained by Matthew, but we can infer from Jesus' answer that they desired a sign that would prove he was who he claimed to be, that he was the Messiah.

Jesus will not be backed in a corner. Jesus tells them, "You are great at reading the weather, but you aren't so great at reading the signs of the appointed times." He cryptically hints that the answer to their sign is in the sign of Jonah. But he leaves it at that. Those of us who know the story recognize that Jesus was speaking of his resurrection. As Jonah was in the belly of the fish for three days, he would be in the earth for three days. This would ultimately become the sign of his kingship. Since he came back from the dead, then he is Lord.

Jesus is the only religious leader in the history of humanity to give verifiable evidence that what he taught was true. He said that he would die and in three days he would come back from the dead. This is something that was easily verifiable. If he is who he claims to be, wait three days after his death and take a look at his body. If he is still dead, then parade his body throughout the streets of Jerusalem and proves his claim of divinity to be false.

But what happens if after three days he is alive? Then his death was a hoax or he is who he claimed to be. Matthew and the other gospel writers demonstrate that his death was not a hoax. Jesus was examined by the soldiers at the cross, buried in a tomb for three days, and guarded by the Romans who would have exposed any wrongdoing. He really did die on the cross, and he really rose from the dead. This makes Jesus unique: different from any man or woman who has ever lived, and also different from any other religious leader in history. Jesus is the only religious leader who gave a challenge for us that would prove his authenticity: kill me and wait three days. If he lives, then everything he said was true. He did rise from the dead, and what he taught is true. This is the significance of the sign of Jonah.

The Yeast of the Pharisees and Sadducees (16:5-12)

⁵The disciples went to the other side of the lake, but they forgot to bring bread. ⁶Jesus said to them, "Keep on your guard against the yeast of the Pharisees and Sadducees." ⁷They disputed with each other, saying, "It is because we did not bring bread."

⁸But Jesus knowing what they were discussing said, "You of little faith, why are you arguing about not having bread. ⁹Don't you get it? ¹⁰Don't you remember the five loaves for the 5,000, and how many baskets were collected? Or the seven loaves for the 4,000, and how many baskets you collected? ¹¹Why can't you understand that I was not talking about bread. Beware of the yeast of the Pharisees and Sadducees." ¹²Then they understood that he had not told them about the yeast of bread, but about the teaching of the Pharisees.

6-7 Jesus uses the word *zuma*, which is translated "leaven" or "yeast." You can see how Jesus used this symbolism before in Matthew 13:33. Here he refers to the teaching of the Pharisees and Sadducees. Fritz Rienecker, a Greek scholar, describes the exact point of Jesus' criticism, writing, "Jesus meant their teaching, the rigid legalism and casuistical sophistry of the Pharisees and the political opportunism and the worldly materialism of the Sadducees."[22] This is the leaven that Jesus criticized.

8 Jesus uses an interesting word to refer to his disciples–*oligopistos*. This is a compound word built from the words *oligo*, meaning "little" or "few" and *pistos*, meaning "faith." The word literally means "little faith." Jesus refers to those who have little confidence in his power to provide them with food. But on a broader plane, he refers to anyone who doubts that he is the Messiah.

Practically Speaking ❧

Remembering God

At this point in the story the disciples get very forgetful. Does this ever happen to you? They forgot to bring bread on their journey across the lake. They forgot that Jesus had already fed two multitudes with just a few loaves. They forgot what Jesus meant by the leaven of the Pharisees and the Sadducees. But most important of all, they forgot who Jesus was. In the next section, Peter will briefly remember who Jesus is, declaring, "You are the Christ the Son of the Living God," but then he will forget it again just as quickly.

The disciples suffer from the same malady that afflicted the Hebrews when they came out of Egypt: forgetfulness. This is the same disease that plagued David in his later years: forgetfulness. It is the same sickness that can cripple us spiritually today: forgetfulness.

We need to remember who God is. We must remember who Jesus is and what he has done for us. Memory keeps us from doubting God's power. Memory keeps us from being people who are *oligopistos*, people of "little faith."

When we forget what God has done for us, we are in a bad place. Failing to remember who Jesus is hurts our faith. From this point on in the gospel story, Jesus will be working on his disciples' memory. He will try to teach them not to forget who he is. When we fail to remember who Jesus is, we lose our faith.

Peter's Statement of Faith (16:13-20)
Cf. Mark 8:27-30; Luke 9:18-21.

[13]*Jesus came into the district of Caesarea Philippi and he asked his disciples, "Who do people say the Son of Man is?"*

[14]*They answered, "Some say John the Baptist, some say Elijah, some Jeremiah or one of the prophets."*

[15]*"What do you think?" he asked.*

[16]*Simon Peter answered, "You are the Christ, the Son of the Living God."*

[17]*Jesus said to Simon, "You are fortunate (blessed), Simon Bar Jonah, because flesh and blood did not reveal this to you but my Father in heaven revealed it. [18]I say to you–you are Peter and on this rock I will build my church and the gates of Hades will not conquer it. [19]I will give you the keys to the kingdom of heaven, and what you bind on earth will have been bound in heaven; what you loose on earth will have been loosed in heaven. [20]Then he sternly warned his disciples not to tell anyone that he was the Christ (the Messiah).*

13 Jesus uses his favorite title of himself here, Son of Man. This term connects Jesus with his humanity. But for the Jew, it was also a Messianic title that emphasized the universal authority and power of Jesus.

14-15 When Jesus asked who people said he was, the response of the disciples was interesting. They only mentioned people who were dead–John the Baptist, Elijah, Jeremiah or one of the prophets. Jesus obviously had a great influence on the people for them to place his name alongside of these great men of Scripture.

16 Peter confessed that Jesus was the Christ, the son of the living God. Christ without the article "the" has the connotation of a personal name. This is why Jesus is later referred to as Jesus Christ. But with the article "the" the name becomes a title. Christ is the Greek equivalent of the Hebrew, "Messiah." This was the Old Testament title for the "anointed one" of God. It also means "King."

This is the only place where the title "son of the living God" is found in the New Testament. Although the phrase "God's son" is often used, "living God" is only found here. In applying this term to Jesus, Peter is underlining the fact that God is at work in the life of Jesus.

17 The phrase "flesh and blood" is only found here and in 1 Corinthians 15:50 and Galatians 1:16. It is a Jewish way of referring to the whole of man, with a special emphasis on his weakness. Flesh and blood is subject to disease, sickness and death. "Heaven" on the other hand, is not subject to such weaknesses. Peter's confession has heavenly insight. After all the times Peter has tripped up, misspoken, and made a fool of himself, he is finally praised by Jesus for his heavenly insight. But as we will see, this insight is short lived.

Jesus called Simon by his Hebrew name, "Simon Bar Jonah" that means "Simon son of Jonah." Peter's father is identified in John 1: 42 as John. Instead of seeing a discrepancy between the two passages, it is better to understand Jonah as a form of "Johanan."

18 Much had been made in Protestant circles between the terms *petra*, meaning rock, and *petros*, meaning Peter. The argument is that *petra* has a feminine ending and means a bedrock, much like the one that Jesus was probably standing on when he had this conversation. The word *Petros*, has a masculine ending and means a small stone or a pebble. Therefore, Jesus was not building the church on Peter (*petros*) but on the rock (*petra*) of his confession that Jesus was the Christ the son of the living God. This argument works in the Greek, but Jesus didn't teach his disciples in the Greek. The Aramaic or Hebrew behind the two terms demonstrates that Jesus used one word for rock here, *kepha*. The Hebrew is found in the other name for Peter in the Bible, *Cephas*.[23] Therefore, we should be careful not to overplay the distinction between *petros* and *petra*. In the Hebrew, Jesus highlights Peter's role in the early church. He was the spokesman of the apostles. But that being said, the distinction that Jesus never meant to found his church on Peter, but on Peter's confession, is clearly discerned from the Greek. If Jesus had wanted to make Peter the head of the church, he could have said, "You are Peter, and on you I will build my church." But he did not say that. Paul also made clear in 1 Corinthians 3:11 that there is only one foundation for the church–Jesus Christ.

19 Much confusion exists over this verse. Is Jesus giving Peter the authority to bind and loose God's decisions on earth? This would make the word of Peter equal with the word of God. But we know that Peter was just a man, and he was fallible. The Greek suggests that Peter could only bind and loose what had already been bound and loosed in heaven. The Greek uses the future tense (*estai*) with the perfect past participle (*dedemenon/lelumenon*) to become the future perfect passive periphrastic, "will have been bound/will have been loosed."[24] That is to say that the binding and loosing has already occurred in heaven. It is the role of the church to demonstrate decisions that have already been made in heaven and not vice versa.

First Century Insights ❧

Caesarea Philippi (Banias)

At the foot of Mount Hermon in northern Israel (1,700 feet above sea level) lies Caesarea Philippi (Banias). A tributary of the Jordan River runs through the ancient city. In this idyllic setting of waterfalls and lush, green vegetation, Herod Philip, the son of Herod the Great, decided to build his capital of the Northern province of Galilee and dedicate it to Caesar–thus the name Caesarea Philippi.

Caesarea Philippi is one of my favorite places to visit in The Holy Land. It is a beautiful park that lends itself to a great nature walk or a time of meditation. It is also rich in Biblical significance, a place that demonstrates how geography and archaeology can illuminate the Biblical text.

As you approach Banias from the parking lot, you walk over a stream (*Nahar Banias*) that runs down from the mountains. You approach a cave that juts into a huge rock cliff. The cliff rises a hundred feet or more above you. Just to the right, as you approach the cave, there is what looks like a huge spinning top located in a sand pit. When you push the top in a circle it makes an impression in the sand. The impression is of the confession that Peter made at Caesarea Philippi some two thousand years ago, "You are the Christ, the Son of the living God." It is in several languages. It stands as a reminder of the great event that once occurred in this city.

At Caesarea Philippi (Banias) a cult existed that worshipped the Roman god of nature, Pan. A temple was built in Philippi in front of a cave that was believed to lead to the gates of Hades, the entrance to the underworld. A spring ran just in front of the cave. As sacrifices were thrown into the cave, the cultic priest watched the waters of the spring for blood. If he saw blood, the gift was accepted. If no blood was seen, the gift was rejected.

Here at Caesarea Philippi, where the gates of Hades existed in local belief, Jesus asked his disciples, "Who do people say I am?" They responded, "Some say Elijah, Jeremiah, John the Baptist, perhaps one of the prophets." Jesus then asked, "What about you? Who do you say I am?" Peter, who usually spoke first, replied, "You are the Christ, the son of the living God." Jesus praised Peter and commented that on the rock of his confession he would build his church, and that even the gates of Hades would not prevail against the church.

Jesus had a double reference in mind. The Gates of Hades refers to Satan and his dominion. It also refers to the influence of pagan religion. Since Jesus is the Christ, he will be victorious over both.

Endnotes

[1] Martin Dibelius, *From Tradition to Gospel*, trans. Bertram Lee Woolf (London: Redwood Press Limited, 1919, p. 110.

[2] Ibid.

[3] Rudolf Bultmann, *Form Criticism*, trans. Frederick C. Grant (New York: Harper and Row, Publ., 1934) p. 39.

[4] Ibid.

[5] Ibid., p. 45.

[6] Rudolf Bultmann, *History of the Synoptic Tradition*, trans. John Marsh (New York: Harper and Row, Publ., 1963), p. 31.

[7] Eduard Schwiezer, *The Good News According to Mark*, trans. Donald H. Madvig (Richmond, Virginia: John Knox Press, 1970), p. 123.

[8] Vincent Taylor, *The Gospel According to St. Mark* (London: Macmillian and Co. Ltd., 1953), p. 298.

[9] Ibid., p. 299.

[10] Xavier Leon-Dufour, ed., *Dictionary of Biblical Theology*, trans. Joseph Cahill (New York: Desclee Company, 1962), p. 189.

[11] William Barclay, *New Testament Words* ((Philadelphia: The Westminster Press, 1964), p. 41.

[12] Alan D. Richardson, ed., *A Theological Word Book of the Bible* (London: SCM Press, Ltd., 1957), p. 172.

[13] *Theological Dictionary of the New Testament*, s.v., "*didasko*," by Tad Rengstorf.

[14] Richardson, p. 153.

[15] Schwiezer, Mark, p 124.

[16] Ibid, p. 123.

[17] Barclay, *New Testament Words*, p. 255.

[18] Taylor, p. 300.

[19] Eduard Lohse, *The New Testament Environment*, trans. John Steely (Nashville: Abingdon, 1971), p. 147.

[20] Lohse, p. 165.

[21] By the end of the first century after the destruction of the temple in Jerusalem, these oral traditions were collected and written down. This collection and codification of rabbinic tradition became the Mishnah. Rabbinic interpretation of the Mishnah was later collected and codified in the Midrash.

[22] Rienecker, p. 49.

[23] Eduard Schweizer, *The Good News According to Matthew,* Translated by David E. Green (Atlanta: John Knox Press, 1975), p. 336.

[24] Reinecker, p. 49.

5

Private Ministry in Galilee
Preparing the Hearts
of the Disciples
Matthew 16:21-18:35

Jesus Foretells His Own Death and Resurrection (16:21-23)
Cf. Mark 8:31-33; Luke 9:22

²¹*From that time on, Jesus began to show his disciples that it was necessary for him to go to Jerusalem and suffer much from the elders, chief priests, and the scribes. He was to be killed and on the third day rise.*

²²*Peter took him aside and began to rebuke him, "May God in his mercy spare you this, Lord. This will never happen to you."*

²³*Jesus turned and said to Peter, "You get behind me Satan! You are a stumbling block to me. You are not thinking of the matters of God, but you are thinking the thoughts of men."*

21 The verb *began* is emphatic. It implies that a new stage in the revelation of Jesus has begun. From this time on, he now moves closer to the cross with every step.

22 Peter's response in the Greek is *ileos*. It is translated in other places as mercy. Here it can mean "Mercy on you, Lord." Other translations say "May God in his mercy spare you," or "May God be gracious to you." But it also contains the idea, "God forbid."

23 "To think" is to set one's mind on, to contemplate. Peter's mind was set on matters of men, not on matters of God.

How quickly Peter's stock goes from the heights to the rock bottom. Jesus had just praised him because he was speaking with spiritual insight. Now Peter gets the worst rebuke that Jesus ever gave anyone, "Get behind me, Satan!" Peter is no longer thinking spiritually. His thinking is worldly. This is his response when Jesus predicts his death.

This topic, the death of Jesus, constantly tripped up the disciples. We will see Jesus predict his death three times over the next several chapters, and each time the disciples fail to understand him. Matthew clearly demonstrates the dullness of the disciples in this matter. He begins here with Peter.

When Jesus predicted his death, Peter was so sure that Jesus was wrong that he took him aside to rebuke him. Imagine that. Peter tells Jesus that this will never happen.

Then Jesus calls Peter something he never called anyone else: Satan. He said that Peter had become a stumbling block to him. How amazing these words stand in contrast to the words of praise for Peter in the last section. The idea is that if you miss the death and the resurrection of Jesus then it doesn't matter how much you understand–you have missed everything. Peter is the portrait of every disciple. We must understand the cross. If we fail to understand the cross, then we fail to understand Jesus.

The use of the term "stumbling block" here is interesting. If you remember a few chapters earlier Jesus dismissed the Pharisees and Scribes because they were not open. Peter approaches Jesus and is concerned that he might have offended the religious authorities. He asks Jesus, "Aren't you concerned that you offended them?" The word "offend" is taken from the same root as the word "stumbling block." The word is *skandalon* and it can mean "offense," "stumbling block," "to scandalize," or "an occasion to sin." The earlier question of Peter must have rung through his mind as Jesus speaks to him, "Peter, you know how worried you were over whether I offended the Pharisees. Realize that you have offended me."

Why was it such an offense? Perhaps Peter was just concerned with the safety of Jesus. When you understand all the nuances of the word *skandalon*, then you see why it was offensive. The word can also mean "an occasion for sin." Peter was presenting Jesus with an occasion to sin. If Jesus had not chosen to die for the sins of the world, he would have sinned. Temptation was real for Jesus. The choice to die on the cross was a struggle for him.

The Cross and Self-Denial (16:24-28)
Cf. Mark 8:34-9:1; Luke 9:23-27

²⁴*Then Jesus said to his disciples, "If you wish to come after me, you must deny yourself and take up your cross and follow me. ²⁵For whoever wishes to save his life will lose it, and whoever wished to lose his life will discover it. ²⁶For what does it profit a man, if he gains the entire world and loses his soul, and what will a man gain in exchange for his soul? ²⁷For the Son of Man will come in the glory of his Father and of the heavenly messengers*

(angels), and then he will repay everyone according to what they have done.
²⁸*Amen, I say to you, that some are standing here who will not die before they
see the Son of Man coming in his kingdom."*

Jesus now looks at his disciples and teaches them about discipleship. Peter had just rebuked Jesus for predicting the cross. Now
Jesus tells his disciples that not only will he die, but they must die as
well. Their death is a matter of self-denial. Aside from the physical
cross and other forms of execution they will face in the future, the
cross Jesus refers to here is figurative, symbolizing the death of one's
own dreams and ambitions. To save your life, you have to lose it. This
will become a major theme of Jesus from this point on. He is teaching
his disciples the cost of discipleship.

Jesus also heightens the role of the Son of Man here. The Son
of Man initiates the judgment scene. He will come with his angels to
judge the deeds of humanity. Since Jesus will oversee judgment, we
must live by Jesus' standard every single day.

Jesus also gives a timeframe for the coming of his kingdom.
It will come while some of the disciples are still alive. Therefore, the
kingdom will come in their generation. This prophecy is fulfilled in
Acts 2 when the church comes into existence.

The Transfiguration (17:1-9)
Cf. Mark 9:2-8; Luke 9:28-36

¹⁷:¹*After six days, Jesus took Peter, James, and his brother John
with him up on a high mountain by themselves. ²And he was transfigured
(metamorphed) before them, and his face was shining like the sun, and his
garment became white as light. ³Then suddenly Moses and Elijah appeared
in front of them, talking with him. ⁴Peter said to Jesus, "It is good for us
to be here. If you wish, I will build three booths here, one for you, one for
Moses, and one for Elijah." ⁵As he was speaking suddenly a bright cloud
overshadowed them, and a voice out of the clouds said, "This is my son whom
I love. I am pleased with him, listen to him." ⁶When the disciples heard this,
they fell on their faces and were terrified.*

⁷*Jesus came and touched them saying, "Get up and don't be afraid."
⁸When they looked up, they saw no one except Jesus. ⁹As they descended the
mountain Jesus ordered them, "Tell no one what you saw until the Son of
Man rises from the dead."*

Jesus chooses an inner circle from the disciples, and he allowed
them to see things that the other nine did not. Peter, James, and John
were taken on a high mountain to witness the transfiguration of Jesus.
A practical point that can be drawn from this scene is that Jesus had

friends, and then he had some special close friends with whom he shared more of his life. We can only get close to so many people. We should have a plethora of friendships in the kingdom. But we should also have some friends that we are close to in a special way. We can share our inmost feeling with these friends. These friends become our counselors. These are the friendships that we trust and value most of all. Although Jesus did not depend on his inner circle in the same way that we do, the fact that he picked out a few from the twelve to share more intimate times with is a principle that we can imitate.

For many years the high mountain of this passage was identified with Mt. Tabor close to the Sea of Galilee. But this is just a traditional site for the transfiguration. Mt. Tabor is barely a mountain, and it certainly is not a high mountain. The last location of Jesus before the transfiguration was Caesarea Philippi in Northern Galilee. There is a high mountain close to Caesarea Philippi, Mt. Hermon. Mt. Hermon is the highest point in Israel, rising up to 9,000 feet above sea level. It is much more likely that this was the site of the transfiguration.

The word for "transfigured" is the Greek *metemorpho*. This word means "to change," or "to transform." We derive our English word "metamorphosis" from this word. It is also used in the Bible to describe the change that occurs in a person's life when they become a disciple of Jesus. We become different.

Moses and Elijah appeared on the mountain with Jesus. The voice of God was heard declaring, "This is my son whom I love. I am pleased with him. Listen to him." Moses represents the law and Elijah represents the prophets. God singles out Jesus and declares that we should listen to him; that is to say, Jesus is above the law and the prophets. For Matthew's Jewish audience, this was a very important point. God is putting his stamp of approval on Jesus here.

When the disciples heard the voice of God, they fell on their faces in fear. Jesus did not want them to be afraid. Jesus consistently attacks fear in this gospel. When people are afraid, he tries to dispel their fears. He told the disciples to get up and keep what they have seen a secret until the Son of Man rises from the dead.

Elijah and the Suffering Son of Man (17:10-13)
Cf. Mark 9:9-13

¹⁰Then his disciples asked him, "Why then do the scribes say that it is necessary for Elijah to come first?" ¹¹Jesus answered, "Elijah is coming and he will restore everything. ¹²I tell you, Elijah has already come, and they did not recognize him but they did to him whatever they wished. Thus also is the Son of Man about to suffer at their hands." ¹³Then the disciples understood that he spoke to them about John the Baptist.

This reference to the Son of Man brings the role of Elijah to the minds of the disciples. They ask Jesus, "Isn't Elijah to come before the kingdom is established?" Jesus answers that he has already come, but he wasn't received like a prophet. Jesus links the fate of Elijah with his own fate, to suffer at their hands. Then the disciples understand. They are dull, but at times the blinders come away from their eyes and they see clearly. Elijah was John the Baptist. John the Baptist had come and gone. The kingdom of God can now come, but Jesus must prepare his disciples for the arrival of his kingdom.

Jesus Cures a Boy with a Demon (17:14-21)

[14]When they came to the crowd, a man came to him and knelt before him, and said [15]"Lord, have mercy on my son because he is an epileptic and suffers greatly. For he often falls in the fire and in the water. [16]I brought him to your disciples and they were not able to heal him." Jesus answered, [17]"Oh unfaithful and perverse generation. How much longer must I be with you? How long must I put up with you? Bring him here to me."

[18]Jesus rebuked the demon in him, and he cared for him and the child was healed from that hour. [19]Then the disciples came to Jesus and asked him privately, "Why were we not able to cast it out?" [20]He answered, "Because you lack faith. I say to you–[21]If you have faith as a mustard seed, you will say to this mountain move from here to there. It will be moved and nothing will be impossible for you."

Jesus faces a hopeless situation. A father brings his son to Jesus asking for a cure. His epilepsy causes him to fall into fire and water and severely injure himself. Jesus' disciples had already tried to cure the man, but were unable. Matthew highlights the fact that Jesus can help in situations that appear to be helpless.

First, Jesus rebukes his disciples for their lack of faith. He calls them unfaithful and perverse. He adds, "How long must I be with you? How long must I put up with you?" Jesus could tolerate many things from his disciples, ingratitude, lack of compassion, pride and selfish ambition, but there was one thing that Jesus could not tolerate: lack of faith.

Why was this? Our lack of faith keeps God from powerfully working in our lives. God often works in spite of our pride. He often works in spite of our lack of compassion. But he will not work through us if we lack faith. Faith is "the" crucial ingredient to allow God to work through us.

Jesus Again Foretells His Own Death and Resurrection (17:22-23)

22As they were gathering in Galilee, Jesus said to them, "The Son of Man is going to be betrayed into the hands of men, and 23they will kill him. But in three days, he will be raised." They were greatly disturbed.

Jesus again predicts his death and resurrection. He will do this several times in the latter half of Matthew. He is trying to prepare his disciples for what is about to come. The fact that Jesus predicts his own death shows that he was not surprised when it happened. He did not start something that went out of control. He was in control of all the events of his life. He wanted his disciples to know what was going to happen. He was very specific and concise here: I will be betrayed, killed, and raised in three days. This greatly disturbed the disciples. But they still did not fully understand what Jesus was talking about. He would predict his death again in an attempt to prepare them for his crucifixion.

Jesus and the Temple Tax (17:24-27)

24When they came into Capernaum, the temple tax collectors came to Peter saying, "Does you teacher pay the temple tax?"

25Peter answered, "Yes."

When he arrived at the house, Jesus spoke quietly saying, "What do you think Simon, from whom do the kings of the earth receive collections and taxes? From their child or others?"

26Peter answered, "From others."

Jesus said, "The children are free, 27but in order not to give them a reason to stumble, go to the lake and cast a hook, and pull in the first fish you catch. Open its mouth and you will find a coin. Give it to them for you and me."

This lesson is still played out today on the banks of the Sea of Galilee. When you order fish (the local indigenous fish is called "St. Peter's Fish") from a restaurant, be sure to check its mouth. The local merchants might have placed a coin in the mouth of the fish to commemorate this story of Jesus.

The Jewish authorities required a half-shekel tax of every male twenty years and older. This was the equivalent of two days pay.

True Greatness (18:1-5)

18:1At that time the disciples came to Jesus asking, "Who is the greatest in the kingdom?" 2And Jesus called a child to him and stood him among them, 3and he said, "Amen I say to you, unless you repent and become like children, you will not enter the kingdom of heaven. ⁴Therefore whoever becomes humble like this child, he will be greatest the kingdom of heaven. ⁵Whoever welcomes a child in my name, welcomes me."

Who is the greatest? This question has posed problems for humanity for centuries. The pursuit of greatness has caused countries to be destroyed. It has led people to cheat and defraud others. It has caused uncountable heartache and ruin.

Greatness in itself is not wrong. Jesus was a great person, and he did nothing wrong. The early apostles were great men. They stumbled at times, but they got back up and accomplished great things for God.

Since not all greatness is wrong, what type of a pursuit of greatness does Jesus tell his disciples to avoid? The pursuit of greatness at the expense of humility. Jesus brings a child into his circle and tells his disciples that they must become humble like a child.

What type of humility does a child have? Many children want to be number one. Haven't you heard children argue over who is going to be first? Haven't you heard them bicker over who is the best? They pursue greatness with the same zeal as adults.

But children tend to get over their hurts quicker than adults. They love to play more than they love to argue. Adults can hang on to grudges for years. They are less humble, it is harder for them to get past their hurt feelings. This brings to mind a conversation I overheard during a family vacation to North Carolina. My family loves to eat at Cracker Barrel. It is a restaurant that originated in Tennessee and serves good southern cooking. We stop at Cracker Barrels whenever we see them.

Once we stopped at a Cracker Barrel in Virginia and had supper. I was paying the bill when someone came to the cash register next to me to return a purchase. She was returning a nice china doll that seemed to be in perfect condition. The woman behind the register asked her if anything was wrong with the doll.

"No, the doll is wonderful," replied the customer.

"Then why are you returning it?" asked the clerk.

The customer answered, "I bought it for the friend of my little girl. It is her birthday. But her mother said something that offended me and now I'm returning this present. Her little girl isn't going to get something this nice."

"That's too bad," said the clerk.

"Too bad for the mother and her girl," said the customer angrily, "I'm never speaking to them again."

As I stood there listening to this exchange, I couldn't help but

Practically Speaking ☞

Go the Distance

No one wants to be pushed around or bullied. When I was in elementary school, I was always one of the shortest kids in my class. Picture a blond-haired, blue-eyed, freckle-faced kid who weighed about twenty pounds less than everyone else in the class and you get the idea of how I looked. I was the perfect target for a bully. Fortunately, my best friend, Bill Cromer, happened to be the tallest, meanest, toughest kid in the entire school. If anyone picked on me, they had to face Bill.

Whenever we feel taken advantage of, we want to stand up for our rights. When attacked, we reciprocate by lashing back. When abused, we demand help until relief comes. Our humanity compels us not to allow ourselves to be pushed around. If anything, we are going to do the pushing.

The story of Jesus and the temple tax grabs our attention from the first reading. Here we learn a lesson from the character of Jesus, his willingness to go the distance for God.

If your father owns a house, then you as the son or daughter are not required to bring a gift when you enter the house. You are usually afforded a key to the front door. Knocking or ringing the doorbell is not required upon entering. You enter freely from the front door, back door, side door, or any open window. You enter freely because it is your father's house. In a sense, the house belongs to you, the heir.

God was owner and resident of the temple at Jerusalem. He ordered it built, laid out the plans, saw the project to completion, and took up residency upon completion. The temple did not belong to Solomon. The temple was God's.

Jesus, as God's son, held complete rights to the temple. He was the heir. Jesus did not have to knock on the door to enter. To ask him to pay a temple tax would be like asking us to pay to enter our own homes. If anything, the temple tax should have been paid to Jesus.

Yet when asked to pay the temple tax, Jesus paid it. If he had not, some would have thought he had contempt for the temple. In order not to offend anyone, he paid the tax.

Jesus could have stood up for his rights. "My father owns this house and I will not pay a tax on it." But Jesus humbled himself and paid the tax. He would pay the tax to bring glory to the Father. Though he was God, he learned obedience. Jesus was willing to go the distance, any distance, to please the Father.

What distance will you go to please God? Is there a stopping point for you in your discipleship? Are you willing to allow someone to step on your pride without retaliation? Do you go the extra hour in prayer? Have your goals reflected the extra-mile character of Jesus? You must "go the distance."

I love the movie *Field of Dreams*. As a Midwestern farmer walks along the rows of corn in his field, a voice whispers, "If you build it, they will come." Upon reflection, the man realizes that if he builds a baseball diamond, then Shoeless Joe Jackson will come play on his field. As he begins to build, neighbors mock him, the crops begin to fail, his wife doubts him, and he even begins to doubt. He hears another voice: "Go the distance!" He puts the doubts to rest, perseveres in spite of the opposition, and sees the project through to completion.

Jesus never stopped short of completely pleasing the Father. He "went the distance," daily. What will it take for you to go the distance?

Note: This story also conveys the power of Jesus over nature. He tells his disciples to look for coins in a fish's mouth. (If only it were that easy for us to pay our taxes today). Jesus did not have even a drachma to pay the temple tax. When he left heaven, he literally became poor for us (2 Corinthians 8:9).

think that the real victims in this story were the little girls. All they wanted to do was play together. One of them would miss the other's birthday because of their mothers' feud.

Our pursuit of greatness can cause us to do some silly things. We can act unapproachable to other people. We can hurt people with our coldness. We can hold on to hurts for years and years. We can crush the spirit of others in an attempt to elevate our own egos. Our pursuit of greatness hurts others and it hurts God.

Relationships within the church (18:6-35)

The rest of chapter 18 deals with relationships within the church and situations that come in those relationships. These situations revolve around sin and forgiveness. Different situations are discussed:

Vss. 6-9   Causing other disciples to sin.
Vss. 10-14 Winning back those who have left the church.
Vss. 15-20 Correcting a disciple who is in error.
Vss. 21-22 Being reconciled to your brother.
Vss. 23   Forgiveness.
Vss. 34-35 The Parable of the Unforgiving Servant.

Causing Others to Sin (18:6-9)

⁶*"Whoever causes one of the little ones who believes in me to stumble, it would be better for him to tie a giant millstone around his neck and be throne into the depths of the sea. ⁷Woe to the world because of stumbling blocks. Stumbling blocks are going to come, but woe to the person through whom they come.*

⁸*If your leg or foot causes you to sin—cut it off and cast it from you. It is better to live life maimed than with two hands and two feet to be thrown into the eternal fire. ⁹Or if your eye causes you to stumble—tear it out and cast it from you—for it is better for you to go through life with one eye than to be cast into the gehenna/hell of fire."*

The "little ones" that Jesus is referring to here are not little children but neophyte believers. He warns those who would cause these "little ones" to stumble that they are doomed to destruction. The giant millstone was a circular stone often five or six feet in diameter. Pulled in a circle by donkeys, the millstone rotated on top of an even larger stone, slowly grinding the grain laid between the stones. Anyone who had a millstone tied to his neck and was cast into the sea would sink straight to the bottom. Jesus warns against being a stumbling block to a young believer.

Jesus then repeats what he said in the Sermon on the Mount (Matthew 5:29-30). He uses hyperbole to stress that we need to get away from anything that might cause us to sin.

Winning back those who have left (18:10-14)

¹⁰*"Be careful that you do not despise one of these little ones. ¹¹For I tell you their angels in heaven continually see the face of my Father. ¹²What do you think? If a shepherd has a hundred sheep and he looses one of them, does he not leave the 99 on the mountain to search for the one that is lost? ¹³If he finds him, I tell you plainly, he rejoices over it more than over the 99 who were safe. ¹⁴So is the will of your Father in heaven that not one of these little ones be lost."*

In the context "these little ones" is still referring to followers of Jesus. Out of context it is easy to think "these little ones" refers to children. Then the following sentence about "their angels" looking continually at the face of God would be a reference to guardian angels. But if this sentence refers to guardian angels, then the context implies that the angels are overseeing young disciples. This idea would fit in well with Hebrews 1:14 that reads, "Are not all angels ministering spirits sent to serve those who will inherit salvation?" Angels are ministering spirits for those of us who are his disciples. I'm not sure

I understand completely what that means, but it makes me happy to know that I have angels watching over me.

Have you ever lost something that was important to you? Have you ever lost something that you desperately needed? How do you feel when you lose these things? I feel frustrated, angry, silly, dumb and agitated. Time and again I seem to misplace my keys. I remember a time when my wife and I had returned from a trip to Johannesburg, South Africa. We unpacked everything and I could not find my keys anywhere, not in the suitcases, not in my pockets, not in the briefcase, not on my dresser. The keys were lost. Not just my house key, but also every key that I owned, including car keys, suitcase keys, house keys and the keys to padlocks. I searched and searched until I finally found the keys. I was not going to stop looking for them until they were found. After much searching, I found what was missing.

God has the same attitude toward anyone who leaves the church. God will not give up on that person. The person who leaves God is the one sheep that has gone astray. God will continue to fight to win back anyone who has left him.

Helping the Brother in Sin (Church Discipline) (18:15-20)

15"If your brother sins against you, go show him his fault — just you and him alone. If he listens to you, you have regained your brother. 16If he does not listen, take one or two others with you — that two or three witnesses may confirm every word. 17If he refuses to listen, tell it to the church, and if he refuses to listen to the church, treat him as an outsider or a tax collector.

18I tell you truthfully, Whatever you bind on earth will have been bound in heaven and whatever you loose on earth will have been loosed in heaven. 19Again I tell you, if two of you agree on earth about anything you ask, the Father in heaven will give it to you. 20For where two or three assemble in my name, there I am in their midst."

It has often been said through the centuries that the church is not perfect. This is true. It is not perfect because it is made up of people who are imperfect. I remember hearing an evangelist preach, "You can search and search and find the perfect church. Then you go and join it. Then guess what — it's not perfect anymore."

We sin. We sin against each other and hurt each other. But when we sin against each other, we are to reconcile our relationships. When I was growing up in Tennessee, I knew of situations in churches where people had hurt each other and were unwilling to forgive. They sat on opposite sides of the church building. They never greeted each other. When they passed, they looked in opposite directions. The church is not perfect. But situations like this should not exist in the church.

15-17 Jesus' directive is if your brother sins against you, you go to him yourself and show him his fault. The directive is not to tell as many people as will listen how you have been hurt. Jesus says your responsibility as the injured party is to go to the person yourself. Tell him your grievance and pray that he will listen to you.

If he will not listen, what is the next step? Jesus directs us to take one or two others with us. This is not to attack the person. The motivation is reconciliation. We want to help the person. Once again, the injured party is to take the lead in reconciliation. We can't get hurt and retreat in a corner and say, "He sinned against me, let him take the first step to reconciliation." In a perfect church that would happen, but the church is full of sinners who are trying to overcome sin. We make mistakes. Sometimes we own those mistakes, and sometimes we need help owning those mistakes.

If the person still won't listen, then we can take the matter before the church. We get more people involved to help the person see his sin. Prayerfully, he will see it and change. If he doesn't change, but continues to cling to his sin, then he is to be treated as an outsider. This doesn't mean mistreat him. But it means that we see him as a person who is outside the fellowship that we need to win back.

18 In context, the binding or loosing has to do with the church's decision to include or exclude the sinful brother from fellowship. Jesus is saying that the church has authority in such matters. It is an authority given to the church by God. With this authority comes responsibility. The church must take these matters seriously, and act in these situations after much prayer and fasting.

19-20 In the context, Jesus is speaking about people agreeing on the course of action to take concerning a brother in sin. Jesus is talking about church discipline. The two or three are coming together in agreement over what must be done with a brother in error. They are to take this matter to God, and he will answer their prayer concerning the situation. He is with them in the midst of this matter.

For us to take this verse out of context and apply it to the prayers of disciples in all situations is bad hermeneutics. God is always with us when we pray. But this verse is speaking only of church discipline, and it should be used only to apply to church discipline.

Forgiveness (18:21-22)

²¹Then Peter approached Jesus and said, "Lord, when my brother sins against me. How often must I forgive him? Until seven time?"

²²Jesus answered, □No, not seven times, but seventy-seven times.□

Peter, the outspoken one, has a question. He wants to know how often he must forgive someone. Rabbinic literature says that we must forgive a person up to three times. If he sins against us the fourth time, then we do not need to forgive him. Peter goes beyond the rabbinical tradition and says "up to seven times."

Jesus tells Peter that we must forgive people an unlimited number of times. Not three times, not seven times, but seventy-seven times. As long as the brother is sincerely asking for forgiveness, our attitude as the injured party must be to forgive.

The Parable of the Unforgiving Servant (18:23-35)

   23"For this reason the kingdom of heaven is like a king who wishes to settle accounts with his slaves. 24As he went over his accounts, a person was brought to him that owed 10,000 talents, and he could not pay. 25The Lord ordered him to be sold with his wife and children and all he owned – so payment could be made. 26The slave fell on his knees saying, 'Have patience with me, and I will repay you everything.' 27And his Lord had compassion on him and released him and forgave his debt.

   28That slave went out and found a fellow slave who owed him 100 denarii's, and he seized him by the throat, saying, "Pay me what you owe." 29The fellow slave fell down and begged him, 'Have patience with me and I will repay you.' 30But he refused, he went and threw him in prison until he could pay the debt.

   31When his fellow slaves saw these events they were disturbed and they went and told the Lord what had happened. 32Then the Lord summoned him and said, 'Evil slave! I forgave all your debt because you pleaded with me. 33Should you not have had mercy on your fellow slave as I had mercy on you?' 34The Lord was enraged and handed him over to be tortured until he could pay his debt. 35So my Father in heaven will do to you if you do not forgive your brother from the heart."

To stress the importance of unlimited forgiveness, Jesus tells the parable of the unmerciful servant. Although there are several lessons that can be drawn from this parable, Jesus states the point of the parable very succinctly, "So my Father in heaven will do to you, if you do not forgive your brother from the heart." It is a parable about forgiveness.

The parable is easily summarized. A king was going over outstanding accounts when he discovered that a man owed him 10,000 talents. D.A. Carson puts this debt in perspective by writing:

> We glimpse some idea of the size of the indebtedness when
> we recall that David donated three thousand talents of gold and

seven thousand talents of silver for the construction of the temple.
Some recent estimates suggest a dollar value of twelve million; but
with inflation and fluctuating precious metal prices, this could be over
a billion dollars in today's currency. This was an overwhelming debt.
The point is that the man could work for the king all his life and still
not repay the debt.[1]

Does that sound familiar? Hopefully it doesn't sound like our personal debt. But it does sound like the debt that we owe God.

The king ordered that the man, his wife, and children should all be sold into slavery to recover the debt. This was in keeping with Old Testament teaching (Exodus 22:3). The man threw himself on the mercy of the throne. His life and the life of his family would not come close to paying the debt as the top price for a slave in that day was about one talent. So the king released him, forgiving his debt. Notice that he did not expect him to work until the debt was paid. He forgave the debt.

This same man finds a fellow slave who owes him 100 denarii. A denarius was a day's pay. So he owed the man one hundred days wages. Instead of forgiving his fellow slave, the man had him thrown in prison. The other slaves were greatly distressed at the man's lack of forgiveness, and they reported the incident to the king. The king arrested the man, had him tortured and thrown in jail. Since he was unwilling to forgive others, he would not be forgiven.

The message is clear: we must forgive others. If we are disciples, we should realize how much God has forgiven us. We are the man who owed 10,000 talents to the king. This is a debt that is beyond our ability to repay. So Jesus paid it for us. How ungrateful for us to then turn around and not forgive others. As God has forgiven us, we must forgive everyone around us.

Endnotes
[1] Carson, p. 406.

6

Ministry in Judea
Turning to Jerusalem
Matthew 19:1-23:39

Teaching about Divorce (19:1-12)

19:1When Jesus finished saying these things, he left Galilee and came to the region of Judea across the Jordan. 2Large crowds followed him and he healed them there.

3The Pharisees came to him testing/tempting him and saying, "Is it lawful for a man to divorce his wife for any cause?"

4Jesus answered, "Have you not read that the one who created them at the beginning, 'He made them male and female,' 5and, 'for this reason a man should leave his father and mother and be joined to his wife and the two will become one flesh.' 6So they are no longer two but one. Therefore what God has joined together, let no one separate."

7They said to him, "Why then did Moses command us--to give a certificate of divorce and allow us to divorce her?"

8He answered, "Because of your hard hearts, Moses allowed you to divorce your wives, but it was not so from the beginning."

9I tell you, "Whoever divorces his wife, except for unfaithfulness (sexual sin) and marries another commits adultery."

10His disciples said to him, "If this is how it is with a man and his wife, it is better not to marry."

11Jesus answered, "Not everyone can accept this teaching, but only those to whom it is given. 12For there are some who are eunuchs from birth, and some are made eunuchs by man, and some made themselves eunuchs for the kingdom of heaven. Whoever is able to accept this, should accept it."

The Pharisees questioned Jesus about divorce. They themselves were divided on the issue. Jesus answered that it was always God's intention that man should marry one woman for life. So the Pharisees wanted to know why Moses allowed for a certificate of divorce. Jesus answered that it was because of the hardness of man's heart. Jesus allows divorce for marital infidelity. This is one of many verses that deal with divorce in the Bible. This is a controversial issue today so let us do an overview of the topic as taught in the Bible.

Practically Speaking ᘒ

Divorce and Remarriage: A Perspective

I grew up in a conservative church in Middle Tennessee. Most people who know me know this. Several ultra-conservative publications governed this part of the church. I was taught to take the most conservative stance on every issue. We accepted the King James Version or the American Standard Version (1901) of the Bible. No pretenders, no other contenders, those were the "authorized" versions.

Later, I went to an extremely liberal seminary, Southeastern Baptist Theological Seminary in Wake Forest, North Carolina. Professors who studied at Tubigen University, Oxford University, Harvard, and Emory trained me. None of these professors accepted the plenary, verbal inspiration of the Bible. A few years after I left, the school went through a purging and all my old professors were asked to leave because they were deemed too liberal. I've seen the left, and I've seen the right. I hope I fall somewhere in the middle.

I will first take a look at the Biblical verses that speak on this issue. After that, I will share my conclusions from my study.

Malachi 2:16 "'I hate divorce,' says the Lord God of Israel." (NIV)

I believe any study on marriage, divorce, and remarriage needs to begin with Malachi 2:16. God's view of divorce is stated clearly and succinctly. Here Malachi warns each husband to stay faithful to the wife of his youth. Obviously this was a problem that had to be addressed. Why stay faithful? Because God hates divorce. Any study of divorce and remarriage must recognize where God stands on the issue. God hates divorce.

We must keep this concept clearly before us. Church members should not view divorce as an option. In premarital counseling, we must stress that God hates divorce. God has a high standard for marriage. We need to keep this standard high.

Another verse that connects at this point is Ecclesiastes 5:4-6, "When you make a vow to God, do not delay in fulfilling it. He has no pleasure in fools; fulfill your vow. It is better not to vow than to make a vow and not fulfill it. Do not let your mouth lead you into sin. And do not protest to the temple messenger, 'My vow was a mistake.' Why should God be angry at what you say and destroy the work of your hands?" Marriage vows must be taken seriously. Anyone who marries within the church must recognize that they are making a vow before God. This vow is sacred and should be kept.

Deuteronomy 24:1-4

But God did allow divorce. In Deuteronomy 24:1-4 a man is instructed that if he finds something indecent (*erwat dabar*) about his wife, then he can give her a certificate of divorce (*seper keritut*). This certificate gave her the right to remarry. The teaching of Jesus helps us understand that God allowed divorce because of the hard-heartedness of humanity. Men were leaving their wives, abandoning them without any rights or privileges. God allowed the certificate of divorce to establish some rights for women in this unjust environment. God loves justice. God's heart for humanity allowed divorce to be established in the Mosaic code.

What is meant here by "something indecent?" Does this mean annoying habits, fading beauty, or undesired actions? One of my old professors, Clyde Woods, comments:

> Thus, this passage does not command divorce as older English versions might be understood, but rather, conceding the custom (compare Leviticus 21:7, 14; 22:13; Numbers 23: 14), the expression seems to connote obnoxious or indecent behavior, thus some serious grounds for divorce. Adultery cannot be meant since that offense merited death (Numbers 22:22). In the day of Moses, God allowed divorce to occur, but he never meant this to be taken as license to divorce for any small, selfish, or trivial matter. "Something indecent" connotes obnoxious or indecent behavior.[1]

The reason for divorce must be a serious matter. It does not mean issues like she is a bad cook or she's not as pretty as she use to be. By New Testament times, the rabbis were divided over this matter. Jesus speaks to this division.

Mark 10:2-12

The beginning of this section is almost identical to Matthew 19. Matthew seems to have borrowed his account from Mark. The ending of Mark (verses 10-12) differs from Matthew. Jesus enters a house and is questioned by his disciples. He answers them from a gender-neutral point of view. If the man or woman divorces and marries again, adultery is committed. There is no exception clause like we see in Matthew. It seems that Jesus is trying to stress the importance of staying married. He allows no "do-overs" in this situation. He stresses the need to work through any problem and stay married. This is the word to his disciples in private–help people work through any problems in their marriages and keep them together. If they separate and remarry, then they commit adultery.

If one of the partners goes against this advice, leaves, and commits adultery, what happens to the other person? According to Matthew 5 and 19, they are free to remarry. But the emphasis in Matthew 5, Matthew 19, and Mark 10 is to stay together–work it out.

We should note that twice, where Jesus refers to the commandment of God, his opponents refer to what is permissible. Jesus is concerned with the will of God, while the opponents are concerned with taking the greatest advantage of what is permissible. We need to guard against this humanistic tendency in our thinking today as well. If we do not accept the high standard that Jesus had for marriage and staying together in marriage, then we allow people to have "shallow thinking" concerning the sanctity of the marriage bond. People will not be committed to each other for life if they do not take their marriage vows seriously.

Luke 16:17-18

Here Jesus talks about the continued obligation of the law. He illustrates it with the example of marriage. Marriage is to be honored. Divorce is not an accepted practice. Jesus upholds the sanctity of marriage by coupling the honor of the marriage vow with the integrity of the law of God. This demonstrates the seriousness of the marriage vow in the mind of Christ. I. Howard Marshall, professor at the University of Aberdeen, writes:

> In any case, Luke's saying goes against Jewish ideas, according to which a husband had freedom to divorce his wife and remarry, and condemns this as adultery. Similarly, the saying condemns the second husband for committing adultery; Jewish law allowed such marriages, except in the case of a woman marrying her co-respondent. Thus the saying sharpens the teaching of the Old Testament law, and in no sense undermines it.[2]

The rabbis were divided on this issue. Some taught that divorce could be easily given, while others taught that divorce could only be given in the case of adultery. Jesus tries to focus on the heart of what was said about divorce in Deuteronomy 24. Divorce is not to be taken lightly. Certificates of divorce should not be written for the least little thing. He takes "something indecent" as meaning adultery. Only in the case of adultery is divorce an option. In his covenant community, this was his rabbinical ruling on the issue. Later, the church would adopt this ruling. Paul would have some clarification on it pertaining to those outside the community.

Matthew 5:31-32

This saying is found in the Sermon on the Mount. It is meant for the covenant community of Jesus. Notice that it is written from a particularly masculine point of view. This is because in the first century Judaism the woman had little rights. Women were being divorced for any reason. The two rabbinical schools of Jesus' day were debating the reasons for a divorce. Shammai believed that divorce could only be given in the case of adultery. Hillel believed that a woman could be divorced for small reasons, including childlessness, cultic offences, and incompetence in performing household tasks like burning dinner. If the husband felt the wife was unsuitable to his desires, then he could write her a "certificate of divorce." This certificate was given to protect her rights.

Jesus attempts to change the situation by telling the men within his community that there is only one reason (*parektos logou*=except for the reason, word, matter) for divorce. The sole reason to give a certificate of divorce is *porneia* meaning any type of sexual unfaithfulness. To divorce her for any other reason is to make her an adulteress. Because of the socioeconomic situation of first century Palestine, the woman would be forced to find another husband to support her. Since she was divorced illegitimately, she would become an adulteress and anyone who married her would become an adulterer.

Jesus teaches that if divorce comes because of marital unfaithfulness, then the one who was faithful could divorce the other party. But what happens to the person who committed adultery? Is he or she able to remarry? Let me again stress that the point of Jesus in his teaching is that divorce should be avoided at all costs. But in the case of marital unfaithfulness, it is permitted. When the divorce occurs, the marriage is over. Therefore, both parties now reenter a state of being unmarried. Therefore, they are both free to remarry.

Jesus underscores the sanctity of marriage for those in his covenant community. His followers are not to take divorce lightly. This is especially true of men who had more rights than women in the first century. Marriage was for life. The only legitimate reason for divorce was adultery/marital unfaithfulness.

Matthew 19:3-12

Although Jesus is answering questions posed by the Pharisees, his statements concerning divorce apply to his covenant community. Jesus harkens back to Deuteronomy 24 to establish the sanctity of marriage. A man and woman become one flesh in marriage. No one should take this lightly. But in Jesus' day people were taking divorce lightly. Divorce was rampant. Jesus tells his followers that he expects a different attitude toward marriage from them. In Jesus' community there is only one reason for divorce: sexual unfaithfulness. Jesus treats marriage seriously. Robert W. Wall, in *The Anchor Bible Dictionary*, comments, "Clearly, the sum of the synoptic tradition argues that Jesus' teaching intended to create among his disciples an intolerance for divorce even though Jewish law tolerated it."[3]

1 Corinthians 7:10-20

The Apostle Paul gives additional teaching on the divorce and remarriage issue. He is attempting to clarify what should happen to the people who have come into the kingdom already divorced and remarried. He also clarifies what should happen if a believer is married to an unbeliever. These are situations that concerned the early disciples and still concern us today. What does Paul say?

First, he says to those who are married to an unbeliever that if they consent to stay married then the marriage remains intact. If the unbeliever decides to leave the believer, then the believer is free to remarry.

Second, he says that everyone comes into the kingdom in whatever condition in which they were called. If they were baptized uncircumcised, they remain uncircumcised. If they came into the kingdom single as a result of divorce, then they are treated as a single person. If they come into the kingdom divorced and remarried, then they are received as married. Each person comes into the kingdom as they were called.

The Early Church

I could not find much material in the Church Fathers regarding divorce and remarriage. If I had, I would have placed little weight on it. By the end of the first century, Gnosticism was growing within the church community. This teaching viewed the body as evil. It also viewed sex as only for procreation. The more spiritual would be expected to abstain from the act; thus church leaders were not married. Tertullian (c. 200) says:

> Christ abolished the commandment of Moses—why then should not the *Paraclete* have cancelled the indulgence granted by Paul? "Hardness of heart" held sway until the coming of Christ; let weakness of the flesh bring its reign to an end with the coming of the *Paraclete*. The New Law abolished divorce—the New Prophecy abolished second marriage.[4]

Conclusion

For those in the church, God gives us a high standard in marriage—we are married for life. Jesus does give one exception: divorce is allowed in the case of marital unfaithfulness (sexual infidelity). If a couple is married in the church, they must recognize they are married for life. They must not break the vows they made before God and his community. He said it as a warning to those who are marrying in the community of believers to hold marriage sacred and holy. We must keep a high standard here. If we do not hold to a high standard, then we by neglect are acting as if Jesus said nothing on this topic.

But even with this high standard, divorce does happen. When someone is unfaithful, their partner can divorce them. When this happens the marriage is over and both parties enter the realm of the unmarried. They can marry again.

If someone marries in the church and falls away from God, then the teaching of Paul comes into play. If the member who falls away wishes to remain with the faithful partner, then the faithful partner must fulfill his or her marriage vows. But if the member who falls away chooses to separate, divorce, or commit adultery, then the faithful member can divorce and remarry. They are not bound in these circumstances.

What if someone falls away, divorces, and then decides to get restored? Can they then remarry? If a person is divorced, the marital bond is broken. The parties are no longer bound by it. Within the church, divorce simply should not happen. But if someone leaves God, then they might decide to get divorced. They come back to the church in whatever state they are in when they decide to repent.

We have to walk the tightrope of teaching what the Bible teaches and counseling people who are hurting themselves and others. Robert W. Wall states:

> Scriptural teaching on divorce underscores two convictions, which form a pastoral dialectic. Following Jesus, there must be a readiness to resist divorce as an evil; divorce is opposed to God's reign, even though the believing community may tolerate it. However, following Paul, there must be a willingness to resist facile solutions, which fail to accommodate concrete and difficult cases presented by our own situations.[5]

Paul gives us room to accept those outside the church into the church in whatever state they are living in when they become disciples. He

Conclusion *(continued)*

does not attempt to change the high standard of Jesus concerning marriage for those within the community of believers.

I believe that we must follow Paul and attempt to make the teaching of Jesus applicable to a secular, pagan, and godless society. But we must be careful to not make the message so accommodating that we forget what Jesus taught. Jesus had something serious to say to his community about marriage, divorce, and remarriage. Are we getting that message through to his community today?

Jesus Blesses the Little Children (19:13-15)

¹³Then little children were brought to Jesus for him to place his hands on them and to pray for them. But his disciples rebuked those who brought them. ¹⁴Jesus said, "Allow the little children and don't stop them, for the kingdom of heaven belongs to such as these." ¹⁵And he laid his hands on them and went on his way.

Jesus loved little children. Here they are brought to him to be blessed by him. The disciples rebuked those who brought them. Perhaps they thought that Jesus was too busy for the little children. Perhaps they didn't want to be bothered with them. Jesus makes it clear that he wanted to be with the children. He did not just tolerate them; he did not just put up with them. He loved children. Do we have a heart for children? Do we take time for them? Not just as parents taking time for our own children, but do we as disciples of Jesus have a heart for children? What about in our children's ministry? Have we volunteered to teach in our children's ministry? What about in the fellowship around church? Do you know the children in your church? Do you take time during fellowship to stop and speak to them or to play with them? Jesus had a heart for children.

Jesus said that children belong to the kingdom of heaven. Many churches teach infant baptism. This doctrine was originally practiced because people were deciding to not be baptized as adults to escape a church tax. If you baptized them as babies, they had to be a part of the church and must pay the church tax. Later, Augustine promoted the doctrine of original sin, that we are all born with sin, to explain the reason for infant baptism. Infant baptism is never taught in the Bible. There is not a single example of infant baptism in the Bible. Baptism is an adult decision. Here Jesus says that children are a part of God's kingdom. He does not say they are in sin and need infant baptism. He received them as part of his fellowship and blessed them.

The Rich Young Man (19:16-22)

[16]*Then someone came to Jesus and said, "Teacher, what good should I do to have eternal life?"*

[17]*Jesus said, "Why do you ask me what is good? Only one is good. But if you wish to have eternal life, then keep the commandments."*

[18]*He asked, "Which ones?"*

Jesus said, "Do not murder, do not commit adultery, do not steal, and do not bear false testimony. [19]*Honor your father and mother and love your neighbor as yourself."*

[20]*The young man said, "I have kept all these; what do I lack?"*

[21]*Jesus answered him, "If you wish to be perfect, go sell your possessions and give them to the poor. You will have treasure in heaven. Then come, follow me."*

[22]*When the young man heard this, he went away sad because he had many possessions.*

The story of the "Rich Young Ruler" is found in all three gospels. He is described as a rich man in all the Synoptics. Luke calls him a ruler, and Matthew mentions that he is young. Thus the designation rich young ruler.

In Mark, the young man approaches Jesus and says, "Good Teacher." In Matthew, he says, "Teacher, what good thing should I do?" Jesus responds in Mark by saying, "Why do you call me good?" and in Matthew by saying, "Why do you ask me about what is good?" The natural way to harmonize the two accounts is to picture the rich man asking the question with the adjective "good" in both sections. For example, "Good Teacher, what good thing must I do to inherit eternal life?" Jesus would then respond to both questions, "Why do you call me good and why do you ask me what is good? Don't you know that God alone is good?"

The man comes to Jesus wanting to know what good thing he could do to inherit eternal life. He has kept the commandments. So he must be looking for something beyond the commandments that would guarantee his salvation. Jesus lets him know that he is thinking the wrong way. The only "good" thing you can do to inherit eternal life is to know the "good" Father who gives eternal life. The young man was looking for a legalistic approach to God. Jesus tells the man that salvation is a matter of relationship, not works.

Since Jesus is God, why does he not accept the designation of "good" as applied to him by the rich, young ruler? Jesus deflects the glory that the man wanted to give him and gives it to God the Father. This was the nature of Jesus to glorify the Father with his life. Here he could have accepted the title "good," but he glorifies God the Father with the title.

But the fact that we have a relationship with the "good" Father does not negate that we must keep the commandments. When the young man asks, "what must I do," Jesus responds by listing the sixth, seventh, eighth, ninth, and fifth commandments while adding, "love your neighbor as yourself." But the young man is quick to check these off his legalistic works list. So Jesus goes to the man's heart. Jesus says, "If you want to be perfect..." "Perfect" means complete. If you want to have a complete relationship with God, then you must do this. What is it that is keeping you from being close to God? What is hindering your relationship with God? For the rich young ruler, Jesus puts his finger on the heart of the issue and says, "Go, sell what you have and give it to the poor."

The rich, young ruler was unwilling to tick this off his legalistic checklist because this was the real issue that was keeping him from having a great relationship with God. D.A. Carson writes:

> He was willing to discipline himself to observe all the outward stipulations and even perform supererogatory works; but because of his wealth, he had a divided heart. His money was competing with God; and what Jesus everywhere demands as a condition for eternal life is absolute, radical discipleship. This entails the surrender of self.[6]

Riches were on the throne of his life. Since riches were there, God could not be on the throne. He loved riches more than God.

Grace and Reward in the Kingdom (19:23-30)

23Jesus said to his disciples, "I tell you truthfully, it is difficult for the rich to enter the kingdom of heaven." 24I'm going to say it again, "It is easier for a camel to go through the eye of a needle than for a rich man to enter the kingdom of God."

25When his disciples heard this, they were greatly astonished and asked, "Who then can be saved?"

26Jesus looked at them and said, "For man these things are impossible, but for God all things are possible."

27Peter said, "We have given up everything to follow you. What will we have?"

28Jesus said to them, "Amen, I say to you, at the renewal of all things, when the Son of Man sits on his throne of glory, you who have followed me will sit on twelve thrones, judging the twelve tribes of Israel. 29Whoever has left his house, or brothers, or sister, or father or mother, or children or field for me will receive a hundred times as much and will inherit eternal life. 30The many who are first shall be last and the last first."

The disciples and most Jews expected the rich to inherit heaven. The Jewish mind embraced prosperity theology. This is the thought that God prospers the individual. Therefore, the more you serve God, the more riches you will acquire. In some ways the Old Testament does support this thinking. The patriarchs all received material blessings from God and were rich, although we also see that their riches did not guarantee happiness. King David and King Solomon were symbols of God's material blessings. But this thinking breaks down in the prophets. The prophets were ordinary people who struggled materially throughout their lives. Amos was a shepherd and sycamore fig tree keeper. Isaiah was a simple priest and so was Ezekiel. Daniel advanced in the Babylonian empire, but don't lose sight that he was an exile, captured in battle and that he was thrown into a lion's den to die. So prosperity theology is not Biblical. Jesus teaches against it here.

Instead of prosperity theology Jesus teaches that is it difficult for the rich to enter the kingdom of heaven. Just as the rich young ruler walked away from Jesus because of his riches; many are drawn away from God by their materialism. This does not mean that the rich cannot enter heaven; that would exclude Abraham, Isaac, Jacob, and King David. Anything is possible with God.

Some scholars over the years have tried to explain away the image of the camel going through the eye of the needle. Even when I was a small boy growing up in church, I heard preachers say that the "eye of the needle" was a gate in the wall of Jerusalem where the camel would have to bend down on its knees and crawl into the city. But this is just not true. There is no gate called "the eye of the needle." Matthew is talking about the eye of a sewing needle. That is how difficult it is for the rich to enter the kingdom of heaven.

The disciples recognized exactly what Jesus was saying, and they balked at it. If it is that difficult for the rich to be saved, then who then can be saved? It is impossible in the eyes of men. But nothing is impossible with God. For the rich to enter the kingdom of heaven, they must turn their lives over to God. Surrender everything to him. This is what the rich young ruler was unwilling to do.

It is what Peter claims that the disciples had done. He says, "We've left everything to follow you." But Jesus lets Peter know that you don't give up anything for God without receiving it back and more. He tells them that at the end of time, when the Son of Man sits on the throne of glory, they will sit on twelve thrones, judging the twelve tribes of Israel. It is difficult to know what Jesus means here. "Judging" can mean "placing judgment on something," or "ruling." Will the disciples sit on judicial thrones or princely thrones?

James and John later request to sit on princely thrones. Perhaps this is where they got the idea. Also, they will judge the twelve tribes of Israel. Is this literally the twelve tribes of Israel or a symbolic image of the church? It seems to me that it is best in this context to take the word "judge" to mean "to pronounce judgment on," and to take the twelve tribes to mean Israel. Since Israel for the most part had rejected Jesus, and the disciples had left everything to follow him, in the judgment their places would be reversed and the disciples would sit as examples of what Israel would have been if Israel had received Jesus as the Messiah.

Jesus also tells the disciples that whoever has left everything will receive a hundred times as much houses, brothers, sister, fathers, mothers, children, fields, and eternal life. This is not prosperity theology. The rewards are not promised in the here and now. They are promised at the renewal of all things. The history of the early church demonstrates that the early Christians did not prosper materially in their lifetime. They were persecuted and rejected by the world. Many suffered death for their belief. Their families were ripped apart. They lost employment and had to flee their homes and fields for their lives. They had to go underground and hide from the authorities. How anyone can develop a prosperity theology based on the teachings of Jesus and the history of the early church is beyond me. Disciples will receive countless rewards, not in the here and now, but in the hereafter.

The Laborers in the Vineyard (20:1-16)

²⁰:¹*"For the kingdom of heaven is like a landowner, who went out early in the morning to hire laborers in his vineyard. ²He agreed with his brothers for the daily wage (a denarius a day). He sent them into his vineyard.*

³*He went out about nine o'clock (the third hour). He saw others standing idle in the marketplace. ⁴He said to them, 'Go into the vineyard, and I will give/pay you whatever is right.' ⁵And they went.*

Again he went out around noon (the sixth hour) and three (the ninth hour) and did the same thing.

⁶*Around five o'clock (the eleventh hour) he went and found others standing and told them, 'Why are you standing around doing nothing for the whole day?'*

⁷*They answered, 'Because no one hired us.'*

He said, 'Go into the vineyard and get to work.'

⁸*When evening came, the Lord of the vineyard said to his manager, 'Call the laborers and pay then their wages, beginning from the last to the first.'*

⁹*When those hired about five o'clock came, they received a daily*

wage – one denarius. *[10]And when the first came, they expected to receive
more, but each of them received a denarius.* *[11]So they grumbled against the
landowner saying,* *[12]'Those who came last worked only one hour, and you have
made them equal to us who endured the day's burden and the scorching heat.'*

*[13]He answered one of them, 'Friend, I am not treating you unfairly,
didn't you agree to work for a daily wage? [14]Take your things and go, I am
going to give the last the same as I give you. [15]Can I not do as I wish with
what belongs to me? Are you envious because I am generous?' [16]Thus the last
will be first and the first last."*

Parables were usually stories based on common events that
everyone could envision. This story is difficult to envision. But Jesus
tells it, and he makes a point about God's generosity from it. It was
common in those days for people to work as day laborers. In fact, that
still happens today. At the corner of *HaNevaeim Rehov* in Jerusalem,
every morning Palestinians line up hoping that cars will stop to hire
them for the day. The common pay in the first century for a day's
work was the denarius. The day would begin early in the morning
and end in the late afternoon. According to Deuteronomy 24:15, you
were to pay the person on the day they worked.[7]

In this story, the landowner hires some workers early in
the morning for a day's work. It seems that the work needs to be
completed that day, so he goes out to hire extra workers throughout
the day. He hires men at nine, at noon, at three and at five. At the end
of the day, he begins to pay the laborers for their work. He pays those
who arrived last, first. He paid them for a full day's work. They were
delighted to receive a full day's pay for an hour of work. They felt the
generosity of the landowner. Those who worked the full day must
have been perplexed. They must have felt that they were going to
receive a wonderful tip for working the entire day.

The landowner pays everyone who started work later in the
day the same wage – a denarius. How could they complain? They
were paid in full, though they only worked part of the day. Then it
came time to pay those who had worked the full day. Those who heard
the parable must have wondered how this story would end. Since the
landowner had been generous to everyone else, certainly he would be
generous to those who had labored the full day. But to their surprise,
they received the same pay as everyone else, a day's salary. They
protested, "How can you pay those who worked only one hour, the
same as those of us who worked all day? We worked through the heat
of the afternoon. They came as the day was cooling down. How can
you do this?" The landowner answered, "You agreed to a day's wage.
If I want to pay the others they same as you, how can you complain?
It is my money, not yours. Are you upset that I am generous?"

It is easy for us to sympathize with those who worked all day. In our minds it certainly seems unfair. Some would try to explain away the actions of the landowner by saying that the one-hour worker did as much in one hour as the others did all day. But you cannot derive that from the story. The workers were all paid the same wage even though some worked longer and harder than others. He did not mistreat or abuse those who worked for the full day. They got what they had settled on as the day began. They were bitter at the landowner's generosity toward the other workers. They did not complain that they did not get paid what they had earned, but they were upset that the others got as much as them.

The point of the story is that God is generous. He is a God of great grace. His grace is never earned. If you work all day or one hour, at the end of the day what God gives, he gives by grace.

In the world, he who works the longest gets the most pay. We understand that. It is difficult for us to understand that in God's kingdom, things work differently. We don't earn our wages in God's kingdom. We don't work to earn grace. Our wages (grace) are given freely and we work because we are delighted that we have received such a wonderful gift. It is the grace of God that makes the last first. He is so generous that it is difficult for us to grasp his generosity. Jesus is helping us to understand the generosity of God through this parable. Because his grace is so radical, we can never truly grasp it. But the more we understand it, the more we appreciate the generosity of God and the more we will want to serve him.

Jesus Foretells his Own Death and Resurrection for a Third Time (20:17-19)

17And Jesus was going up to Jerusalem he took his twelve disciples aside on the road and said to them, 18"You can see that I am going up to Jerusalem and the Son of Man will be handed over to the chief priest and scribes and they will condemn him to death 19and he will be mocked, scourged/ flogged, and crucified and on the third day he will be raised.

Jesus predicts his crucifixion for the third time. Each time he adds new details hoping to help his disciples understand what he is talking about. Jesus tells his disciples that he was "going up" to Jerusalem. He turns his face toward Jerusalem and gets ready for his crucifixion. "Going up" is a term used throughout the Bible in reference to Jerusalem. Jesus is north of Jerusalem; should he not say, "going down to Jerusalem?" But Jerusalem is a city set on a hill. It is 2,500 feet above sea level. From any direction that you approach the city you have to "go up" to Jerusalem. Also, theologically, since

Jerusalem is the Holy City, the City of David, you go up to Jerusalem.

When he arrives in Jerusalem, he will be handed over to the chief priests and scribes. The Jewish authorities will arrest him and condemn him to death. He will suffer much in Jerusalem–he will be mocked, scourged, and crucified. Only the Romans could crucify Jesus. So although he would be arrested and condemned by the Jews, the Romans would also play a part in his death. But the disciples are not to be discouraged, because on the third day he will rise from the dead.

The Request of James and John's Mother (20:20-28)

20Then the mother of the songs of Zebedee came to him with her sons and kneeling before him she asked a favor of him.

21He said to her, "What do you want?"

She replied, "Say that my sons will sit--one on your right and one on your left – in your kingdom."

22Jesus answered, "You do not know what you are asking, are they able to drink the cup that I am about to drink?"

They said to him, "We are able."

23He said to them, "You will indeed drink my cup, but those places are for those that my father purposed it for."

24The twelve heard this and were angry with the two brothers. 25But Jesus called them to him and said, "You know that the rulers of the Gentiles rule with absolute authority over them and their great ones have authority over them. 26It is not to be this way with you. Whoever wants to be great among you, he must be servant 27and whoever wants to be first must be your slave. 28For the Son of Man did not come to be served, but to give his life as a ransom for many."

Jesus has just predicted his death. You would expect his disciples to be empathetic at this point. Shouldn't they approach Jesus with encouraging words? But notice the contrast between the two stories that follow the story of Jesus predicting his death. James, John and their mother approached Jesus asking for a favor, to be given positions of authority in Jesus' kingdom. What type of response is this to the prediction of Jesus? They are blind. They still do not understand the type of Messiah that Jesus is or what his prediction meant.

Then look at the two blind men. Even though they have no physical sight, they see Jesus for who he is—the Son of David, the Messiah. Although blind, they could see more clearly than the disciples. So Jesus heals them and they follow Jesus. Follow him where? To Jerusalem, where he would die.

Mark has James and John approaching Jesus without their mother. Matthew has all three approaching Jesus, but there is no inconsistency. They all three asked Jesus to give them positions of prominence. Matthew 27:56, compared with Mark 15:40, gives the mother's name as Salome. She could have been the sister of Mary, the mother of Jesus (John 19:25). This would have made her the aunt of Jesus, and James and John his cousins. Thus they were not just looking for seats of prominence, but they might have expected it as a family favor.

Jesus lets them know that they are under a false impression. His kingdom would be a glorious kingdom, but not in the way they were thinking. He had just predicted his death. But they missed that point. He asks them, "Can you drink my cup?" The cup of Jesus was the cup of suffering. Anyone who wished to follow Jesus must drink that cup.

They answer, "We can drink your cup." They still don't understand Jesus. Later on they will. They will both drink his cup. James would be the first apostle to be martyred (Acts 12:2), and John would suffer exile on the Isle of Patmos.

When the other ten disciples learned of James and John's request, they were indignant. Jesus brings them all together and uses the situation as an opportunity for teaching. They still do not understand the nature of kingdom. They are thinking too much like the Greeks and Romans. In their kingdoms, the rulers lord it over the subjects. Caesar was to be worshipped as a god. To rule in God's kingdom is a different matter. To be great in God's kingdom, you must learn to serve, you must learn servant leadership. Jesus did not come to be served as king, but he came as king to serve. His kingdom was radically different from the kingdoms of the world. He came to offer himself as a ransom for many. "Ransom" (*lytron*) is used in the New Testament as the purchase price for a slave or to buy back prisoners of war. Jesus came to serve and also to be the purchase price for slaves.

Jesus Heals Two Blind Men (20:29-34)

²⁹*As they were leaving Jericho, a large crowd followed him.* ³⁰*Two blind men were sitting by the road and heard that Jesus was coming, they cried out saying, "Have mercy on us, Lord, Son of David."*

³¹*But the crowd rebuked them telling them to be quiet. So they cried even louder, "Have mercy, Lord, Son of David!"*

³²*Jesus stood still and called them to him saying, "What do you want me to do for you?"*

³³*They answered, "Lord, open our eyes."*

³⁴*Jesus had compassion on them and touched their eyes, and immediately they regained their sight and followed him.*

Luke says that Jesus was "going into" Jericho when he met the blind men. Mark and Matthew have Jesus leaving Jericho to go to Jerusalem. Some clarify this by saying that there were two Jericho's in the first century (just as people today refer to Old Jerusalem or New Jerusalem, two different geographic areas in Jerusalem). Luke makes reference to the new Jericho that was known by the Romans, and Matthew and Mark refer to the old Jewish Jericho. Others see Luke's miracle occurring as Jesus entered Jericho. The blind man told his friend about the miracle and two other blind men approach Jesus as he leaves Jericho.

The point of the story is that the blind men who cannot physically see are able to see Jesus more clearly than his disciples. They see Jesus as the Son of David, the Messiah. When the crowd rebukes them for crying out to Jesus, they cry out louder. They know who Jesus is and will not leave him alone until they receive a blessing from him. He cures their blindness. They follow Jesus, Mark adds, "on the way." Where was Jesus going? To Jerusalem and to his death. The way of Jesus was the way of suffering. The blind men were willing to follow Jesus to his death.

The Passion Week (21:1-28:20)

Jesus' last week was spent in and around Jerusalem. The time is April, six days before the Passover. He entered Jerusalem from the old Jericho road, which ascends from 1,300 feet below sea level to 2,500 feet above sea level and is seventeen miles long. He entered Jerusalem during the day, teaching and preaching. During the night, he stayed in Bethany on the southeastern slope of the Mount of Olives. This was the home of Lazarus, Mary and Martha. It is very likely that he stayed at their home during this last week. Bethany afforded Jesus a beautiful view of the city of Jerusalem. It is still the most spectacular entrance to the city. He arrived in Bethany on Friday before the Sabbath, and made his triumphal entrance into Jerusalem on Sunday, the day after Sabbath.

The Triumphal Entry (21:1-11)

[21:1]*When they came near Jerusalem, they came into Bethany located on the Mt. Olives. Jesus sent two of his disciples* [2]*saying, "Go into the village and immediately you will find a donkey tied there and a colt with him. Untie them and bring them to me.* [3]*And if anyone says anything to you, just say to him, 'the Lord needs them.' And he will immediately send them.* [4]*This happened that the word of the prophet might be fulfilled:*
[5]*Tell the daughter of Zion,*

> Behold the King comes to you
> Humble and riding on a donkey
> And on a colt, the foal of a donkey.

> ⁶*His disciples went and did just as Jesus directed them.* ⁷*They brought the donkey and the colt and placed garments on them and he sat on them.* ⁸*A very large crowd spread their garments on the road, and others set branches from the trees and spread them on the road.* ⁹*The crowds that went ahead of him and followed him cried out, saying:*

> Hosanna, to the Son of David.
> Blessed is he who comes in the name of the Lord.
> Hosanna in the highest.

> ¹⁰*And he went into Jerusalem. The whole city was in turmoil, asking, "Who is this?"* ¹¹*And the crowds declared, "He is the prophet, Jesus of Nazareth in Galilee."*

On Sunday of Passover week, Jesus enters Jerusalem from Bethany. He sends two of his disciples ahead to Bethpage to acquire a donkey and a colt. Since the colt was young, the older animal was needed to guide it. Jesus is preparing for his entrance into Jerusalem. When someone inquired about the animals, the disciples were to respond, "The Lord has need of him." This implies that the owner of the animals was also a disciple of Jesus.

This event must be taken as a prophetic symbol of the king entering his capital. But Jesus enters Jerusalem as a Messianic king that the people were unprepared for. He came humble and riding a colt, whereas the people wanted a military king who would ride before a conquering army on a warhorse. Rulers sometimes rode donkeys in time of peace. Jesus is a Messiah of peace. Jesus was riding in fulfillment of scripture. The beginning of the verse is from Isaiah 62:11 and the remainder is from Zechariah 9:9. It was common in the first century for rabbis to combine verses like this. The verse emphasizes the humility of Jesus.

The passage goes on to say that the donkey and colt arrived, garments were placed on the animals, and Jesus sat on them. I had a professor in college that made light of this scene asking how could Jesus ride on two animals? Was he a circus performer that had one foot on each animal? But the antecedent to the pronoun "them" is garments. Jesus wasn't riding both animals; he was riding on several garments that were placed on the animals.

Other garments were spread on the road while people also cut branches from trees and set them on the road. This was a traditional way to greet a king or an august visitor into a town. They also cried out *Hosanna*, which literally means "Save us." By the first century this term had become a note of praise, "Praise to the God who saves."

The title "Son of David" shows that there were some who understood that Jesus was the Messiah. The phrase "one who comes in the name of the Lord" also points toward the messianic nature of Jesus. Since the crowds change these shouts of joy to shout of derision in a few short days, it is clear that they did not understand the type of Messiah that Jesus was. "Hosanna in the highest!" is praise to God for sending Jesus.

Jesus probably entered the city at what is today known as St. Stephen's Gate or the Lion Gate on the northeastern corner of the city. The crowds were stirred in excitement as he entered the city and many wanted to know who he was. The followers of Jesus identified him as a prophet from Nazareth in Galilee.

Matthew has pointed out the kingship of Jesus throughout his gospel. He has clearly demonstrated that Jesus is the Messiah, the Chosen One of God. Now he begins the coronation of the King. But the coronation leads not to a golden throne in a majestic palace on a hill of Jerusalem, but to a cross. He crown would be a crown of thorns. Jesus would become king through his suffering.

Jesus Cleanses the Temple (21:12-17)

12Jesus went into the temple and he cast out all who were buying and selling in the temple, and he turned over the tables of the moneychangers and the seats of those selling doves. He said to them, 13"It has been written:

'My house shall be called a house of prayer
But you have made it a den of robbers.'"

14The blind and the lame came to him in the temple, and he healed them. 15The chief priest and scribes saw the amazing things he did and heard the children crying out in the temple: "Hosanna to the Son of David." They became angry and said to him, 16"You hear what they are saying!"

But Jesus said to them, "Yes. Have you not read – out of the mouths of children and infants you have prepared praise?" 17And he left them. He went out of the city to Bethany and spent the night there.

The Synoptics place the cleaning of the temple at the end of Jesus' ministry, while John places this event at the beginning of the ministry of Jesus (John 2:13-22). Most scholars believe that Jesus only cleansed the temple once, and John placed the cleansing at a different place in his gospel for theological reasons. But Jesus could have cleansed the temple twice. He could have cleansed it to inaugurate his ministry, and three years later he could have cleansed it again to begin the Passion Week. We do know that the testimony that convicted Jesus of a capital crime had to do with the destruction of the temple. It is likely that he cleansed the temple twice.

The outer court of the temple was the Court of the Gentiles. It is the only place where the Gentiles (God-fearers) could go to worship in the temple area. But the outer court of the Gentiles had been transformed from a place of prayer to a market. The religious authorities placed money tables and market stalls close to the Royal Stoa at the southern wall of the temple. The moneychangers exchanged Greek and Roman coins into temple currency. They would charge for this exchange. They also sold sacrifices that were required of the pilgrims who had come to worship. Many brought their own sacrifices on the journey to the temple. They were animals that they had raised and were affordable sacrifices. But these would be found unworthy. The pilgrims would then be charged exorbitant prices for worthy sacrifices. Thus the temple had become a "den of robbers" instead of a "house of prayer."

After cleansing the temple, the blind and lame came to Jesus to be healed. After Jesus healed them, they praised God saying, "Hosanna to the Son of David." This infuriated the chief priests. They wanted Jesus to quiet the crowd. Jesus answers them by referring to Psalm 8: 2–God has prepared this praise to come from children and infants. So who are they to try and stop it? Jesus then goes to Bethany to spend the night.

Jesus Curses the Fig Tree (21:18-22)

[18]*In the morning, when he returned to the city, he was hungry.* [19]*He saw a fig tree on the side of the road and he approached it and found nothing on it except leaves, and he said, "May you never bear fruit again." Immediately the fig tree withered.*

[20]*When the disciples saw this, they were amazed and said, "This tree withered immediately. How is that possible?"*

[21]*Jesus answered, "I tell you the truth–If you have faith and do not doubt, not only will you do what was done to this fig tree, but you can say to this mountain, 'Go be thrown into the sea,' and it will be done.* [22]*Whatever you request in a faithful prayer, you will receive."*

Matthew places the cursing of the fig tree on the morning after the cleansing of the temple. Mark splits the story in half as a framework for the cleansing of the temple. According to Mark, Jesus curses the fig tree, cleanses the temple, and then teaches about the withered fig tree. Some scholars believe that Mark is following an exact chronology of the events where Jesus visits the temple on Sunday and cleanses the temple on Monday. They think Matthew is using a topical approach and condenses the events.

Which Gospel writer is correct, Mark or Matthew? Both are correct. Mark is right chronologically and Matthew is correct topically. We use the same freedom in our writing today. Other scholars say that Matthew agrees with Mark and places the cleansing of the temple on Monday. But Matthew does not mention the cursing of the fig tree on the day before; he includes the cursing and the withering of the fig tree together on Tuesday morning. His lack of concern for the exact chronology does not mean he is mistaken. He is trimming, condensing and abbreviating Mark's account for topical reasons.

Jesus was hungry, and he approached a fig tree looking for fruit. By April, the fig tree should have begun to produce fruit that would ripen by August. Although this fruit was not highly desirable, it was edible. D.A. Carson writes:

> That it was not the season for figs explains why Jesus went to this particular tree, which stood out because it was in leaf. Its leaves advertised that it was bearing, but the advertisement was false. Jesus, unable to satisfy his hunger, saw the opportunity of teaching a memorable object lesson and cursed the tree, not because it was not bearing fruit, whether in season or out, but because it made a show of life that promised fruit yet was bearing none.[8]

Because the tree was barren, Jesus cursed the fig tree, and it immediately withered. The disciples were astonished at how quickly the tree withered. They wanted to know how the tree withered so quickly. Jesus used this occasion to teach them about faith. If they had faith and didn't doubt, they could do what he did. In fact, they could say to a mountain "be thrown in the sea," and it would happen. This is the power of faithful prayer.

Many wonder why would Jesus curse the fig tree. Jesus performed a prophetic symbol here. He acted out a parable. He used the fig tree to teach his disciples about faith. Jesus had the right and the power to do this. The barren tree represented barren Israel. They should have had faith in him, but they didn't. Since they didn't, God would curse them. But those who believed (had confidence) in Jesus would be able to do amazing things.

Jesus and the Religious Authorities Square Off (21:23-22:46)

This is one of my favorite sections in the gospel. The religious authorities attempt to trap Jesus by asking him questions. The questions come from many different directions. Different types of religious authorities question him. Each time Jesus baffles them with his answer. At the end of their questions, Jesus asks them a question. He goes on the offensive. This shuts them up completely. Mark places these questions on Tuesday of the Passion Week.

The Sects of Judaism

The Religious Sects	Stance	The Political Sects
Sadducees	Moderates	Herodians
Pharisees	Extremists	Zealots
Essenes	Radicals	Sicarii

The Authority of Jesus Questioned (21:23-27)

²³When Jesus entered the temple courts, the chief priest and the elders of the people came to him as he was teaching and said, "By what authority are you doing these things and who gave you this authority?" ²⁴Jesus answered, "I will ask you a question. If you answer me, I will tell you by what authority I am doing these things. ²⁵The baptism of John–from where did it come–heaven or man?" They argued with one another saying, "If we say, from heaven, he will say to us–why did you not believe him? ²⁶If we say, From men–we fear the people for they think of John as a prophet." ²⁷So they answered Jesus, "We don't know." He said to them, "Neither will I tell you by what authority I do these things."

The chief priests and elders approached Jesus seeking his authority for actions —like the triumphal entry, cleansing the temple, healing in the temple court. They represented the Sanhedrin who had authority over the temple area. Jesus used the rabbinical formula and answered a question by asking a question. He asked them if the baptism of John was from heaven or from man. The religious authorities had to withdraw and discuss how to answer his question. Jesus had left them no out. If they said "from heaven," then they should have followed John. Also, John pointed to Jesus so they should follow Jesus. If they said "from men," then the crowd would be upset. So they answered, "We don't know." Since they couldn't answer Jesus' question, he will not tell them by what authority he had done these things.

The Parable of the Two Sons (21:28-32)

²⁸"What do you think? A man had two sons. To the first he said, 'Son, go today and work in the field.'

²⁹The son answered, 'I will not!' But he later changed his mind and went.

30He went to the other and said the same thing. He answered, 'I'll go, sir, but he did not go.'

31Which of the two did the will of the Father?

They said, 'The first.'

Jesus said, 'I tell you honestly that the tax collectors and the prostitutes are going into the kingdom of heaven before you. 32For John came to you in the way of righteousness and you did not believe him, but the tax collectors and prostitutes believed him. And after you saw it, you did not repent and believe him."

Jesus now directs three parables at the religious authorities. The first is the parable of the two sons. Which son did the will of the father? The first son who told the father he would not work in his field only to later change his mind and do it, or the second son who said he would go, but did not go? The first son did the will of the father. The first son represents the people that the religious authorities snubbed their noses at: the tax collectors and the prostitutes. They changed their minds and followed John (and also followed Jesus). The second son represents the religious authorities that saw all that John did, but did not believe him and did not repent. Imagine how shocked the religious authorities must have been that this parable was directed at them. The religious Jews considered the tax collectors and prostitutes the lowest class. Yet Jesus says that they were accepted into the kingdom of heaven before the religious leaders.

The Parable of the Wicked Tenants (21:33-46)

33"Listen to another parable. There was a landowner who planted a vineyard and he placed a fence around it. He dug a winepress and built a tower. Then he leased the vineyard to some farmers and went to another country.

34When time for harvest arrived, he sent his servants to the tenants to collect his portion of the harvest. 35Then tenant seized the servants and they beat one and killed another and stoned a third. 36Then he sent other servants and they did the same to them. 37Finally, he sent his son saying, 'They will respect my son.'

38But the tenants saw the son and said, 'This is the heir. Let's kill him and steal his inheritance.' 39And they took him and cast him outside the vineyard and killed him.

40When the owner of the vineyard arrives back home, what will he do with those tenants?"

41They answered him, "He will take those evil men and destroy them and lease the vineyard to other tenants who will give him his portion of the harvest."

[42]Jesus said to them, "Have you never read in the Scriptures:
The stone the builder rejected
Has become the headstone
This is what the Lord has done
And it is amazing in our eyes.
[43]Because of this I say to you, the kingdom of God will be taken from
you and given to the people (the nations, Gentiles) who will produce fruit.
[44]The one who fell on this stone will be broken to pieces, but it will crush the
one it falls on."

[45]And when the chief priests and Pharisees heard this parable, they
knew that he was speaking about them. [46]And they desired to arrest him, but
they feared the crowds, for they regarded him as a prophet.

This second parable is even more directly aimed at the religious
leaders. Jesus describes a landowner who took great pains to grow a
vineyard.[9] He built a stonework fence around it to protect it from animals. He built a winepress for the harvest and a tower to guard his
investment. He then rented his vineyard to some farmers and went
to a foreign land to live. At harvest time, it was customary to send
someone to collect his share of the harvest (one-third or one-fourth of
the harvest). But the farmers refused to pay the owner. The owner sent
three servants to the tenants, and each was mistreated. He sent other
servants, and they were treated the same way. So the owner sent his
son, thinking they would respect him. But they killed the son.

Jesus then presses the audience for the meaning of the parable.
What should happen to the tenants when the owner returns? They answer, "He will kill the evil tenants and give the vineyard to other tenants." Jesus quotes Psalm 118 speaking of the stone that the builders
rejected. This stone has become the capstone. He directs the parable to
the religious authorities, "The kingdom of heaven will be taken from
you and given to the Gentiles who will produce fruit." They have rejected the message of the prophets. They have now rejected the message of the Son. In fact, in a few days they were going to take the Son
and kill him. God was going to take what was meant for them and
give it to the Gentiles.

The chief priests and Pharisees could not miss the meaning of
the parable. They wanted to arrest Jesus on the spot, but they were
afraid of the crowds. The crowds regarded Jesus as a prophet.

The Parable of the Wedding Banquet (22:1-14)

[22:1]Again Jesus spoke to them in parables, saying, [2]"The kingdom of
heaven is like a king who is preparing a wedding feast for his son. [3]He sent
his slaves to call the invited guests into the banquet, but they did not want

to come. ⁴*Again he sent other servants saying, 'Say to the guests, behold the feast is ready, my oxen and finest calves have been slaughtered and everything is prepared. Come to the feast.'*

⁵*But they did not respond and went away: one to his farm, another to his business, and* ⁶*the rest seized his servants and mistreated them and killed them.*

⁷*The king was filled with anger and sent his soldiers to destroy those murders and burn their city.* ⁸*Then he said to his servants, 'The wedding is prepared, but the invited guests did not come.* ⁹*Therefore, go into the main street and whoever you see invite them to come to the banquet.'*

¹⁰*The servants went into the streets and gathered everyone they found, the wicked and the good – and the wedding hall was filled with guests.*

¹¹*But the king came in and saw a man not dressed in a wedding robe. He asked,* ¹²*'Friend, how did you get in without a wedding robe?' But he was silent.*

¹³*Then the king said to the attendants, 'bind him hand and foot and cast him into the outer darkness where there is weeping and gnashing of teeth.* ¹⁴*For many are called, but few are chosen.'"*

Jesus directs a third parable toward the religious authorities–the parable of the wedding feast. When compared with Luke's parable of the wedding banquet, several differences are striking. In Luke, Jesus tells the story about a man and not a king. In Luke, the people who are invited make excuses. In Matthew they don't want to come. In Matthew, the king sends soldiers to destroy those who were invited and didn't come. Luke does not include this. The stories are so different that they should be taken as different parables told on separate occasions.

Here the kingdom of heaven is compared to a marriage feast. A king prepares a marriage feast for his son and sends his servants to call the invited guests to the feast. This was common practice in the first century. The guests would be called to the feast when final preparations were completed. But these guests, who had already accepted an invitation to the feast, refused to come. The king sent his servants a second time and explained that everything is prepared and it is time to come to the feast. The guests are given more than one chance to be a part of the feast. This time the guests seize the king's servants, mistreating and killing them.

The king is enraged by this action. He sends his soldiers to destroy the men who acted in such an evil manner. He then sends his servants into the streets to invite anyone to the wedding feast. Those who respond to this invitation fill the hall. But the king notices that someone has entered the feast without a wedding robe. He orders his attendants to cast him out of the feast. Many are called, but few are chosen.

It is obvious that Jesus has in mind the Jews who had not received him as the Messiah. They had been invited to the feast, but they did not want to attend. Now the feast would be open to anyone–tax collectors, prostitutes and Gentiles.

In verse eleven, the parable takes a sudden and unusual turn. Someone attends the feast, but he is not dressed for the feast. Jesus is no longer speaking of the Jews who had rejected him. He speaks of those people who act like they belong in the feast, but are frauds. They are not true disciples. God passes judgment on them in the same way that he judges the Jews who do not accept Jesus as the Messiah. To be a part of God's wedding feast you have to live the life of discipleship. What are the wedding garments at God's feast? They are the fruit of a changed life. Discipleship must be lived out. Many are called, but few are chosen.

The Question about Paying Taxes (22:15-22)

15Then the Pharisees went and planned how they might trap Jesus in his words. 16And they sent their disciples, with the Herodians, saying, "Teacher, we know that you are honest and you teach the way of God in truth and you are not anyone's pawn because you are not partial to anyone. 17Tell us, therefore, what do you think – is it lawful to pay taxes to Caesar or not?"

18But Jesus knew the evil they planned, and he said, "Why do you test me, you hypocrites. 19Show me the coin used for the tax." They brought him a denarius. 20He asked them, "Whose image is this and whose inscription is on it?"

21"Caesar's," they answered.

"Then give to Caesar what is Caesar's, and to God what is God's," he said.

22When they heard this, they were amazed. And they departed from him.

Jesus has told three parables directed at the Jewish religious authorities. They now bombard Jesus with questions. Different sects of the Jews attempt to trap Jesus by questioning him. They hope to engage him in an argument that will expose some falseness about him. The word "trap" was used in hunting referring to trapping or snaring an animal. Each time the leaders engage Jesus in debate, Jesus answers their questions and leaves his critics baffled.

The Pharisees and the Herodians were the first to lay their trap. These two groups are strange bedfellows. The Pharisees were anti-Rome. The Herodians supported the alliance with Rome. The

Sadducees worked closely with the Herodians, but the Pharisees did not. That these two groups should come together against Jesus demonstrates that a cross-section of Jewish leadership was against Jesus.

The opponents of Jesus begin by flattering Jesus. They address him as "Teacher" or "Rabbi." They speak of his integrity and his teaching the truth of God. They say that Jesus was not concerned with being popular with people. Then they ask the question that is meant to ensnare Jesus: Is it right to pay taxes to Caesar or not?

The trap is obvious. If Jesus says no, it is not right, then the Herodians who are in favor of Rome will report him to the Roman authorities. If he says yes, then the Pharisees will announce to the people that Jesus is pro-Rome. He will then lose his audience, because how could the Messiah be pro-Rome?

But Jesus answers their question with great wisdom. He asks them to show him a coin that was used for the Roman poll tax. This tax had to be paid in Roman currency by every foreign subject from puberty until sixty-five. It was a reminder that the nation was under the rule of the Roman Empire. They handed Jesus

The Herodians

The Herodians were a political sect of the Jews. This sect began in AD 6 when Archelaus was dethroned. They desired the restoration and perpetuation of the Herodian dynasty. They wanted their government to coexist with the Roman government. Mark 3:6, 12:13; Mt. 22:16 refers to them.

a silver denarius, a coin equal to a day's wage. Jesus asks whose image is on the coin, and what was inscribed on it. The coin bore the image of the Emperor's head along with an inscription. The inscription read, "Tiberius Caesar, son of the divine Augustus on one side," and "*pontifex maximus*" which means high priest on the other. It is easy to see why this coin offended the Jewish people. The Emperor is referred to as being divine and as being the high priest.

Jesus then makes his rabbinic pronouncement, "Give to Caesar what is Caesar's, and to God what is God's." One of the greatest aspects of true biblical Christianity is that it can exist under any political system. This will come as a shock to many politically charged believers, but Christianity is apolitical. Jesus did not come to overthrow the government. He was not concerned with sweeping social reform. He was concerned with individuals. Jesus wanted to better the lives of people, one person at a time. Thus he spent his days in the backwaters of the Roman Empire, a secluded part of Judea known as Galilee. He never spoke to the Roman Senate or appeared before Caesar.

But Jesus also adds, "Give to God what is God's." When the government comes in conflict with an individual's ability to serve

God, then the individual must serve God. For a while the early church enjoyed the favor of all the people. They did not attempt to stir things up politically. They went around helping individuals. But in time the Roman government started to clamp down on the freedom of the early church to worship Jesus. They demanded that the Christians bow to Caesar and worship him. At this point, the Christians had to rebel against the government. They had to give their allegiance to God.

The Herodians and Pharisees saw the wisdom of Jesus' statement and were amazed by it, and left.

The Question about the Resurrection (22:23-33)

²³On the same day the Sadducees came to him saying--there is no resurrection. They asked him, ²⁴"Teacher, Moses said, 'If a man dies without children, his brother should marry his wife and have children for his brother.' ²⁵There were seven brothers, and the first married and died without children, leaving his wife to his brother. ²⁶Likewise the second and the third--until the seventh. ²⁷Finally, the woman died. ²⁸Now in the resurrection, out of the seven brothers, whose wife will she be? For all had been married to her."

²⁹Jesus answered them, "You are wrong because you do not know the Scriptures or the power of God. ³⁰For in the resurrection they are neither married nor given in marriage, but are all as the angels in heaven. ³¹But concerning the resurrection of the dead, have you not read the word of God when it says, ³²'I am the God of Abraham, the God of Isaac, and the God of Jacob.' God is not the God of the dead, but of the living." ³³And when the crowd heard this they were astounded at his teaching.

It was now the Sadducees' turn to attempt to trap Jesus. The Sadducees believed in the Pentateuch, the first five books of the Old Testament. They were the high class, more influential leaders. They did not believe in angels or the resurrection. They asked Jesus a question that was used to stump people who believed in the resurrection. They brought up the law of levirate marriage. This was a law that was established to take care of widows. It was part of the Old Testament social system (Deuteronomy 25:5-10). If a man died and left his wife without a son, then his brother must marry her, beget a son and raise the child. The book of Ruth is an illustration of this principle at work.

The question that the Sadducees posed to Jesus was hypothetical. What if a married man had seven brothers? He died, leaving his wife alone to fend for herself. His brother now would become her husband. What if this happened seven times? We would certainly feel sorry for this woman and her bad luck. We might investigate the situation to see if any foul play occurred. But the Sadducees ask, "Since she was married seven times, who will be her husband in heaven?"

How many times had the Sadducees trapped advocates of the resurrection by this question? Jesus answers them directly: you are wrong on two counts; you don't know the Scriptures or God's power. In heaven, they are like the angels. This argument would trouble the Sadducees, since they did not believe in angels. When we die, we are transformed. Life as we know it changes. Marriage is no more. This does not mean that God will wipe away all memories of our marriages or our children. The Bible doesn't really speak to this issue. It is possible that all pleasant thoughts of our past life will exist with us in heaven. Love will exist in heaven. Since we will be in the presence of God, our love will be perfected. We will love on a level that we have never experienced.

Jesus then turns to the Scripture to answer the Sadducees. Since they only believed the books of Moses (the Pentateuch), Jesus answers using the book of Exodus. God says, "I am the God of Abraham, the God of Isaac, and the God of Jacob" (Exodus 3:6). Jesus bases his argument on the tense of a verb (present tense, "I am the God"). This shows that Jesus believed in the inspiration of Scripture. He is willing to base his argument for the resurrection on the tense of a verb. The thought is that Abraham, Isaac and Jacob are still alive, and God is still their God. Since they are alive, the resurrection is true. God is the God of the living. Those righteous who died are still alive with God.

Matthew mentions that the crowds were amazed at the teaching of Jesus. The exclusion of the Sadducees' response leads us to assume that they were less than impressed with the teaching of Jesus. This is another example of their rejection of Jesus as the Messiah.

The Greatest Commandment (22:34-40)

34When the Pharisees heard that he had silenced the Sadducees, they gathered together and 35one of them, a lawyer, questioned him (putting him to the test). 36"Teacher, which is the greatest commandment in the law?"

37He answered him, "Love the Lord your God with the whole of your heart and with the whole of your soul and with the whole of your mind. 38This is the greatest and the first commandment. 39And the second is similar--Love your neighbor as yourself. 40These two commandments sum up all the law and the prophets (all the Scriptures)."

Jesus had answered the questions of the Herodians, the Pharisees, and the Sadducees. Now it was time for the scribe-lawyers to question him. The scribes were well versed in the laws. They knew several languages and copied official documents for the people. The lawyer asked him about the law: what is the greatest commandment in all the law? This was a typical inquiry of the scribes. But many scribes taught that all aspects of the law were equal, therefore, there could not be a "greatest" command.

Jesus answered them by quoting the opening of the *Shema Israel*. This was a prayer that was prayed three times a day by religious Jews. It is found in Deuteronomy 6:4-5. The greatest command was to love God with all your heart, soul and mind. The heart is the seat of the emotions or our will. The soul is what makes us an individual. The mind is our intellect. Together these are to be taken as the whole of man. We are to love God with our whole being. This is the greatest commandment.

But after this, Jesus goes on to talk about the commandment that is the next greatest: to love your neighbor as yourself. The religious authorities were quick to point out the need to love God with our whole being, but they would often mistreat their neighbor. Jesus shows that loving people must follow our love for God. Jesus is perhaps the first to combine these two commandments in this way. Jesus closes by saying that the law and the prophets can be summed up in these two commandments.

The Question about David's Son (22:41-46)

⁴¹*While the Pharisees were gathered together, Jesus asked them a question, saying —* ⁴²*"What do you think of the Christ/the Messiah? Whose son is he?"*

They said to him, "David's."

⁴³*Jesus replied, "How then did David by the Spirit call him* ⁴⁴*'Lord,' saying:*

> *Say to my Lord*
> *Sit at my right hand*
> *Until I put your enemies*
> *Under your feet.*

⁴⁵*If David calls him Lord, how is he his son?"*

⁴⁶*And no one was able to answer his question, nor did anyone dare ask him more questions from that day.*

Jesus had answered the questions of the religious authorities, and now he goes on to ask them a question. Jesus did not stay on the defensive. He let his attackers ask him questions, but he also asked them a question. I think this concept is very important for us in today's world. Christianity is always being attacked. Science, philosophy, and the media all attack it. Instead of staying on the defensive against these attacks, as Christians we should go on the offensive. We should ask science, "If the world just evolved over time, then how do you explain morals and ethical values?" We should ask the philosophers, "If you have all the answers, then show us how humanity can get along with humanity." We should ask media, "You constantly attack Christianity, but do you even know what you are attacking? Have you ever read the Bible or studied the teachings of Jesus?" Jesus defended himself, then he took a stand. We must be willing to stand for the truth.

Jesus asked, "What do you think of the Messiah? Whose son is he?" They answered, "David's." Jesus then adds, "Then why did David call him Lord." Since he is the Lord of David, he is greater than David. The religious leaders rejected the type of Messiah that Jesus represented. They wanted a Messiah along the lines of King David, a military king who would bring a powerful political kingdom into existence. But Jesus is a Messiah who is greater than David. Since he is greater, his kingdom will be superior to David's. It will not be a military kingdom, but a spiritual kingdom.

Jesus' question to his critic shuts them up. They have no more questions for him. He has answered them brilliantly on every turn. He posed a question to them that made them think about their views of the Messiah. He has proven that he was both the Son of David and the Lord of David. Jesus is the Messiah. Jesus is King.

Seven woes on the teachers of the law and the Pharisees (23:1-36)

Matthew 23 begins the last of the five major discourses of Jesus as recorded by Matthew. This last discourse runs through chapter 25. Structurally, Matthew 23 concludes the material that precedes it–the conflict between the Jewish religious authorities and Jesus.

Warning to the crowds and to his disciples (23:1-12)

23:1Then Jesus said to the crowds and to his disciples, 2"The scribes and the Pharisees sit on Moses' seat. 3Therefore whatever they say to you, do and keep, but do not do their works for they do not do what they say. 4They tie up heavy burdens and put them on men's shoulders, and they are unwilling to lift a finger to move them. 5They do all their works to be seen by men; they make their phylacteries wide and their tassels long. 6They love to have the place of honor at banquets and the best seats in the synagogue. 7They love to be greeted in the marketplaces and be called, 'Rabbi.'

8But you are not to be called – Rabbi. You have one teacher. You are all brothers. 9Call no one father on earth, your Father is in heaven. 10Neither call them instructor, because you have one instructor–the Christ. 11The greatest of you will be your servant. 12Whoever wants to exalt himself will be humbled, and he who humbles himself will be exalted."

Jesus takes time to warn his followers about the scribes and the Pharisees. These two groups represented religious leaders who were legalistic in their approach to God. They were known for their self-righteousness (believing that people had to do things exactly like them to be right) and their hypocrisy (saying one thing and doing another). They believed not only in the written Law of Moses, but also in an oral law that was handed down by the rabbis. The point of the oral law was to build a hedge or fence around the written law so that you would never get close to breaking a written law. For example, the law says not to lift a burden on the Sabbath. The oral law would define exactly what a burden was. If you had a cotton swab in you ear, and it fell out on the Sabbath, you could not pick up the swab because that would be lifting a burden on the Sabbath. Although at face value the oral law appears to be a good thing, it ended up being a list of legalistic requirements that kept people from thinking about the purpose of the law. It became a burden to the people.

Jesus recognizes the authority of the scribes and Pharisees. They sat on Moses' seat. This was a literal seat in the synagogue that was reserved for people of authority. Jesus warned his followers to listen to the instruction of the Pharisees and scribes, but not to follow their example. They did not do what they said. They were hypocrites. Their oral traditions had become a burden to people, and they were unwilling to remove those burdens. They did their works to be seen by men. They wore their phylacteries wide and their tassels long. Phylacteries were small leather boxes that contained Scriptures. The idea for this came from Exodus 13:9, 16. But until after the Babylonian exile, it was just an idea. Following the exile, religious Jews began to wear phylacteries. The tassels were worn on the corners of their garments (Deuteronomy. 22:12). These tassels were later applied to the prayer shawl. The broadening and lengthening could refer to a practice that the phylacteries were worn outside of the designated times of prayer by the Pharisees. Jesus is speaking of their desire to be seen by men to receive the praise of men.

The Pharisees and scribes also loved to sit in prominent seats to be seen by men. They loved to be called "Rabbi." The word "rabbi" comes from *rab* meaning "great" and from *bi* meaning "my." So it could be translated as "my great one." This is certainly a huge title for any man to wear. Jesus teaches his followers not to call men rabbi. God is to be "their great one." They are to be of equal rank. Jesus teaches his followers not to have an ecclesiastical hierarchy. They are not to call people "father" and "teacher" as honorific titles. God is to be their father and Jesus is their teacher. This does not take away from the fact that Jesus gave a role in the early church for the teacher.

The Rabbi

In the Hebrew *Rabbi* means "my great one." The role of the Rabbi developed during the Babylonian exile. During the exile, the priest could not offer the daily sacrifices (because the altar for sacrifices was in Jerusalem). In place of these daily sacrifices, people began to gather together to read the scriptures. This gathering became the "synagogue." *Synagogue* literally means gathering or assembly. The leader at this meeting took on the role of rabbi. Originally, the rabbi was a respected teacher who instructing people in God's word. Later, they were called upon to settle disputes between people. To settle the disputes the rabbi's would quote scripture, quote the oral law, and quote different rabbis' interpretation of the oral law. When they were ready to pronounce their judgment, they would preface it by saying, "Amen, I say to you." After this, they would give their judgment. Their judgment became binding. Thus the role evolved from an instructor to a highly authoritative person who settled disputes.

Over time, many of the rabbis became experts in the law. This group developed into the scribes of the first century. They knew several languages and would translate legal documents for people.

Ephesians 4:11-14 reads, "It was he (Jesus) who gave some to be apostles, some to be prophets, some to be evangelists, and some to be pastors and teachers, to prepare God's people for works of service, so that the body of Christ may be built up until we all reach unity in the faith and in the knowledge of the Son of God and become mature, attaining to the whole measure of the fullness of Christ."

Matthew 23:11-12 can help us understand the way "teacher" is used in Matthew 23 verses the way "teacher" is used in Ephesians 4. Jesus says "the greatest among you must be your servant." When we use honorific titles to exalt people, this is wrong. If we use titles to recognize the works of service that people are doing for God, then this is fine. The evangelists, teachers, pastors in our churches have roles of service within the church. We must be careful not to exalt these positions to ones of greatness. This is harmful for the individuals being exalted and for the church. The one who attempts to exalt himself will be humbled. And God will exalt those who choose to be humble.

God wants us all on an equal playing field. In the New Testament there was no clergy/laity system. Everyone was a *diakanos*, a servant. Once I went on a trip (actually it was a teacher's conference) to Athens, Greece. Athens is the birthplace of democracy. While there we visited a cemetery that dates to the Archaic Period, 7th/6th century BC. The monuments for the graves during this time were amazing, beautiful sculptured marble that paid homage to the deceased. One sculpture was so amazing it almost seemed to be alive. It was a sculpture of a mother lovingly holding her sick child. The cemetery was very impressive.

But in another corner of the cemetery there were no monuments, no elaborate statues chiseled in marble. Instead, there were plain circular columns about four feet high that all looked the same except for the inscription on the face of the column. These columns raised my curiosity. So I went up to one of the security guards and asked their meaning. She said they were from the fifth century BC, the Classical Period. This was the time of the rise of democracy in Greece. During this time, one of the governors of Greece decided that it was not right for the rich to be buried with huge statues and monuments erected to them while the poor would have nothing or a simple marker for their graves. He ordered that everyone be buried in the same manner with a simple 3 to 4 foot tall column to mark their grave. He was attempting during life and during death to level the playing field.

Jesus does the same thing here with the use of titles. He says, "Let's not build monuments to each other with titles like Rabbi, Teacher, Instructor, Father." Let's level the playing field and call each other *diakonos*, servant.

The Seven Woes (23:13-36)

Jesus now issues seven woes on the scribes and Pharisees. A "woe" can be a warning or a condemnation. In this context, the "woes" seem to be the later. Jesus, as judge, pronounces judgment on the religious authorities that have burdened the people. In doing this he stands in the tradition of the great prophets of the Old Testament who had very strong things to say to leaders who led their people harshly (Ezekiel 34).

The First Woe
You Stand as Barriers to God's Kingdom (23:13-14)

¹³*"Woe to you, scribes and Pharisees, you hypocrites, because you shut the kingdom of heaven to men. ¹⁴For you do not enter nor do you allow others to enter."*

In order to help people into God's kingdom, you must accept the kingdom yourself. The scribes and Pharisees were unwilling to do that. They denied that Jesus was the Messiah. They did not accept his Messianic reign. They stood outside God's kingdom. Therefore it was not possible for them to help people into God's kingdom. In this way they stood as a barrier to other people. They shut the kingdom of heaven in men's faces. Bad enough that they would not enter the kingdom themselves. Worse yet that they stood as a barrier to other people's entrance into the kingdom. This behavior warrants the first "woe" from Jesus.

The Second Woe
You convert people to your oral traditions (23:15)

> [15]*"Woe to you, Scribes and Pharisees, hypocrites, you travel across land and sea to make a single convert, and when he converts you make him twice the son of hell* (Gehenna) *you are."*

The scribes and Pharisees were mission minded. Jesus did not mind that. But they were not working to bring people into God's kingdom. They were peddling their form of Pharisaic Judaism to people. They would travel far and wide to gain one convert to their cause. They had zeal, but it was zeal without knowledge. What made the Scribes and Pharisees different from the other sects of the Jews was their adherence to an oral tradition–established and guarded by the Pharisees. These commands were not part of the Old Testament, but were created by men to be a protective fence around the law. But the traditions became burdens to the people.

The Pharisees failed to see how their strict legalism was a heavy burden on the people. The people were smothering under the legalistic requirements of the Pharisees. Jesus gave this stinging condemnation: when someone becomes a convert you make him twice the son of hell as you are. Their converts became even more adept at practicing the legalism of the Pharisees than their teachers. In doing so they gave up their freedom. They lost sight of mercy and grace. They lived by a self-righteous standard. Most importantly, they failed to accept Jesus as Messiah.

The Third Woe
You are blind guides who swear false oaths (23:16-22)

> [16]*"Woe to you, blind guides, who say, 'Whoever swears by the temple – it is nothing. Whoever swears by the gold of the temple – he is bound.' [17]You blind fools! Which is greater–the gold or the temple, which makes the gold sacred? [18]You also say, 'Whoever swears by the altar it is nothing, but whoever swears by the gift on the altar he is bound.' [19]You are blind. Which is greater–The gift or the altar that makes the gift sacred? [20]Therefore whoever swears by the altar swears by it and everything on it.*

²¹*Whoever swears by the temple swears by it and the one who dwells in it?*
²²*The one who swears by heaven swears by the throne of God and he who sits
on it."*

Jesus calls the Pharisees and scribes "blind guides." How can
they lead people when they are blind? That is foolish. Jesus discloses
an example of how they are blind guides: the swearing of oaths. The
Pharisees had built a tradition that taught proper and improper ways
to swear oaths or make promises. Jesus put aside this foolishness and
demanded that everyone simply tell the truth (Matthew 5:33-37).

What did the Pharisees teach about the swearing of oaths?
They taught that an oath had to be said in a particular fashion to be
binding. To swear by the temple was not binding, but to swear by the
gold of the temple was binding. To swear by the altar was not binding,
but to swear by the gift of the altar was binding. You had to be a part
of the circle of the Pharisees to understand these rules. Therefore, the
Pharisees could easily deceive anyone outside their circle by stating
an oath that was not binding. They could swear by the temple (which
any non-Pharisee would think is binding since it was the most important symbol in Judaism) and the oath not be binding. If their oath was
challenged, then they would explain why it was not binding ("I swore
by the temple, but not the gold of the temple"). This is much like the
game we played as kids where if we made a promise with our fingers
crossed, then the promise was void. Crossing your fingers invalidated
the promise. But the Pharisees and scribes were not children. They
had established a system that was used to deceive people. They were
dishonest and disingenuous.

No wonder Jesus had such hard words for them—"blind
guides," "blind fools," "blind men." Jesus disclosed the foolishness of
their system and turned it on its ear. He declared that the images that
are truly binding are the temple, the altar, and heaven. Jesus was not
establishing a new system of oath taking. He was overturning their
system the same way he overturned the money tables in the temple.
He had already stated his teaching on the taking of oaths in the Sermon on the Mount–don't swear. He now teaches that we should always be honest. If we do promise something, then we should follow
through on our promise.

The Fourth Woe
You neglect the more important matters of the law like justice and mercy and faith (23:23-24)

²³*"Woe to you, Scribes and Pharisees, hypocrites. You tithe mint,
dill, and cumin, and have neglected the more important matters of the law like
justice and mercy and faith. You should do these things without neglecting
the others.* ²⁴*Blind guides, you strain at the gnat and swallow the camel."*

The Old Testament law taught the practice of tithing (Deuteronomy 14:22-19). The Pharisees were keen on making sure that all of the laws on tithing were strictly enforced. Although Jesus and the early church never taught the practice of tithing, Jesus does not fault them for that practice here. He does challenge their strict adherence to tithing while showing laxity toward weightier matters of justice, mercy, and faithfulness. What good does it do for you to strictly adhere to some parts of the law while neglecting other parts? What good does it do for you to strictly tithe, and then treat people harshly?

The weightier matters of the law can also be translated the "more important" matters of the law. These are matters that are closer to the heart of God. This teaching is in line with the teaching of the prophets. They taught that God desired mercy more than sacrifice. The Pharisees had gotten matters reversed. This is easy to do because it is easier to see a tithe given than it is to see mercy extended to someone. Legalism favors the physical, things that can be touched and seen. They majored in minors like hand washing, oath taking and tithing. Although these things are not wrong when practiced properly, the Pharisees practiced these legalistic acts while negating the need for justice, mercy and faithfulness.

Justice, mercy and faithfulness all have to do with how we treat other people. Tithing can be practiced without any concern for others. Justice means to treat people fairly. Mercy means to show people forgiveness. Faithfulness means to be a trustworthy person. How we treat others is central to the heart of God.

Jesus did not say that we should practice justice, mercy, and faithfulness to the exclusion of tithing. We should not neglect either one. The Pharisees failed to see the heart of God. They strained at the gnat, but were choked by the camel. They would filter their wine to keep from swallowing an unclean gnat. But in treating people without justice, mercy, and faithfulness, they were swallowing the camel. They had missed God's heart. In doing so they also blinded themselves to the true nature of Jesus–he was the Messiah.

The Fifth Woe
You clean the outside, while the inside is filthy (23:25-26)

[25]*"Woe to you, scribes and Pharisees, hypocrites, you clean the outside of the cup and plate, but inside you are full of greed and self-indulgence. [26]Blind Pharisee! First clean the inside of the cup so that the outside may also be clean."*

What was important to the Pharisees and scribes? Keeping oral traditions was important. Being seen by men was important. Practicing the externals was important. Legalism was important. They missed the importance of heart and attitude. They failed to challenge and nurture the inner person. They cleaned the outside of the cup–the externals, while the inner cup remained filthy–the heart. They kept their oral laws while their hearts were filled with greed and self-indulgence. They should have started with the heart, the inner man. They should have cleaned out the greed and selfishness. After doing this, the outside would be clean. The way to clean the outside is to clean the inside.

The Sixth Woe
You are whitewashed tombs–beautiful on the outside, but full of dead men's bones on the inside (23:27-28)

[27]"Woe to you, Scribes and Pharisees, hypocrites because you are like whitewashed tombs that look beautiful on the outside, but on the inside are full of dead men's bones and all uncleanness. [28]Thus you look righteous to men on the outside, but inside you are full of hypocrisy and wickedness."

Jesus reiterates what he just said: clean the inner man. The Scribes and Pharisees were like whitewashed tombs. Before the Passover, the Jews would whitewash the graves around Jerusalem so that they would stand out to the pilgrims traveling to the city. This way they could avoid the graves and not become ceremonially unclean. These tombs would look pretty on the outside, but inside they contained the bones of dead men.

Jesus compares the Scribes and Pharisees to these graves. This would have been particularly offensive to these leaders since Jesus was comparing them to something unclean. The religious leaders were like tombs in that they looked good on the outside, but their hearts were dead. Inside they were full of hypocrisy and wickedness. This is a biting condemnation of the Pharisees and scribes.

The Seventh Woe
You act as if you would not have killed the prophets (23:29-32)

[29]"Woe to you, Scribes and Pharisees, hypocrites, you build tombs of the prophets and decorate the graves of the righteous. [30]You say, "If we lived in days of our fathers, we would not have taken part with them in the shedding of the blood of the prophets. [31]Thus you testify against yourselves that you are descendants of those who murdered the prophets. [32]And you shall fulfill the measure of the sin of your forefathers."

The Scribes and Pharisees built memorials for the prophets of the Old Testament. They did this to testify that they would not have murdered the prophets had they been living back then. But the prophets of old would have rebuked the Scribes and Pharisees just as harshly as they rebuked the false prophets of their own day. The Scribes and Pharisees were the true descendants of the people who killed the prophets. The memorial that they built stood as a testimony to their guilt. Their decision to deny Jesus as the Messiah also testified to this.

Conclusion (23:33-36)

33"You snakes! You offspring of vipers! How will you flee from the condemnation of Gehenna? 34I am sending you prophets and wise men and teachers. Some you will kill and crucify; others you will flog in your synagogues and pursue from village to village. 35So on you will come all the blood of the righteous that has been shed on the earth–from the blood of righteous Abel to the blood of Zechariah son of Berekiah, whom you killed between the temple and the altar. 36I tell you truthfully, all this will come upon this generation."

Jesus calls the Scribes and Pharisees snakes. They are snakes and the offspring of vipers. How could they expect to escape from the condemnation of Hell? Jesus would prove that they were just like their forefathers. He would send them prophets, wise men, and teachers whom they would crucify and flog. The blood of all the righteous martyrs would be on their heads, from Abel to Zechariah, from the opening to the close of the Old Testament. But the blood of the righteous would not just be on the heads of the Scribes and Pharisees. The blood would be on "this generation." In other words, anyone who follows the Scribes and Pharisees would share their fate.

Jerusalem, Jerusalem (23:37-39)

37"Jerusalem, Jerusalem, the city that kills the prophets and stones those sent to it. How often I wished to gather your children as a hen gathers her chicks under her wings, but you would not allow it. 38See, your house is left to you desolate. 39I tell you, you will not see me again until you say, "Blessed is the one who comes in the name of the Lord."'

Jesus now says a lament over the city of Jerusalem. This is the city that he loved, but it is also the city where he would die. Jerusalem had a history of mistreating the messengers that were sent to her. Jesus wanted to gather Jerusalem to him and bless the city. The image of the hen gathering her chicks under her wing for protection is a beautiful image. Jesus wanted to protect Jerusalem, but she would not allow it. Since she rejected Jesus, Jesus would reject her. Her house would be left desolate. This is a prediction of the destruction of the city in AD 70 by the Romans.

Endnotes

[1] Clyde Woods, *The Living Way Commentary on the Old Testament*, Volume Two, Leviticus-Numbers-Deuteronomy (Shreveport, Louisiana: Lambert Book House, 1974), pp. 266-267.

[2] I. Howard Marshall, *Commentary on Luke*, New International Greek Testament Commentary (Grand Rapids: Wm. B. Eerdmans Publishing Co., 1978), p. 631.

[3] Robert W. Wall, "Divorce," in *The Anchor Bible Dictionary*, Vol. 2 (New York: Doubleday, 1992), p. 128.

[4] *The Early Church Fathers*, edited and translated by Henry Bettenson (Oxford: Oxford University Press, 1956), p. 132.

[5] Wall, p. 219.

[6] Carson, p. 424.

[7] Ibid., p. 445.

[8] Carson, p.445.

[9] If you ever have the opportunity to go to the Holy Land, be sure to visit The Jesus Village in Nazareth. They have done a nice job restoring a first century farm like the one in this story.

7

Ministry in Judea
Teaching about the Future
Matthew 24:1-25:46

He who loves the coming of the Lord is not he who affirms it is far off, nor is it he who says it is near. It is he who, whether it be far or near, awaits it with sincere faith, steadfast hope, and fervent love.

–Augustine of Hippo, theologian

We must never speak to simple, excitable people about "the Day" without emphasizing again and again the utter impossibility of prediction. We must try to show them that impossibility is an essential part of the doctrine. If you do not believe our Lord's words, why do you believe in his return at all? And if you do believe them must you not put away from you, utterly and forever, any hope of dating that return? His teaching on the subject quite clearly consisted of three propositions. (1) That he will certainly return. (2) That we cannot possibly find out when. (3) And that therefore we must always be ready for him.

–C. S. Lewis, British author and literary critic

The Long Apocalypse (Matthew 24:1-51)

In Matthew 24, Matthew gives a longer, fuller description of Jesus' teaching concerning the destruction of the temple. Here Jesus answers two questions: when will the temple be destroyed and when will time end? The key in this passage is to understand where he stopped answering the first question and began answering the second question.

The two questions appear in verse three. First the questioners want to know when the temple will be destroyed. Second, they want to know the signs concerning his coming and the end of the age. In verses 4-35, Jesus describes the events surrounding the destruction of the temple. In verse 36 he makes a transition to his second coming and the end of the age. Notice how closely verses 4-35 tie into the description given by Mark concerning the destruction of temple. Jesus mentions the following signs: false messiahs, wars and rumors of wars, famines, earthquakes, persecution, increase of wickedness, the gospel preached to the whole world as a testimony to all nations, the abomination of desolation, the sun and moon darkened, stars fall and planets shake, the Son of Man comes in the clouds, angels gather the elect.

Some of these signs seem to speak to the second coming of Jesus; namely, the gospel preached to the whole world, Jesus coming in the clouds, and the angels gathering the elect. But, two sayings place these events in the context of the first century. First, the disciples are told to flee to the mountains of Judea when they see these signs (verse 16). These signs were given to the early Christians as a warning to get out of town and save themselves when the Roman army approached Jerusalem. Second, "all these things" were to happen in their "generation." These signs were given to their generation, not our generation.

In verse 36, Jesus makes a transition to answer the second question posed by the disciples. When would he come and when would time end? Verse 37 states that Jesus is describing how it will be "at the coming of the Son of Man." First, it will be sudden, unexpected, no signs given. He would come as a thief. No need to try to predict the second coming of Jesus. The angels know nothing of that time so do not ask them. The Son does not even know anything about that time, so he cannot tell you. Only the Father knows. This is obviously different from what was just described with the destruction of the temple. Now there is absolute secrecy, no signs, no clues. Since only the Father knows, who are we to presume to predict this date. What arrogance on the part of any minister to claim to know what the angels or the Son does not know!

Second, this event is described in terms of the resurrection as described in 1 Thessalonians 4. "One will be taken and the other left" describes how those who are alive when Jesus comes will be caught up in the clouds with Jesus. This is not the Rapture described by the premillennialists, but it is part of the resurrection process. Those who are left are not left to get another chance at judgment. They are not to begin to build a millennial kingdom for Jesus. Those who are left will then be taken to judgment where they will face the weeping and gnashing of teeth described in verse 51.

It should also be said that Matthew 24 includes images and language that are apocalyptic in nature. *Apokalypto* is a Greek word that means "to reveal what is hidden, to make known." Apocalyptic writing uses symbols and metaphors to disclose information to a specific group of people who were usually undergoing persecution or in need of encouragement. Apocalyptic literature is full of images that are highly symbolic. The initiated can understand the symbols, but for those outside the circle of the initiated, the symbols have no meaning.

Imagine if you don't know anything about baseball and you turn on the radio to hear, "With two men out, it's a three-two pitch; the runner steals a base and now he's on his way home!" There is a sort of code language being used that is readily understood by anyone who follows the game of baseball. However, a visitor from another century, having no knowledge of the sport, would find the words mysterious or downright incomprehensible. Taken literally, does "two men out" mean that two fellows are unconscious or simply away from their desk? Does a "three-two pitch" refer to the 32-degree slope on a roof? Isn't "stealing" wrong? And what is the guy going to do in his house once he reaches "home?" Or perhaps reaching "home" refers to heaven. As you can see, the broadcast is nonsense if you don't understand the "code language" of the game.

In the same way, the symbols and numbers, images and references of apocalyptic literature may seem strange to us, but they were familiar to their intended audiences in the first century. Once you have a basic grasp of the "game," in this case the culture of Jewish apocalyptic writings, then the "code language" is easily understood as well.

What do we learn here? When Jesus comes to judge the world, it will be without warning, without signs or omens, he will come as a thief. There is no need to attempt to predict when this will happen. In fact, it is simply arrogant to do so. We must be ready at all times. We must always be prepared to meet Jesus.

The destruction of the temple foretold (24:1-2)

24:1Jesus came out of the temple and was walking away, when his disciples approached him and pointed out the buildings of the temple to him. 2Jesus asked them, "Do you see all these buildings? I tell you truthfully, not one stone will be left here on another. All will be cast down."

The temple in Jerusalem was one of the wonders of the ancient world. Herod the Great (37-4 BC) began reconstruction of the temple complex in 20-19 BC. The reconstruction went on for some eighty years. The new temple complex was completed only a few years before it was destroyed in AD 70. Herod's temple is known as the second temple though in actuality it is the third temple. It was viewed as a reconstruction of the temple of the exiles, but the changes and expansion to the temple and the temple site were so vast under

Herod that it is best to think of Herod's temple as a completely new
structure. He expanded the temple on the north, west, and south side;
the eastern edge of the temple fell too steeply into the Kidron Valley
to allow any expansion on that side. Herod completely buried any
remains of Solomon's temple or of the Post-Exilic temple as he rebuilt
the new one. The new temple mount covered 35 acres. It was larger
than the Acropolis in Greece. It was an impressive site, one of the
wonders of the ancient world.

When the disciples left the temple, they pointed out to Jesus
the beautiful buildings of the temple complex. Jesus predicted that
the temple would be destroyed. Not a single stone would be left on
another. This prediction came true in AD 70 when Titus, general of the
Roman army, marched into Jerusalem and destroyed the temple.

The Signs of the End of the Age (24:3-8)

*3As Jesus was sitting on the Mount of Olives, his disciples came to
him in private, saying, "Tell us, when will this happen and what will be the
sign of your parousia and of the end of the age?"*

*4Jesus answered, "See that no one deceives you. 5For many will come
in my name saying, 'I am the Messiah,' and will deceive many. 6You will hear
of wars and reports of wars. Do not be alarmed. It is necessary for these things
to occur. But the end is still to come. 7For nation will rise up against nation,
and kingdom against kingdom, and there will be famine and earthquakes in
various places. 8All of this is the beginning of the birth pains."*

The disciples approached Jesus later as he was sitting on the
Mount of Olives and asked him two questions. It is important to see
that they asked two different questions because Jesus spent the rest
of chapter twenty-four answering not one, but two questions. The
first question had to do with the destruction of the temple and when
this would happen. The second question had to do with the second
coming (*parousia*) of Jesus, the sign of the second coming and the end
of the age.

He began by answering the first question: when would
the temple be destroyed? Verses four thru thirty-five answers this
question. Before the temple is destroyed many false prophets will
appear. They will say they are the Messiah. These people will deceive
many. But Jesus lets them know that the time for the destruction
of the temple is not to come just yet. There will also be famines
and earthquakes in various places. All of these are signs that the
destruction is still to come.

Persecutions Foretold (24:9-14)

[9]"Then you will be delivered over to be tortured and killed. You will be hated by all the nations because of my name. [10]And many will stumble and betray one another, and hate one another. [11]And many false prophets will rise and deceive many [12]because of the increase in lawlessness. The love of many will grow cold, [13]but the one who perseveres to the end will be saved. [14]And this good news of the kingdom will be heralded to the whole world as a witness to all nations, and then the end will come."

"Then you will be delivered over to be tortured and killed," refers to the disciples. This would come before the destruction of the temple. By the time the temple was destroyed in A.D. 70, almost all of the original twelve disciples of Jesus had died as martyrs because of their faith in Jesus. They were hated by all nations. Many of the early followers stumbled when persecution first hit the church. But those who faced their end with faith would be saved. The whole world would hear the proclamation of the kingdom before the end (of the temple) would come. According to Paul, the gospel was preached to every creature under heaven in his lifetime (Colossians 1:23).[1]

To make it to heaven takes resiliency. Only he who perseveres to the end will be saved. You might remember from United States history that Lewis and Clark were commissioned by the United States government to find a passage to the Pacific Ocean. After two years they saw a river with a huge bluff just beyond it. They believed that just beyond the bluff was the Pacific Ocean. As they climbed the bluff they looked out and saw the unexpected. They did not see water; they saw the Rocky Mountains. They had only reached the Missouri River. The toughest part of their journey was ahead of them. But through their resilience they were the first non-native Americans to see the Rocky Mountains. Later they would be the first non-native Americans to travel overland across the United States to the Pacific Ocean.

Resiliency is necessary in many areas of our lives. None more so than our spiritual lives.

The Abomination of Desolation (24:15-28)

[15]"When you see 'the abomination that causes desolation' standing in the Holy Place, spoken through the prophet Daniel, let the reader understand. [16]Then those in Judea must flee to the mountains. [17]The one on his roof must not go down to take anything from his house. [18]The one in the field must not go back to get his coat. [19]Woe to the pregnant women and the nursing infants in those days. [20]Pray that your flight may not be in winter or on a Sabbath. [21]For then there will be great tribulation like has not been from the beginning of the world until now and never will be."

²²*And if those days had not been cut short, no one would survive, but for the sake of the elect those days will be shortened.* ²³*Then if anyone says to you, 'Behold, the Messiah is here' or 'There he is!' Do not believe it.* ²⁴*For false messiahs and false prophets will appear and give great signs and miracles to deceive, if possible, the elect.* ²⁵*Look, I have told you ahead of time.*

²⁶*"Therefore if anyone says, 'Look, he is in the desert!' Do not go there. Or, 'Look, he is in the inner rooms!' Do not believe it.* ²⁷*For as lightening comes from the east and shines in the west, so will be the* parousia *of the Son of Man.* ²⁸*Wherever the corpse is, there the vultures will gather. "*

The Seleucids were the Syrian governors who controlled the territory north of Palestine. After the reign of the Ptolemies, they controlled Palestine from 198-143 BC. At the beginning of the second century, Antiochus III (the Great) wrested control of Palestine from Egypt. Once in control the Seleucids continued the policies of the Ptolemies allowing the high priests to control Palestine.

In 175 BC, Antiochus IV (Epiphanes) began to rule in Syria. Epiphanes means "the manifest god," and the Jews made a play on this word calling the ruler Antiochus Epimanes meaning "the insane." At this time, Onias a devout observer of the law was high priest. Onias' brother, Joshua, opposed Onias as high priest. Joshua was in favor of the Greek culture, a proponent of Hellenization. The Greeks so heavily influenced him that he even changed his name to Jason. Jason convinced Antiochus IV to strip Onias of the high priesthood and give it to him. Thus Jason became high priest and began an intense Hellenization campaign across Jerusalem. He built a gymnasium in Jerusalem where the participants would compete naked, as was the Greek tradition. During these games the Greeks would make fun of the Jews who had been circumcised. Many of the Jewish participants, including some priests, tried to have their circumcision surgically reversed in order to escape ridicule (1 Maccabees 1:15).

Later, a Jew named Menelaus offered the Syrian governor a higher bribe for the high priesthood. Thus, Menelaus replaced Jason as high priest, and the office became open to the highest bidder.

In 169 BC, Antiochus IV Epiphanes entered Jerusalem to replenish his treasury, which had been depleted in battles with Egypt and Rome. He plundered the Jerusalem temple taking with him: the altar of incense, the seven-branched lamp stand, and the table of showbread (1 Maccabbees 1:20-24).

A short time later the Syrians and Antiochus IV entered Jerusalem with the purpose of enforcing Hellenization upon the Jews. They decided to destroy the Jewish communities and their indigenous way of life. They tore down the walls of Jerusalem, built a fortress on the hill of the ancient city of David (the Acra), forbid the Jews on pain of death to keep the Sabbath or to circumcise their sons, erected a pagan altar on the site of the altar of burnt offerings, and offered a pig upon the altar of Yahweh as a sacrifice to the supreme god, Olympia Zeus (167 BC).

This act became known as the "abomination of desolation" spoken of by the prophet Daniel (11:31, 12:11). Mark also refers back to this event in his gospel as one of the signs, which would surround the destruction of the temple in Jerusalem. In the apocryphal book, 1 Maccabees 1:54-64, this event is described:

> Now on the fifteenth day of *Chislev,* in the one hundred and forty-fifth year, they erected a desolating sacrilege upon the altar of burnt offering. They also built altars in the surrounding cities of Judah, and burned incense at the doors of the houses and in the streets. The books of the law, which they found, they tore to pieces and burned with fire.
>
> Where the book of the covenant was found in the possession of any one, or if any one adhered to the law, the decree of the king condemned him to death. They kept using violence against Israel, against those found month after month in the cities. And on the twenty-fifth day of the month they offered sacrifice on the altar, which was upon the altar of burnt offering. According to the decree, they put to death the women who had their children circumcised, and their families and those who circumcised them; and they hung the infants from their mother's necks.
>
> But many in Israel stood firm and were resolved in their hearts not to eat unclean food. They chose to die rather than to be defiled by food or to profane the holy covenant; and they did die. And very great wrath came upon Israel.

Pious Jews died rather than defile themselves according to the orders of Antiochus IV. The Jews in the countryside outside of Jerusalem were especially antagonistic toward the Syrians. Some of these rebels banned together under the leadership of an old priest named Mattathis. This lead to the Maccabean revolt.

Much has been written about "the abomination of desolation." Those who believe that Jesus is speaking of the end of the world in this section are still looking for the abomination of desolation. We must remember that we are reading apocalyptic literature here. It is highly symbolic. We should also remember that Jesus is still answering the first question here: when will the temple be destroyed? Taking these thoughts in consideration, what is the abomination of desolation? It refers back to a prophecy in Daniel 11:31 that was fulfilled by Antiochus Epiphanes in 168 BC when this Selucid ruler erected an altar to Zeus over the altar of burnt offering in the temple area. He then offered a pig (an unclean animal) on this altar. This was the "abomination of desolation." This was to happen again before the temple was destroyed. It happened when Titus and the Roman army marched into the temple courts. Before the temple was burned to the ground, Titus took a look in the Holy of Holies. This was the most sacred room of the temple that could only be entered by the High Priest, and even he could only enter it once a year on the Day of Atonement. When Titus looked into the Holy of Holies, the abomination of desolation had occurred.

The early Christians heeded Jesus' words and when the Roman army came into Jerusalem, they fled. They went across the Jordan River and established several communities, one at Pellum. Because they understood, trusted, and obeyed the words of Jesus they escaped the Roman sword. The Jews who did not heed Jesus' warning, stayed behind and were executed. Josephus, the Jewish historian, notes that the Romans killed so many Jews at the temple that the blood flowed in streams.

God had pity on the elect in those days. He allowed them to flee. But they still had to be aware of the many false Messiahs that would come to deceive them. Jesus came in judgment on Jerusalem in that day. It was not the day of final judgment.

The Coming of the Son of Man (24:29-31)

> [29]"*Immediately after the suffering of those days:*
> *The sun will be darkened*
> *The moon will not give its light*
> *The stars will fall from heaven*
> *The powers of heaven will be shaken.*
> [30]*Then the sign of the Son of Man will appear in heaven, and all the nations of the earth will mourn, and they will see the Son of Man coming on the clouds of heaven with power and great glory.* [31]*And he will send his angels with a loud trumpet call, and they will gather his elect from the four winds, from one end of heaven to the other.*"

Jesus now uses apocalyptic language to describe the suffering that goes on in the days before and following the destruction of the temple. Did the moon darken? Did stars fall from heaven? Did the Son of Man appear on the clouds of heaven? Were the angels sent to gather the elect? Perhaps not literally, although we weren't there and don't know. But let's not overlook the fact that this is figurative, apocalyptic language. These are words of judgment. The prophets of the Old Testament used this same type of language to symbolize the judgment of God on Israel.

In this case, God judged the city of Jerusalem in AD 70. In that way, the Son of Man did appear. He appeared as the judge over Jerusalem, temple worship and the Jewish system, all which had failed to receive him as the Messiah. He came in power and great glory and judged Jerusalem. The elect were gathered away from Jerusalem and were spared the judgment of the city.

The Parable of the Fig Tree (24:32-35)

32"Learn from the parable of the fig tree:

As soon as its branches become tender and its leaves come out, you know the summer is near. 33Even so, when you see all these things, you know that it is near, right at the gates. 34I tell you the truth, this generation will not pass away until all these things have occurred. 35Heaven and earth will pass away, but my words will not pass away."

The parable of the fig tree reminds the hearers to pay attention to his words. When they see the signs that he has spoken, they must flee the city. When these signs occur, destruction is at the gate. Verse 34 is the key to seeing that everything said up to this point was speaking of the destruction of Jerusalem. It reads, "I tell you the truth, this generation will not pass away until all these things have occurred." These events must happen in "this generation." Many want to take "generation" to refer to this present age—the Christian age. But the word does not mean that. It meant a generation of people, a 20 to 40 year generation. D.A. Carson writes, "'This generation'–can only with the greatest difficulty be made to mean anything other than the generation living when Jesus spoke."[2] Jerusalem was destroyed within 40 years of Jesus' prediction of its destruction.

During Passover of AD 70, Titus, Emperor Vespasian's son, led the Roman army against the city of Jerusalem. Because of the holiday season, Jerusalem was swollen in size. Titus laid siege to the city. Jewish resistance fighters were nailed to crosses on the banks outside the city in order to intimidate those who remained inside. The intensity of the Zealots held strong, but the Romans were stronger.

The Romans pushed into the city and set fire to the holy temple. Titus entered the Holy of Holies just in time to seize the seven-branched candlestick and the table of showbread. They marched these emblems back to Rome as trophies of war. The temple was left in ruins. The most holy symbol of Judaism had now been destroyed.

After the destruction of the temple, Titus initiated two actions. First, he deported as many Jews as possible back to Rome as slaves. Second, he renamed the land Palaestina, Land of the Philistines. The Jews despised this name because they despised the Philistines.

Be Alert (24:36-44)

³⁶*"Concerning that day and hour no one knows, neither the angels of heaven, nor the Son, only the Father. ³⁷For as the days of Noah were, so will be the parousia of the Son of Man. ³⁸For as in those days before the flood they were eating and drinking, marrying, and giving in marriage until Noah entered the ark, ³⁹and they knew nothing until the flood came and took them all away, so it will be at the parousia of the Son of Man. ⁴⁰Two will be in a field, one will be taken and one left. ⁴¹Two women will be grinding meal, one will be taken and the other left.*

⁴²*Therefore keep alert, because you do not know on what day your Lord will come. ⁴³But understand this–if the owner of the house had known in what part of the night the thief would come, he would have stayed awake and not let his house be broken into. ⁴⁴Then you must also be alert, because the Son of Man will come at an unexpected hour."*

Now Jesus moves on to answer the second question: what will be the sign of your second coming and the end of the age? Jesus says that no sign will be given. No one knows the day or the hour when he will come. The angels don't know. The Son doesn't even know. Only the Father knows. Since only the Father knows the day or the hour of the Son of Man, it is ludicrous of us to attempt to predict when Jesus will come. He will come as a surprise. Like the flood surprised the people in Noah's day, people will be surprised when Jesus comes. Two will be taken in a field and one left. When Jesus comes, the elect will meet him in the air. Those "left" does not refer to a group that will be left behind to face the anti-Christ. It means they will receive judgment after God judges the elect.

The point of Jesus is that we should be alert. We should always be alert. Since we don't know when he will come, we should be ready at any moment for his return. He will come as a thief, unannounced. No matter how hard we try or how much we would like to predict when Jesus will return, it simply is not possible. Jesus will come as a thief; he will surprise us. Therefore, we must be vigilant. Always ready for his return.

The faithful or unfaithful slave (24:45-51)

⁴⁵*Who then is the faithful and wise slave, who the master put in charge of the servants of his household to give them food at the proper time?*

⁴⁶Blessed is that slave whom his master finds at work when he arrives. ⁴⁷I tell you the truth, he will put him in charge of all his possessions. ⁴⁸But if the wicked slave says in his heart, 'My master is delayed,' ⁴⁹and he begins to beat his fellow slaves, and eats and drinks with drunkards. ⁵⁰The master of that slave will come on a day when he does not expect him and at an hour he does not know. ⁵¹He will cut the slave to pieces and put him with the hypocrites, where there will be weeping and gnashing of teeth.

Who is the faithful and wise servant? The one who is always ready for his master's return. Whenever the master returns, he finds him at work. This servant will be put in charge of all the master's possessions. The wicked servant sees the delay of his master as an opportunity to be wicked. He beats his fellow servants, eats, and gets drunk. He doesn't think the master will catch him. But the master will, and will punish him for his indiscretion. The point of the parable is that we all must stay alert for the second coming of Jesus because we do not know the day or the hour when he will come.

Jesus speaks about the end of time (Matthew 25:1-46)

Jesus continues his thoughts concerning the end of time into chapter 25 of Matthew. Remember the early copies of the Scriptures had no chapter divisions; there would have been no break between chapters 24 and 25.

Jesus tells two parables that each have something to say about the end of time. The Parable of the Ten Virgins (25:1-13) is a reminder to always be on watch for the return of the Messiah. He will return unannounced to surprise those who are not ready for his coming.

The Parable of the Talents (25:14-30) reminds us that we will be judged according to how we have used the gifts that God has given us. Have we made good use of our gifts, or have we used them selfishly? The Messiah will have something to say about how we have used our talents when he returns.

Jesus gives us his greatest portrayal of the final judgment scene in verses 31-46. Here Jesus (the Son of Man) sits upon a throne of judgment before all of humanity. He divides everyone into two groups: the sheep and the goats, based upon how they treated others while they were living. Jesus says, "I was hungry and you gave me something to eat, I was thirsty and you gave me something to drink, I was a stranger and you invited me in, I needed clothes and you clothed me, I was sick and you looked after me, I was in prison and you came to visit me." The goats will go away to eternal punishment and the righteous to eternal life.

This is the scene of final judgment. There is no hint of a second chance or purgatory here, and certainly no mention of surviving a "rapture" and getting a second chance. You live your life, you die and then you face judgment.

Parable of the Ten Bridesmaids (25:1-13)

25:1"Then the kingdom of heaven will be like ten bridesmaids who took their lamps and went to meet the bridegroom. ²Five of them were foolish and five wise – ³for the foolish took their lamps, but did not take any oil with them. ⁴But the wise took jars of oil with their lamps. ⁵As the bridegroom was delayed, all of them became tired and fell asleep.

⁶At midnight there was a shout, 'Look, the bridegroom is here! Come out and meet him!'

⁷Then all the bridesmaids woke up and trimmed their lamps. ⁸The foolish said to the wise, 'Give us some of your oil, our lamps are going out.'

⁹But the wise answered, 'No. There will not be enough for you and us. Rather go to the dealers and buy some for yourselves.'

¹⁰But while they were going to buy it, the bridegroom came. Those who were ready went in with him to the wedding banquet, and the door was shut.

¹¹Later the others came, 'Sir! Sir! Open up for us.'
¹²But he answered, 'I tell you the truth, I do not know you.'
¹³Keep alert then, because you know not the day, nor the hour."

Following Jesus' proclamation that the second coming would be unannounced and that he would come as a thief, he gave three parables about the second coming. The first is the parable of the ten maidens (25:1-13). The second is the parable of the talents (25:14-30). The third is the judgment scene (25:31-46).

"At that time" joins this parable of the ten maidens with the preceding story of the second coming of Jesus and the fact that Jesus will come at an unexpected time. "At that time the kingdom of heaven will be like" is to say that this is how it will be for those in the kingdom when Jesus comes; some will be ready and some will not. The story portrays a wedding procession. The maidens were to walk with the bridegroom to the wedding banquet. They were to carry lamps to light the way in this procession. The bridegroom was delayed and the ten maidens had to wait for him before they could go to the banquet.

Five of the maidens were foolish. They took their lamps, but did not take any extra oil with them. Lamps in the first century were generally small and did not burn for a very long time (only a few hours) before they needed to be refilled with oil. The foolish maidens should have planned ahead and taken extra oil. The wise maidens did plan ahead. They took extra oil. They were prepared for the bridegroom to come at any hour. The bridegroom was delayed in his coming, and all the maidens fell asleep while waiting for him.

At midnight, the cry rang out, "Here comes the bridegroom!" He came unexpectedly, while they were all asleep. The maidens woke up and began to trim the wicks of their lamps to make them ready. They would now fill the lamps with extra oil. The foolish maidens were out of oil. Their lamps would not burn. They asked the wise maidens to give them some oil. But the wise refused, realizing they did not have enough oil for themselves and for the others. This was not selfishness on their parts. There comes a time when you have to be able to say "no" to people. People can be helped up to a point, then they must help themselves. For their own good and the good of the foolish maidens, the wise maidens had to say, "No, you go find some oil." The foolish maidens went to find more oil at the nearby shops. But while they were gone, the bridegroom arrived and took the wise maidens into the banquet with him.

Later, the foolish came to the door and begged, "Open the door for us!" They were invited to the banquet, but they came too late. They were unprepared when the bridegroom arrived. The bridegroom said to them, "I don't know you." They weren't ready when the bridegroom arrived so they missed the banquet. So that we don't miss the point of the parable, Jesus makes it abundantly clear by adding, "Therefore, keep watch, because you do not know the day or the hour." We must always be prepared for Jesus to come.

The Parable of the Talents (25:14-30)

14"For it is as a man going on a journey who called his slaves and entrusted his property to them. 15He gave one five talents of money, another two, and another one — each according to his ability. Then he left. 16The one who received the five talents left and traded with them, and made five more talents. 17Likewise, the one with two talents of money made two more. 18But the one who received the one talent went and dug a hole in the ground and hid his master's money.

19After much time, the master of the slaves returned and settled accounts with them. 20The one who had received the five talents of money came forward and brought five more saying, 'Master, you gave me five talents. See, I have made five more.'

21His master said to him, 'Well done, good and faithful servant, you have been faithful in the little things, I will put you in charge of many things. Enter into the joy of your master.'

22The man with the two talents came forward and said, 'Master, you gave me two talents, see, I have gained two more.'

²³*His master said, 'Well done, good and faithful servant, since you have been faithful in the small things, I will put you in charge of many things. Enter into the joy of your master.'*

²⁴*The man who was given one talent came forward, saying, 'Master, I knew you were a hard man, reaping where you did not sow, and gathering where you did not scatter.* ²⁵*I was afraid and went and hid your talent in the ground. See you have what is yours.'*

²⁶*His master answered him, 'You wicked and lazy servant! You knew I reap where I have not sown and gather where I have not scattered.* ²⁷*Then you should have put my money in the bank, so when I returned I would have received it back with interest.'*

²⁸*'Take the talent from him and give it to the one with ten talents. For to all who have, they will be given more. And he will have in abundance.* ²⁹*Whoever does not have, even what he has will be taken away.* ³⁰*And cast this worthless slave in the outer darkness, where there will be weeping and gnashing of teeth."*

The parable of the talents also highlights the importance of using the time before the *parousia* wisely. Just before a landowner takes a journey, he leaves his money in the care of his servants. To the first servant he gives five talents, to the second he gives two talents, and to the third he gives one talent. In our day a talent would be worth about a thousand dollars. Not a small sum of money.

The first and the second servants each doubled their master's money. But the third took his and hid it in the ground; (in the first century, this was a common way to protect money from thieves). When the landowner arrived back from his journey, he praised the first two servants for using the money wisely. But he sternly rebuked the third servant, taking his money and giving it to the first, and casting the servant into the darkness where there was weeping and gnashing of teeth, (a common image for hell).

While awaiting the second coming of Jesus (the *Parousia*), the servants of Jesus must stay busy. This parable comes to life in the church of Thessalonica. Some of the Christians heard that Jesus was going to return quickly. So they quit their jobs, starting mooching off the other disciples, and sat around waiting for Jesus to come. Paul told them to get busy. He told them to find jobs or to starve. The faithful servant will keep busy until the Lord returns. We must take advantage of every opportunity that God gives us to advance the kingdom until Jesus returns.

The Sheep and the Goats (25:31-46)

³¹*"When the Son of Man comes in his glory and all the angels with him, then he will sit on his throne of glory. ³²All the nations will be gathered before him, and he will separate the people one from another as a shepherd separates the sheep from the goats. ³³He will put the sheep on his right hand, and the goats on his left.*

³⁴*Then the King will say to those on his right, 'Come you blessed by may Father, inherit the kingdom prepared for you from the creation of the world. ³⁵For I was hungry and you gave me food, I was thirsty and you gave me drink, I was a stranger and you welcomed me, ³⁶I was sick and you cared for me, I was in prison and you visited me.'*

³⁷*Then the righteous will answer him, 'Lord, when did we see you hungry and give you food, or thirsty and give you drink? ³⁸Or when did we see you as a stranger and welcome you in, or naked and clothe you? ³⁹And when did we see you sick or in prison and visit you?'*

⁴⁰*The King will answer, 'I tell you the truth, when you did it to one of the least of these brothers of mine, you did it to me.'*

⁴¹*Then he will say to those on his left, 'you accursed ones, depart from me into the eternal fire prepared for the devil and his angels. ⁴²For I was hungry, and you gave no food, I was thirsty and you gave me no drink, ⁴³I was a stranger and you did not welcome me in, naked and you gave me no clothing, sick and in prison and you did not care for me.'*

⁴⁴*They will answer, 'Lord, when did we see you hungry or thirsty or a stranger or naked or sick or in prison, and did not care for you?'*

⁴⁵*He will reply, 'I tell you truthfully, when you did not do it for one of the least of these, you did not do it for me.'*

⁴⁶*Then they will go away to eternal punishment. But the righteous into eternal life."*

Matthew 25:31-46 is one of the most grand and inspirational passages of the entire New Testament. One of my seminary professors, Dr. Richard Spencer, called it "the Mount Everest of the New Testament."[3]

31-33 In verse 31, the use of the title, "Son of Man," has received much discussion in Biblical studies. It is understood in some Old Testament passages as just another word for man. In Ezekiel, it is used to show the ordinary nature of the prophet as a man, but also the greatness of his call and service. Daniel sees the term as a Messianic one. How did Jesus apply this title to himself? J.Y. Campbell writes, "It seems probable that the old understanding of the phrase, as a reference to the real humanity of our Lord, contains an essential element of truth."[4]

The word "throne" is used in Semitic literature to symbolize authority and power. The provocative claim of Jesus here is that he will sit upon the throne of glory and judge the world alone. This concept is without parallel in Biblical literature, and it demonstrates the high Christology of Matthew. As we have seen throughout Matthew's gospel, he demonstrates that Jesus is King. At the end of time, Jesus will sit on his throne as the King and judge the world.

In verse 32, "all nations" can be translated "all Gentiles," and it refers to all humanity. The "gathering together" and "separating" are technical terms used in shepherding. The shepherd here is the keeper of a mixed herd of sheep and goats. Concerning their separation, a New Testament theologian, Joachim Jeremias writes, "The sheep and the goats would feed together during the day, but the shepherd would separate them at night because goats are more susceptible to cold and have to be kept warmer than sheep, which like fresh air at night."[5]

The sheep represent the saved either because of their white color or because of their helplessness and absolute dependence upon the shepherd. The right side is a place of honor in Jewish literature; therefore, the sheep are placed on the right.

34-36 In these verses, the king offers the inheritance of a kingdom prepared from the foundations of the world to those who minister to the needy, as if they were serving Jesus. To inherit is to enter into the possession and enjoyment of something. The acts of charity are based upon Jewish acts of charity, but the list neglects two acts which were looked upon highly by the Rabbis: to lament for the dead and to bury the dead. It suggests that Jesus is more concerned for the living than the dead. The Rabbis did not include the visiting of prisons in their lists, and this is probably foreshadowing the Christian persecution and imprisonment.

37-40 Matthew refers to those on whom Jesus pronounced his blessing as "righteous." This is one of Matthew's favorite terms. The theme of righteousness is central to this Gospel's message. Jesus sets the righteousness of his followers against the righteousness of the Pharisees who calculated their acts of charity and performed them to be seen of men. A German scholar, Gottlob Schrenk writes, "The righteous in the last judgment in Matthew 25:37,46 are those who have attained to true righteousness by practicing love in unconscious acts of kindness to the Son of Man."[6]

The righteous acted out of a sense of love and commitment to their Lord, and they are to be blessed with an inheritance prepared since the foundation of the world.

The key issue in verse 45 is what does Jesus mean when he speaks of the least of the brothers? George Eldon Ladd gives three possibilities on what "the least" could mean.[7] The first is a view commonly held by premillennial dispensationalists. This view sees "the brothers" as Christians in tribulation, and judgment is of the Gentiles nations "to decide who will enter the millennial kingdom, and who will be excluded."[8] This view is based upon a presuppositional bias, which is taken to the text and worked into each pericope dealing with eschatological passages.

Another view identifies "the brothers" as Jesus' disciples. Jesus speaks of disciples as brothers in Matthew 12:48-79; 28:10. In Matthew 10: 40-42, Jesus sends out his disciples to preach and comments that whoever receives them in turn receives him. The judgment is upon the "yes" and "no" to the worldwide preaching of these messengers, as displayed in their actual treatment of them.

A third option attempts to look at the full theology of Matthew. In Matthew 5:43-48 the command is given by Jesus to love one's enemies. This runs counter to the type of congregative and distinctive love, which is, expressed when one equates the brothers with disciples. Why is the word "brothers" left out of verse 45? There it seems the least of the hungry, the naked, the sick is being expressed. Paul S. Minias comments:

> Jesus' parable does not measure "leastness" in terms of economic destitution alone, but includes social dereliction as well. There are sick people; in the Bible sickness connotes sin and contagion. There are naked people; in the Bible nakedness connoted powerlessness and disgrace. More important still, the parable mentions strangers and convicts. These least are folk who are overlooked or ostracized, who possess no significance, prestige, or power.[9]

The decision of which of these last two positions is more tenable is difficult. With the background of Jewish ethic being considered and Matthew's theology of being careful not to demonstrate love and righteousness with a bias, it seems the last position is to be preferred.

41-43 These verses are parallel to the preceding verses except for the use of the negative particle and the destination of the accursed ones. The same preparation that was expressed concerning the kingdom given to the righteous is now stated along with the eternal fire. The original preparation of this eternal fire was for the Devil and his angels, but now it is considered to be open to the ones on the left. The picture given in this verse is that the ones who did not minister to the needs of the helpless have sided with the Adversary and are doomed for the same judgment he faces.

44-46 These verses are also set in direct parallel to the preceding answer of the righteous ones. Neither group had seen the Lord as the needy, but the righteous went ahead and gave help anyway. Jeremias comments on the lot of the unrighteous, "Their guilt does not lie in the commission of gross sins, but in the omission of good deeds."[10] By leaving out their ministry to the helpless, they had placed themselves on the side of the Devil and his angels.

The concluding verse is also a summary the verse of reward and punishment given to the righteous and the unrighteous. The word "eternal," (*aionion*), is used here to describe both the punishment and the reward. We must be consistent and translate eternal life and eternal punishment equally. The restoration scholar, J.W. McGarvey states, "It is admitted on all hands that in the expression, 'everlasting life' the term has the full force and therefore it is idle and preposterous to deny that it has the same force in the expression, 'everlasting punishment.'"[11] This is the punishment prepared for the Devil and his angels. The punishment is by fire and the duration is eternal.

Conclusion

This judgment scene gives the disciples of Jesus a revelation as to what God means for his people to be. If a person strives for righteousness, then he must pay strict attention to the lesson taught in this passage. William Barclay writes, "The lesson is this–that God will judge us in accordance with our reaction to human needs."[12]

Our concept of a relationship with God can get so warped by carrying on traditional standards of what it means to be a Christian, that we can forget the example of Jesus and his definition of righteousness. New Testament professor Malcolm Tolbert comments:

> Sometimes we equate faithfulness to Jesus with attendance on religious services and giving money to support the institution. We honor Jesus who never said anything at all about building buildings by erecting larger and more magnificent structures. If we do take his words seriously, we shall surely testify to it by a shift of our emphasis from statistics and buildings to people in their need. The Lord is not going to ask, 'How many buildings did you build?' According to the passage, he is going to ask: How many hungry people did you feed? How many sick people did you visit?[13]

Jesus' words should help us focus our gaze to the helpless, poor and suffering.

Whenever we find it difficult to get out of ourselves and meet the needs of others, then Jesus' words should come ringing into our ears. Dr. Martin Luther King, Jr. has written, "When we, through compassionless detachment and arrogant individualism fail to respond to the needs of the underprivileged, the Master says, 'Inasmuch as ye have done it not to one of the least of these my brethren, ye have done it not unto me.'"[14] We search and find the eyes of Jesus in every poor and helpless person.

Even though we look for the poor and rejected person, the true Christian is not searching to gain credit for himself. Christian service is to be uncalculating. We should be able to ask, "Lord, when did we see you in need?" Human suffering should awaken our compassion to the point of service, but our motives should be to minister and help without any type of ulterior motive. Our response to the needy must be instinctive within our own Christian character for it to be pleasing to God.

Someone looks and sees the tears of loneliness
    As they trickle down the corner of
    Bright blue eyes.
Another gazes and sees the cold, blank,
    Disease-ridden stare of death in
    Dark brown eyes.
Still another looks and wipes crusted
    Sleep from brilliant, newborn,
    Hazel eyes.
And someone stares into dimly lit
    Uncontrolled and functionless
    Almost colorless eyes.
Look closer into these eyes.
    Someone looks back.
And they call him, Jesus.

                      —GSK

Endnotes

[1] Paul died in the persecutions of Nero around the year A.D. 65. This was before the temple of Jerusalem had been destroyed.

[2] Carson, p. 507.

[3] Taken from notes in Dr. Richard Spencer's New Testament Survey class at Southeastern Baptist Theological Seminary in 1983.

[4] *A Theological Wordbook of the Bible*, ed. Alan Richardson (New York: Macmillan Publ. Co., Inc., 1976), s.v., "Authority" by J.Y. Campbell, p. 232.

[5] Joachim Jeremias, *"poikilos, polupoikilos"* in *Theological Dictionary of New Testament*, vol. VI, eds., Gehard Kittel and Gerhard Friedrick, trans. Geoffrey W. Bromiley (Grand Rapids: Wm. B. Eerdmans Publ. Corp., 1968), p. 493.

[6] Gottlob Schrenk, *"dikaios,"* in *Theological Dictionary of the New Testament*, vol. II, eds., Gehard Kittel, Trans. Geoffrey W. Bromiley, (Grand Rapids: Wm. B. Eerdmans Publ. Co., 1968), p. 190.

[7] See George Eldon Ladd's, "The Parable of the Sheep and the Goats in Recent Interpretation," in *New Dimensions in New Testament Studies*, ed. R.E. Longenecker and M.C. Tenney *Grand Rapids: Wm. B. Eerdmans Publ. Co., 1974) p. 191-ff.

[8] Ibid.

[9] Paul S. Minias, "The Coming of the Son of Man," *Theology Today* IX (October 1952); p. 490.

[10] Joachim Jeremias, *The Parables of Jesus*, Trans. S.H. Hooke (New York: Charles Scribner's Sons, 1954), p. 207.

[11] J.W. McGarvey, *Commentary on Mark* (Delight, Arkansas: Gospel Light Publ. Co., 1875), p. 221.

[12] William Barclay, *New Testament Words* (London: SCM Press Ltd., 1964) p, pp. 36-37.

[13] Malcolm O. Tolbert, *Good News From Matthew* (Nashville: Broadman Press, 1975), p. 213.

[14] Martin Luther King, *Strength to Love* (Glasgow: William Collins Sons and Co., 1964), p. 19.

8

The Death and Resurrection
of Jesus
Matthew 26:1-28:20

E verything in Christ astonishes me. His spirit overawes me, and
his will confounds me. Between him and whoever else in the
world, there are not possible terms of comparison. He is truly
a being by himself. I search in vain in history to find the similar to Jesus Christ, or anything, which can approach the gospel. Neither history, nor humanity, nor the ages, nor nature, offer me anything with
which I am able to compare it or to explain it. Here everything is extraordinary.

—Napoleon

Matthew, in his final chapters, describes the most pivotal event
in human history: the death and resurrection of Jesus. This is "the
crowning of the king." It is a coronation like none other. Jesus is given
a crown of thorns and as his first act of royalty he stretches out his
arms and they are nailed to the cross. He dies for the sins of humanity.
But death cannot hold him. So the king returns. He breaks the bonds
of death and reigns with the Father for eternity. No event has changed
the world like this one event. It is the heart of the gospel. It must be in
the heart of every disciple.

The Passion Narrative (26:1-27:66)

Crucifixion to the World by the Cross of Christ
(Galatians 6:14)

When I survey the wondrous Cross
Where the young Prince of Glory died,
My richest gain I count but loss,
And pour contempt on all my pride.

Forbid it, Lord, that I should boast
Save in the death of Christ, my God;

All the vain things that charm me most,
I sacrifice them to his blood.

See from his head, his hands, his feet,
Sorrow and love flow mingled down;
Did e'er such love and sorrow meet?
Or thorns compose so rich a crown?

His dying crimson like a robe
Spreads o'er his body on the Tree,
Then am I dead to all the globe,
And all the globe is dead to me.

Were the whole realm of nature mine,
That were a present far too small;
Love so amazing, so divine,
Demands my soul, my life, my all.
                    –Isaac Watts (1674-1748)

As with Mark, Matthew's passion narrative describes the culmination of the ministry of Jesus. Everything that he has been doing up to this point, has been leading to the cross. Philip Yancey, author of *The Jesus I Never Knew*, comments:

> Of the biographies I have read, few devote more than ten percent of their pages to the subject's death--including biographies of men like Martin Luther King Jr. and Mahatma Gandhi, who died violent and politically significant deaths. The Gospels, though, devote nearly a third of their length to the climactic last week of Jesus' life. Matthew, Mark, Luke, and John saw death as the central mystery of Jesus.[1]

The two longest chapters in Matthew deal with the crucifixion. And yet, one of the details that I appreciate most about the crucifixion story is its brevity of detail. The Gospel writers were masterful in saying volumes with few words.

Matthew places a special emphasis on certain aspects of the passion story. David Hill writes:

> Important features of Matthew's Passion story are: (i) the interpretation of the events as controlled by God (26:2, 18; 27:62ff.; 28.11ff., (ii) the fact that it is the Son of God who suffers and dies (27:40, 43), and whose humility is thereby underlined; (iii) this humiliation is voluntary, and therefore an act of obedience fulfilling the will of God.[2]

Matthew follows the basic outline for the passion story that Mark used in his gospel. But he tells the story from his own point of view as eyewitness to the event.

First Century Insights ᑐ

Crucifixion in the Ancient World

How did the ancients view crucifixion? What type of stigma did a crucified person bear? The early Christians worshiped a man who had been crucified. How did the Jews and Greeks react to this? Until recently I had never thought much about this. I knew what Paul wrote in 1 Corinthians 1:23, "the cross is foolishness (*moria*) to the Gentiles and a stumbling block (*skandalon*, a scandal) to the Jews." But I never investigated how foolish the Gentiles viewed the cross or how much of a scandal the cross was to the Jews. Martin Hengel's book, *Crucifixion*, opened my eyes to the folly of the message of the cross in the ancient world.[3]

How did the ancient world view crucifixion? First, the story of the cross is unique in ancient literature. No other religion was based upon a leader (or a god) who had been crucified.[4] In fact, although many of the Greek gods had foibles, the Greeks celebrated the immortality of their gods. Yet the Christians worshipped a God who had died. He not only died, but their deity died the shameful death on a cross. It was difficult for the Greek mind to accept this. How could a god die? Why would a god die such an ignoble death? This distinguished Jesus from all other religious leaders, all other gods. To the Greco-Roman mind, this was foolishness. They could not grasp it.

Another aspect of this foolishness was the fact that Jesus willingly accepted this shameful death. He did not fight against it. He predicted it would happen. He willingly accepted his arrest. He did not defend himself at his trial. He humbly and obediently accepted death. Humility and obedience did not characterize the pagan pantheon. That Jesus had these characteristics was foolishness to the Greeks.

As a side note, Jesus was not just the only religious leader/ deity to be crucified; he was also the only religious leader/deity to predict his resurrection. This is another distinguishing mark of Christianity. Jesus placed his claims of deity and messiahship on the line when he said, "Crucify me and three days later, I will rise from the dead," something that is easily verifiable. If he does not rise from the dead, produce the body. Parade the dead body of Jesus around Jerusalem and his teachings die. The Jewish leaders knew of his prediction and planned on spoiling it. This is why they placed guards (their own guards) at Jesus' tomb. After three days, they would be ready to produce his body and prove his claims false. But Jesus did rise from the dead. How could the early disciples get over the foolishness and scandal of the cross? The resurrection. They knew it was foolish and scandalous to worship a crucified God, but it was right to worship a resurrected Lord.

Second, the early church was attacked because of the cross. The first major controversy that almost split the church wide open was the Jew/Gentile controversy. This was an immediate problem. Many Christian Jews believed that for a Gentile to become a Christian, he or she had to become a Jew first. They did not welcome the Gentiles into the fellowship. The Jerusalem Council met in AD 49 to settle this dispute.

The second major attack on the church came from the Gnostics. The Gnostics were a group of philosophers who accepted Plato's teaching that the material world was evil. How then is it possible that God could come into the evil world and take on the evil flesh through the incarnation? How is it possible for God to die through the crucifixion? Gnostics taught that Jesus only seemed to be human (docetism). They also taught that Jesus did not die on the cross, he only seemed to die. Gnostics felt that Jesus must have escaped before his arrest or before the crucifixion. Someone else (a replacement) endured the suffering of the imprisonment and crucifixion of Jesus. To them the cross was foolishness. It was impossible that God would suffer as Jesus had suffered.

One such Gnostic was Celsus. He wrote many polemics against the church. Writing against Jesus he said, "And you, do you not believe that the son of God sent to the Jews is the most ridiculous makeshift of all?"[5] Celsus believed that Jesus had the perfect opportunity to demonstrate his divinity at his trial. If he had transported himself away from the suffering, he would have proven his deity. By staying, he disproved it, since no god would undergo the physical torment that Jesus went through. To Celsus, the story of the cross was illogical. Martin Hengel notes the protests of the Gnostics:

> To believe that the one pre-existent Son of the one true God, the mediator at creation and the redeemer of the world, had appeared in very recent times in out-of-the-way Galilee as a member of the obscure people of the Jews, and even worse, had died the death of a common criminal on the cross, could only be regarded as a sign of madness.[6]

To the mind of the Gnostic, the cross was unacceptable.

The early church was ridiculed because of its teaching of the cross. A discovery by archaeologists illustrates this. Archaeologists found a first century drawing of a man being crucified. In the drawing the crucified man was wearing a donkey's head. Underneath this drawing was the inscription, "Alexamenos worships god."[7] This graffito poked fun at the Christian belief that the Jesus who died on the cross was God. This belief was foolishness to the Gentile and a scandal to the Jews.

An interesting note here: many Muslims do not believe that Jesus died on the cross. They worship Jesus as a great prophet, but do not believe in the crucifixion of Jesus. The cross is foolishness to them. Although this is not taught in the Koran, many believe that a substitute for Jesus went to the cross, and that the substitute was Judas. They believe that Judas died on the cross instead of Jesus. I learned this teaching from speaking to many Muslims about the crucifixion when I lived in Jerusalem.

Third, the crucifixion was the most barbaric means of execution in the ancient world. If Jesus were God, why would he undergo this type of death? This death was meant for extreme criminals. It was meant to humiliate the criminal and to make an example of him. It was the supreme demonstration of Roman domination. Crucifixion began with the Persians, but it was used all over the Mediterranean world. It was death without dignity. You are stripped naked and suspended on wood at a major intersection. You are hung in the air for all to see. This was to be the grand deterrent to crime. It was a torturous death, the severity of the torture dependent only on the whim of the executioners. Seneca wrote, "I see crosses there, not just of one kind, but made in many different ways: some have their victims with head down to the ground; some impale their private parts; others stretch out their arms on the gibbet."[8]

The Romans excelled at executions. To keep the Roman Peace (*Pax Romana*), they ruled with an iron fist. Romans listed the ways they executed criminals and placed crucifixion at the top of the list calling it the "*summun supplicium*" (the supreme Roman penalty).[9] After crucifixion, the Romans used burning and decapitation as means of execution. Decapitation was looked upon as a more humane means of execution. It was illegal to crucify a Roman citizen. When a Roman citizen was executed, he was decapitated. This was the penalty inflicted upon the Apostle Paul in Rome. Hanging was also looked upon as a more humane punishment than crucifixion. Isidore of Seville wrote, "But hanging is a lesser penalty than the cross. For the gallows kills the victim immediately, whereas the cross tortures for a long time those who are fixed to it."[10] Crucifixion was the supreme penalty handed out to the lowest class of society. It was for non-Romans. As the gladiatorial games in Rome, crucifixion was often used for entertainment. The crosses were placed at public venues, often outside city gates or at major intersections, so that many people could witness the execution. The executioners were professionals. They knew how to keep a person alive for hours so that multitudes could witness the execution.

Crucifixion was often saved for high crimes and for treason. The Romans wanted to make an example of the most severe criminals, and no crime was more severe than treason. Therefore an added stigma was placed on crucified people: you were more than a common criminal—you were an enemy of the state. Hengel writes, "Crucifixion was also a means of waging war and securing peace, of wearing down rebellious cities under siege, of breaking the will of conquered peoples and of bringing mutinous troops or unruly provinces under control."[11]

The Romans viewed crucifixion as punishment for slaves. In fact "the slaves' punishment" is found in ancient literature to describe crucifixion. When slave owners could not control their slaves, they often had them crucified. This was done as an example to other slaves. If a slave owner was murdered, every slave in his house was executed by crucifixion. That way, any murderous talk among slaves was more likely to be reported by a slave who wanted to protect himself. They typical punishment for a rebellious slave was crucifixion. After the slave rebellion of Spartacus was crushed, six thousand slaves were crucified on the *Via Appia* (Appian Way) between Rome and Crassus.[12]

The knowledge that crucifixion was viewed as the slaves' punishment adds meaning to Philippians 2:6-11. Paul teaches that Jesus willingly became a slave (*doulos*). Jesus also became obedient to death, even death on the cross, the slave's punishment. How far was Jesus willing to go with his acceptance of slavery? He went all the way with it, even unto death. He embraces slavery to the ultimate, most radical degree, death on a cross. But this slave who died a slave's death is no longer a slave. He is now the Lord of the universe. He has been crowned King.

Conclusion

To the first century mind, crucifixion was the most barbaric, degrading, dehumanizing, and humiliating death that a person could suffer. It was saved for the lower classes. It was inflicted on traitorous criminals. It was "the slave's punishment." To the Roman, crucifixion was the "*summum supplicium,*" the supreme penalty. The Greco-Roman mind could not conceive of a deity undergoing this punishment. To them it was just foolishness to think this way.

To understand how the ancients thought about this, think about how the same idea would strike us today. Imagine someone who had been arrested on the suspicion that he wanted to start a revolution and topple the United States government. After 9/11, it is not difficult to imagine this happening. He is tried and convicted of a capital crime against the United States of America. He appeals to all the sources that he can appeal to, but he is still found guilty. It seems that some evidence was trumped up, but the conviction stands. He is executed for treason.

But you know the man. You know he is not guilty. You know that he wanted the best for America and the American people. Some of his words had been taken out of context and he was executed unjustly. You take up his cause. You parade around the country telling everyone that the man who was arrested, tried, convicted, and executed as a traitorous criminal was actually a good man. It is a tough sell. You take it a step further. You declare that this man who was killed by the authorities was not a man at all, that he was the Son of God, he was divine. Imagine how people would react to this. They would think you were insane. Many reacted to the early disciples in the same way. The message of the cross was foolishness to the Gentiles and a stumbling block to the Jews. How did the early church find any converts with this message? It was their commitment to the message that won many people over.

What can we learn from the cross?

1. Jesus literally became a slave for us, and in response we must become a slave for him. Philippians 2:5-8 reads:

> *Your attitude should be the same as that of Christ Jesus:*
> *Who, being in very nature God,*
> *Did not consider equality with God something to be grasped,*
> *But made himself nothing,*
> *Taking the very nature of a servant,*
> *Being made in human likeness.*
> *And being found in appearance as a man,*
> *He humbled himself*
> *And became obedient to death*
> *Even death on a cross!*

Jesus did not just act the part of a slave; he literally became a slave for us. He served humanity in everything he did. He gave himself to humanity everyday. But the ultimate example of his servant nature was his willingness to die the slave's death on the cross.

In Luke 9:23, Jesus directs his disciples, "If anyone would come after me, he must deny himself and take up his cross daily and follow me." What does he mean by "take up his cross daily?" In our culture today, we can water this down until it is meaningless. But in the time of Jesus to take up a cross meant one thing–to die. But not to die just any death; no, it meant to die the slave's death. We must be a slave for Jesus every single day and crucify our selfish nature every day. Some might protest that Jesus was directing this message to his closest circle of disciples. But he begins the sentence by saying, "If anyone would come after me..." The call of discipleship is the same for everyone. You cannot follow Jesus without a cross. The cross is for death, a slave's death. To follow Jesus you must die to yourself everyday and become a slave for him.

2. He died on the cross for us.

The Apostle Paul in Romans 8:32 states, "He who did not spare his own Son, but gave him up for us all–how will he not also, along with him, graciously give us all things?" Hengel comments on Paul's statement,

> Jesus did not die a gentle death like Socrates, with his cup of hemlock, much less passing on old and full of years like the patriarchs of the Old Testament. Rather, he died like a slave or a common criminal, in torment, on the tree of shame. Paul's Jesus did not die just any death; he was given up for us all on the cross in a cruel and a contemptible way.[13]

If we do not stumble at the cross or mock it as foolish, then the cross makes us appreciate the sacrifice of Jesus all the more. Jesus did not die for himself; he died for us. He took our place. We deserve the criminal's death on the cross, but Jesus did it for us.

The plot against Jesus (26:1-5)

> 26:1*After Jesus had finished saying all these things, he said to his disciples,* 2*"You know that in two days, the Passover begins, then the Son of Man will be handed over to be crucified.*
>
> 3*Then the chief priests and the elders of the people gathered in the palace of the high priest named Caiaphas and* 4*plotted how to arrest Jesus secretly and kill him.* 5*They said, "Not during the feast, because the people may riot."*

1-2 Jesus predicts his death for the last time, adding the manner in which it would happen: "the Passover is two days away–and the Son of Man will be handed over to be crucified." This was spoken on the Mount of Olives, late on a Tuesday evening; for the Jews this would be early Wednesday morning.

3-4 The chief priests and elders assembled in the palace of the high priest Caiaphas. The Greek word *aule* can be translated as "courtyard," "farm," "temple court," or "palace." The high priest and high-level Sadducees lived in the nicer part of Jerusalem, which today is located across from the Zion Gate. Archeologists have uncovered many of the ruins in this area and it is safe to say the houses in this neighborhood were palatial. You can visit the ruins today and see how the upper class Jewish elite lived.

Luke lists Annas as the high priest; Matthew and John mention Caiaphas. Annas was the father-in-law of Caiaphas. The Romans ousted Annas in AD 15. Caiaphas took over the high priesthood in AD 18 and was high priest until his death in AD 36. In the Jewish tradition, the high priest was to rule until his death. Since Annas was still alive, many continued to view him as the high priest. When they were both alive, Annas heavily influenced the decisions of the Sanhedrin, the Jewish ruling council. It was as if these two men were co-regents overseeing the affairs of the Jewish population.[14]

5 The Jewish leaders feared that if they moved on Jesus at the wrong time, it might provoke a riot. They might have remembered Jesus' triumphal entry into Jerusalem and the wonderful greeting he had received a few days earlier (Matthew 21). During the festival days it was common for Jerusalem to swell to five times its normal population. Messianic expectations were extremely high during those festival days. The Jewish leaders did not want a riot on their hands, but they did want to deal with the perceived threat of Jesus.

The anointing at Bethany (26:6-13)

⁶While Jesus was in Bethany in the house of Simon the leper, ⁷a woman came to him with an alabaster jar of costly ointment. She poured the ointment on his head as he reclined at the table.

⁸When the disciples saw this, they were angry, saying, "Why this waste? ⁹This ointment could have sold for a large price, and the money given to the poor."

¹⁰Jesus knew what they thought and said, "Why are you troubling this woman? She has performed a good service for me. ¹¹You will always have the poor with you; you will not always have me. ¹²By pouring this ointment on my body she has prepared me for burial. ¹³Listen carefully to me, wherever the gospel is preached in the whole world, what she has done will be told as a testimony of her."

Concerning this story, Jesus himself comments, "Wherever this gospel is preached throughout the world, what she has done will also be told, in memory of her." It is true; all Four Gospels include this story.

But are the Gospels recording one story of the anointing or two? D.A. Carson suggests that we have two stories in the Gospels—one in Galilee (Luke) and the other in Bethany (Matthew, Mark, and John). He comments:

> The stories do differ in several aspects: (1) in Luke the woman is a sinner. The other writers do not mention this. (2) John names her as Mary of Bethany. (3) Luke's setting is Galilee in the home of a Pharisee. Matthew's setting is Bethany in the home of Simon the leper. (4) Here the disciple's criticize her actions; in Luke the host criticizes the woman. (5) Matthew mentions that the woman anointed Jesus to prepare him for burial. In Luke, the story occurs much earlier in Jesus' ministry (Luke 7:36-50), and Jesus contrasts the way the woman welcomed Jesus as compared to the Pharisees' welcome.[15]

Matthew, Mark, and John have small details in their three presentations of the anointing that differ, but they are still the same story. John places the story before the Triumphal Entry and seems to be locating the story chronologically in the passion narrative. Matthew and Mark place the story thematically and not chronologically. Matthew and Mark tie the answer of Jesus to the disciples' criticism of the waste of the ointment to a possible motive for Judas' betrayal.

6-7 The setting is Bethany, a small village on the eastern spur of the Mount of Olives. Jesus often stayed in Bethany when he visited Jerusalem, usually at the home of Lazarus, Mary and Martha. During this last week, he would have entered Jerusalem during the day and stayed at their home in Bethany at night. On this occasion, he was having supper in the home of Simon the Leper. Simon must have been healed from leprosy, or else everyone there was breaking the Mosaic code by eating with him. Archaeologists have discovered a leper colony that existed in Bethany. Many who were healed of leprosy continued to live in the area after their cure because the stigma of leprosy would have stayed with them. Jesus was pushing the limits of social convention by staying in this community. But Jesus always pushed the limits of social convention.

The ointment/perfume was very expensive. In fact, the alabaster flask that contained the fluid would have been pricey. John mentions that the ointment costs a year's wages, for a workingman—three hundred denarii. The ointment was most likely from a nard plant that was native to India. This ointment was especially used for anointing the dead. Jesus relates the anointing to his imminent burial. We cannot be sure if the woman had this in mind when she anointed Jesus or if she was just trying to honor him.

8-9 The disciples question the action of this woman and the willingness of Jesus to accept her gift. John has Judas questioning the act, and Mark that some of those who were present questioned it. It seems that everyone there, except the woman (Mary of Bethany) missed the fact that Jesus was soon to die.

The fact that Jesus knew what they were talking about could imply a supernatural knowledge or that their whisperings carried to the side of the table where he heard what was being discussed. He defends the actions of the woman calling it "a beautiful thing."

Jesus comments, "the poor you will always have with you," has been taken by some as a defense for not meeting the needs of the poor. But Jesus is actually underscoring the fact the poor will always be there and they should be taken care of. But even with all the other needs that are pressing upon us, a selfless, yet extravagant act of kindness shown to Jesus is acceptable.

Judas' plot to betray Jesus (26:14-16)

[14]Then one of the twelve, Judas Iscariot, went to the chief priest [15]and said, "what will you give me if I deliver him over to you?" They paid him 30 pieces of silver. [16]And from that moment he searched for a good opportunity to betray him.

Up to this point in the Gospel, Judas Iscariot has only been mentioned in the list of the disciples. Now he takes a major role–the betrayer of Jesus. Judas was a common name in the first century Jewish community. There are several suggestions as to what Iscariot might mean: (1) the town of Kariot, thus Judas from Kariot, (2) a derivative of the word sacarri, a radical group of zealots who wanting to oust the Romans from the land by any means necessary, (3) from the Aramaic word for "deceiver" *sheqavya*, (4) perhaps a resident from Jericho or (5) from an Aramaic word for "red" used as a nickname describing Judas' red hair or ruddy appearance. The exact meaning of the term is unknown. All things considered, the best possible guess is Judas from the town of Kariot.

The Bible does not give a clear motivation for the actions of Judas. Why did he betray Jesus? Three of the Gospels closely link the betrayal with the story of Mary anointing Jesus with ointment. Could Judas' anger at what he considered an extravagant waste have prompted him to betray Jesus? If Judas was a *sacarri*, then he might have joined Jesus hoping he would lead them in a military revolution. When that revolution fails to occur, he could have become a traitor to Jesus. It might have been a motive of greed. Thirty pieces of silver was not a vast amount of money, but it was worth about 120 denarri or one-third of a year's salary for an average man (it was also the price of a slave).

Whatever the motivation, Judas did betray Jesus. He planned a time when Jesus could be arrested apart from crowds or people. He would later regret his actions, but for now he was committed to give Jesus over to the Roman authorities.

The plot, the anointing, and the betrayal: a summary (26:1-16)

Throughout his ministry Jesus foretold what was going to happen to him at the Passover. He confirms it with his disciples with a saying that could not be mistaken, "the Passover is two days away — and the Son of Man will be given over to be crucified." But still not everyone understands the nature of Jesus' death. That will come only to those who have eyes of faith. The religious leaders (Sadducees, Pharisees, and Scribes) did not have eyes of faith. They plotted to kill Jesus. Because of jealousy and hatred, they wanted to get Jesus out of the way.

Judas did not have eyes of faith. He plotted with the religious leaders to find a way to arrest Jesus. They settled on a price of thirty silver coins as the price of betrayal. For thirty silver coins, Judas sold his soul. Do you have a price for your soul? Would you betray Jesus if the price were right? Judas and the religious leaders should have recognized Jesus as King of Kings, but they were blinded by their own sin and ambition. Judas had been with him for three years, yet he failed to understand who Jesus was.

One woman did see Jesus with eyes of faith. This woman approached Jesus at the home of Simon the Leper carrying an alabaster jar of very expensive perfume. She began to anoint Jesus with this oil. She broke many social customs by doing this. As a woman, she had no right to enter the meal to be with Jesus. As a woman, it was not her place to anoint him. The disciples were more concerned at the expense of the oil than with her lack of social convention. They failed to see with eyes of faith. With eyes of faith, they could have seen what the woman was doing. She alone had eyes of faith. Jesus complimented her on her gift. He recognized that she saw clearly. She was anointing him for burial. She was giving him his flowers before he died. Kings were anointed as they were crowned. She was crowning the king before his death. She alone saw Jesus clearly. Her act of devotion stands for all time as a testimony of faith. Do we have this type of faith so that we can see Jesus clearly? Let's pray to have the faith of this woman who anointed Jesus for burial.

The Last Supper (26:17-25)

[17]On the first day of the feast of Unleavened Bread, Jesus' disciples came to him, saying, "Where do you want us to prepare to eat the Passover with you?"

[18]He answered, "Go into the city to a certain man and say this to him. The teacher says, 'My time is near, I want to celebrate the Passover with my disciples at your house.'" [19]So the disciples did as Jesus directed, and they prepared the Passover.

[20]When evening came, Jesus was at the table with the twelve, [21]and while they were eating, he said, "I tell you truthfully — one of you will betray me."

[22]They became disturbed and each said to him, "Not I Lord!"

[23]Jesus answered, "The one who has dipped his hand into the bowl with me will betray me. [24]The Son of Man goes just as it has been written about him, but woe to the man who betrays the Son of Man! It would be better for him to have not been born."

[25]Then Judas, who betrayed him, said, "Not I Lord!"

Jesus answered, "Yes, you have said so."

Jesus gets ready to have a last meal with his disciples. The room is prepared and they recline to eat. They are still blind. They do not recognize that this is their last meal with Jesus. Even though he specifically told them that he would be crucified on the Passover, the next day, they miss it. How blind can they be? Judas, who has already established the price for betrayal at thirty silver coins, denies that he will betray him. Jesus confronts him saying, "It is you."

Was the Lord's Supper the Passover Meal or was it the meal before the Passover? This question has troubled many students as they attempt to reconcile the Synoptic accounts of the crucifixion with the account in John. Matthew 26:17 connects the Lord's Supper with "the first day of the feast of Unleavened Bread." This was the Passover, Thursday the 14th of Nisan. D.A. Carson explains:

> It seems, then, that Jesus' disciples entered the city shortly after noon on Thursday, 14 Nisan, procured the room, took a lamb to the temple court and killed it, roasted it with bitter herbs (Exodus. 12:8-9), and made other arrangements for the meal, including the purchase of

wine and unleavened bread. Matthew 26:19 explicitly says that they
"prepared the Passover." After nightfall on Thursday evening, when it
was 15 Nisan, Jesus joined his disciples and they ate the Passover.
On these points the Synoptics agree; and this places Jesus' death on
Friday, 15 Nisan, probably about 3:00 p.m.[16]

The Synoptics agree here, but can we reconcile this with the Gospel
of John?

John's account reads, "It was the day of the Preparation of
Passover Week, about the sixth hour. "Here is your king," Pilate
said to the Jews" (John 19:14). John lists the day of the crucifixion
as "the Preparation of Passover Week" (*paraskeue tou pascha*). Many
have taken this phrase to mean "Passover." But it is not the Passover
(*tou pascha*); it is the preparation of the Passover (*paraskeue*). The
Passover was observed on Thursday the 14th of Nisan. The word
"preparation" (*paraskeue*) had over the years become a technical term
that was synonymous with preparation for the Sabbath. The phrase
"preparation of the Passover Week" means the Friday preparation
day for the Sabbath of the Passover week. So John does not have Jesus'
crucifixion on the Passover, but on Friday, the day after Passover.

1 Corinthians 5:7 reads, "Get rid of the old yeast that you
may be a new batch without yeast–as you really are. For Christ, our
Passover lamb, has been sacrificed." Paul calls Christ "our Passover
Lamb." Does this not mean that Jesus had to be crucified on Passover
and not on Friday, the day after Passover? Gleason L. Archer, a
professor at Trinity Evangelical Divinity School, clarifies this:

> It simply needs to be pointed out that the lambs referred to here are
> not those that were slaughtered and eaten in private homes–a rite
> Jesus had already observed with His disciples the night before–but
> the lambs to be offered on the altar of the Lord on behalf of the whole
> nation of Israel. These were all known as Passover sacrifices, since
> they were presented during Passover week.[17]

18-22 Jesus mentions that his appointed time (*kaipos*) is near.
This is of course referring to his crucifixion. He gives his
disciples specific orders concerning the Passover meal. The disciples
follow those directions; they sit down to have the Passover meal together. Jews were to eat the meal inside the city of Jerusalem. That is
why it was important to find a space. We know that the disciples in
an upper room celebrated the meal. A traditional site for this location
has been found in the Old City of Jerusalem close to the Zion Gate.
This was a part of the city where many early Christians lived and
they seem to have held this room in special honor. We have no way of
knowing if this room was the exact location of the last supper.

During the meal, Jesus reveals the shocking news, "One of you will betray me." They all reacted to his statement claiming that they would not betray him.

23-24 Jesus identifies his betrayer as the one who dipped his hand in the bowl with him. The bowl contained some type of dip like hummus, and it would be scooped out with bread. Jesus is referring not only to the physical act or dipping the bread with him, but also to the fact that his betrayer is a friend, one of his immediate circle.

25 Judas attempts to protest his innocence, but Jesus removes all doubt saying, "Yes, it is you."

Jesus' institutes the Lord's Supper (26:26-30)

26As they were eating, Jesus took bread and after blessing it, he broke it and gave to his disciples, saying, "Take, eat, this is my body."

27Then he took the cup and after blessing it, he gave it to all of them saying, "Drink from it, all of you, for 28this is my blood of the covenant which has been poured out for many for the forgiveness of sins. 29I say to you, I will never drink of this fruit of the vine until I drink it new with you in my Father's kingdom."

30After singing a hymn, they went out to the Mount of Olives.

26-27 Jesus institutes the Lord's Supper here. He connects the bread with his body and the fruit of the vine with his blood. Wars have been fought over whether Jesus meant that the bread would literally become his body and the fruit of the vine his blood. But Jesus was not teaching cannibalism. He was setting up a memorial by which we would remember the importance of his death.

28 Jesus speaks of the fruit of the vine as being his "blood of the covenant which is poured out for many for the forgiveness of sins." The blood of Jesus was poured out "for the forgiveness of sins." This is the exact same phrase found in Acts 2:38 in connection with repentance and baptism. Peter says, "Repent and be baptized everyone of you in the name Jesus Christ for the forgiveness of your sins and so that you will receive the gift of the Holy Spirit." Why do people teach that the forgiveness comes before baptism? No one would say that forgiveness came before Jesus poured out his blood. Why would he die if sin had already been forgiven? No, Jesus died so that we could be forgiven. In the same way, baptism is for the purpose of forgiveness of sins and so we might receive the gift of the Holy Spirit.

Practically Speaking ❧

The Lord's Supper—To Remember

Jesus establishes a memorial during his last supper with the disciples. At the Passover feast, unleavened bread and sweet wine were served. Jesus takes the bread and breaks it. The bread represents his body. He passed a cup of wine around and asks all his disciples to drink from it. It represents his blood that would be spilled on the cross. This memorial is still celebrated today when we take the communion, the Lord's Supper. Whenever we take the Lord's Supper, we should reflect back to the cross of Jesus and remember what he gave so we could have forgiveness. This memorial should help us keep our eyes open to who Jesus is and what he did on the cross for us.

When my family lived in Israel, we found it to be a country of memorials. The Israeli people do not want to forget. The Holocaust Museum is a memorial for all the Jews who perished in World War II under the Nazi regime. It also stands a reminder to the Jews and the world that this type of atrocity must never happen again. When you drive from Tel Aviv to Jerusalem, you pass several burned out shells of supply trucks and army vehicles that were used during Israel's War of Independence in 1948. These trucks were left where they were destroyed by Arab artillery. They serve as a reminder to the people of the struggle for independence. This struggle must not be forgotten.

The most telling example of Israel's establishment of memorials is a national Day of Remembrance that has been established. On this day, the country is to remember everyone who fought for the independence and survival of Israel. In the United States we have Veteran's Day, but it is not taken as seriously as the Israelis take their Day of Remembrance. At one point during the day, a siren sounds from locations around the country and the country comes to a standstill. I was walking down Jaffa Road in Jerusalem when the siren sounded. People stopped walking and stood at attention. People stopped their cars in the middle of the street and got out and stood silently beside their cars. People who were eating dropped their knives and forks and stood beside their dinner table. People who were in the middle of a conversation or the middle of a laugh or haggling with someone over a price, stopped and became silent. It was an eerie feeling. The whole street came to a standstill out of respect. It was a memorial. People were to remember what others had given for their freedom

The Lord's Supper is the same type of memorial for us. We are to remember what Jesus did on the cross for us. The memory is to stay fresh. We must not forget. It is not good enough to remember the cross once a year or once a quarter. The Lord's Supper is taken every first day of the week so we will keep his memory fresh. The cross is an event that we must never forget.

Jesus predicts the disciple's denial (26:31-35)

³¹*Then Jesus said to them, "All of you will fall away because of me this night for it has been written:*

> *I will strike the shepherd,*
> > *And the sheep of the flock*
> > *Will be scattered.*

³²*But after I have risen, I will go ahead of you into Galilee."*

³³*Peter replied, "If all fall away because of you, I will never desert you."*

³⁴*Jesus said to him, "This is the truth, tonight before the rooster crows, you will deny me three times."*

³⁵*Peter said to him, Even if I must die with you, I would never deny you." And all the other disciples said the same.*

Jesus predicts that all the disciples would fail to see with eyes of faith and would not stay with him through the crucifixion. Peter, as usual, spoke up first saying that if everyone else left, he would still stay with Jesus. Jesus predicts that Peter would deny him three times before the night was over. Peter says he was ready to die with Jesus. All the disciples said they were ready to die with Jesus. What would you have said? Are you ready to die with Jesus? The call of discipleship is the same today as then. We must be ready to die with Jesus. How do we know if we are willing to die with him? Answer this–do you die every day to your selfish nature and live a selfless life for Jesus? If you are not willing to die in the little ways every day to your selfishness, then you would not be willing to die physically for Jesus. Jesus knew his disciples would deny him because they were selfish by nature. They failed to have eyes of faith and see him as the King of Kings. Are you willing to die for Jesus? How you live your life today will answer that question.

31 Jesus predicts that all of his disciples would "fall away, stumble, be deserters" because of him. The Greek word is *skandalidzo* from which we get our word "scandal." He says the action of the disciples' desertion would fulfill Zechariah 13:7, "Strike the shepherd and the flock will be scattered." Jesus is the shepherd and the disciples are the flock.

32 Here Jesus predicts his resurrection and the fact that he will reacquaint himself with his disciples in Galilee. Matthew will return to these two themes often in the next two chapters. Although he has predicted their desertion, he gives them hope as he speaks of reuniting with them in Galilee.

33 The rooster's crow refers to a time between midnight and 3 a.m. Some scholars have conjectured that in Palestine the rooster crows at 12:30, 1:30 and 2:30 A.M.

Mark refers to this second crowing of the rooster. The Romans referred to the time between midnight and 3 a.m. as the "cock-crow" watch. This would mean that Jesus was awake during this time before his crucifixion. It is safe to say that Jesus got very little sleep the night before his crucifixion, and it is probable that he got no sleep.

Gethsemane (26:36-46)

36Then Jesus went with them to a place called Gethsemane and he said to the disciples, "Sit here while I go there and pray." 37He took Peter and the two sons of Zebedee and began to be sorrowful and troubled. 38He said to them, "My soul is deeply grieved to death. Stay here and stay awake with me."

39Going a little farther, he fell with his face to the ground and said, "My Father, if it is possible, take this cup from me. Yet not as I wish, but as you wish."

40After returning to his disciples, he found them sleeping and said to Peter, "Are you not able to stay awake with me one hour? 41Watch and pray that temptation will not come. The spirit is willing, but the flesh is weak."

42He went a second time to pray, saying, "My Father, if it is not possible for this to pass unless I drink it, your will be done."

43He returned again and found them sleeping, for their eyes were heavy. 44So he left them for the third time to pray, saying the same words again.

45Then he returned to his disciples and said, "Are you still sleeping and resting? Behold the hour is near and the Son of Man will be handed over into the hands of sinners. 46Rise, let's go. See, my betrayer is here."

The lesson of Gethsemane is the lesson of prayer. Jesus teaches us the need to pray to bolster our courage before times of suffering and distress. It is also the beginning of the agony for Jesus. Before he endured the physical abuse of his arrest and crucifixion, he endured the emotional distress of Gethsemane. The phrase "my soul is overwhelmed with sorrow" can also mean "so sorrowful that it is to the point of death." Fritz Rienecker writes, "It implies a restless, distracted, shrinking from some trouble or thought of trouble, which nevertheless cannot be escaped."[18] Jesus was in anguish. Which is more painful, the physical pain or the emotional pain? They were equally draining. Gethsemane was a dark night for Jesus.

36 Gethsemane is an olive garden just across the Kidron Valley from Jerusalem. The word "Gethsemane" means "olive press." It is located on the slope of the Mount of Olives east of the Golden Gate in Jerusalem. There was located an olive grove with a small cave containing an olive press. From this spot you could look upon the city of Jerusalem. Jesus would have been able to see the Temple of Jerusalem as he prayed in the garden.

Part of the garden still exists today and is a "must see" for anyone who visits Jerusalem. When our family lived in Jerusalem, it was one of our favorite spots to visit. It is still the favorite site of my wife and daughter. My daughter, Chelsea, visited it so often that she picked an olive tree that she would climb into and perch on a limb to pray. We named that tree "Chelsea's tree."

Just outside of the garden of Gethsemane is a small grotto or cave that contained an olive press in the first century. Jesus might have gone into this cave when he separated himself from his disciples to pray. This cave can be visited today.

38-39 These verses demonstrate the emotional turmoil that Jesus was suffering the night before his crucifixion. He went to Gethsemane for strength. He received strength through prayer. But, unfortunately, the disciples were of no help to him. Instead of encouraging Jesus this night, their actions were discouraging.

Jesus struggles to surrender his will to the will of the Father. Perhaps he is not asking for a way out, but for another way to accomplish what must be accomplished. Is there another way to redeem the world? His agony in the garden demonstrates that Jesus understood that the crucifixion would be an agonizing death. He voluntarily endured the agony of the cross for us. He had to set his mind for the events that were about to transpire.

40-46 Three times Jesus prays the same prayer to the Father. Each time he returns to find his disciples asleep. How disappointing it must have been for Jesus to find his disciples sleeping. Has anyone asked you to stay awake with them during a traumatic time? Perhaps they are in the hospital where they are afraid and need encouragement. What if your wife is up all night having labor pains because she is about to deliver your child? Do you go to bed and let her endure the pain alone? You find a way to stay awake. You pace back and forth, throw cold water on your face, or make a pot of coffee. But these three, Jesus' closest friends, were tired. Their eyes were heavy. But it isn't that difficult to stay awake for a few hours. (Apparently it was not even midnight). The fact that they fell asleep shows that they still did not understand what Jesus was about to endure. He came to them with his "soul overwhelmed with sorrow," and they were callous to his condition. Let's pray that our hearts will never be so callous.

Practically Speaking ଓ

The Courageous Path

The agony of the cross began for Jesus long before he was nailed to it. The last week of Jesus' life is called the "passion" week because he suffered all week long. It was a week with long hours and little rest. It was a week where he tried to get his disciples to understand what he was about to endure, but they never really understood it until after the resurrection. It was a week of disappointment in the people that were closest to him. We see his agony in Gethsemane. Jesus was overwhelmed to the point of death. He knew what he was about to endure. If there had been a way out, he would have taken it. He submitted to the will of the Father. He did not want to die, but he had to die to pay the price for forgiveness. He willingly paid the price.

Have you every stayed up the entire night in prayer? On several occasions, I have. It is not easy an easy task, but you can do it. It becomes easier when you have people doing it with you. If one of you starts to fade, the others simply help that person to stay awake.

Do you think that if you asked a friend to stay awake while you prayed that they would honor your request? If you asked three friends, that would make it even easier. If one of them were about to fade into sleep, then the other friends would punch them to keep them awake. If only one of the three had a conviction that they needed to stay awake, then he could shout, scream, stomp, or splash them with water to keep the others awake. All three disciples did not fathom the agony that Jesus was experiencing. They slept soundly while he struggled in prayer. This again illustrates how blind the disciples were to the mission and plan of Jesus. They were not good friends to him. Before we get too hard on them, let us ask ourselves, how many times have we been sleeping when we should have been awake?

At any moment in the process of his trial and crucifixion, Jesus could have called twelve legions of angels to rescue him. As he was being mocked, beaten, spit upon and nailed to the cross, all he had to say was the name of the archangel, "Michael." Twelve legions of angels would have arrived. And how do you fight an angel? Jesus had an out. He was not tricked into dying on the cross. Jesus willingly went to the cross for us. He had a way of escape. Instead of escape, he chose to die on our behalf. He took the most courageous path that anyone has ever taken, the path to the cross. The way of suffering for Jesus was the path to our forgiveness.

The Arrest (26:47-56)

⁴⁷*While he was speaking, Judas, one of the twelve, arrived with a large crowd who were carrying swords and clubs. This crowd was sent by the chief priests and elders of the people.* ⁴⁸*The betrayer gave them this sign, "The one I kiss is the man, arrest him."* ⁴⁹*And immediately he approached Jesus saying, "Greetings, Rabbi" and kissed him.*

⁵⁰*Jesus said to him, "Friend, do what you came to do."*

Then they came and seized Jesus and arrested him. ⁵¹*Suddenly, one who was with Jesus put his and on his sword, drew it, and cut off the ear of the high priest's slave.*

⁵²*Jesus said to him, "Put your sword back in its place. All who take the sword will die by the sword.* ⁵³*Do you think that I cannot ask my Father and he will send me at once more than twelve legions of angels?* ⁵⁴*How then would the scriptures be fulfilled that say it is necessary for this to happen?"*

⁵⁵*At that time Jesus said to the crowd, "Am I an insurrectionist that you come with swords and clubs to arrest me? Every day I sat in the temple teaching and you did not arrest me.* ⁵⁶*These things have happened so the writings of the prophets might be fulfilled." Then all the disciples abandoned him and fled.*

47 The crowd that arrived to arrest Jesus was the temple guard used by the Sanhedrin and not the Roman guard.

48-49 Many pilgrims would have been in the garden that night, and so it was necessary for Judas to identify Jesus with a sign. The kiss was on the hand or foot and was a kiss of honor. R.T. France elaborates on the Judas' choice to betray Jesus with a kiss:

> For a Rabbi's disciple to kiss his master (on hand or foot) was not an everyday greeting, but a mark of special honor. Nor dare the disciple take this initiative uninvited; to do so was a "studied insult." The greeting of Jesus as Rabbi in this context is therefore heavily ironical (see vs. 35, the only other use of this address in Matthew, again by Judas). Judas' action thus not only identifies Jesus to the arresting party, but also marks his own public repudiation of Jesus' authority.[19]

50 Jesus responds to Judas with the word "friend." Instead of resisting, he invites Judas to hurry and finish what he has started. The scene demonstrates that Jesus is in charge of what is occurring. He has set his mind in prayer and is ready for the events that are about to transpire.

51-52 One of Jesus' disciples grabs a sword and cuts off the ear of one the high priest's servants. John lets us know that it was the impulsive Peter who cut off the ear of Malchus. The proverb "all who draw the sword will die by the sword" must be taken in context. It is not a blanket statement teaching pacifism, but is a way that Jesus restates that he did not come to begin an armed revolution.

53 Jesus was not trapped into going to the cross. He always had a way out. At any moment, he could have called the angels to come rescue him. A legion is 6,000 soldiers. He withstood the pain of the cross willingly; he was not a helpless victim. He was following the will of the Father by allowing the guard to arrest him.

55-56 Jesus again demonstrates that he is one who is in control at his arrest. He asked, "Why have you come to arrest me like an insurrectionist?" He reminds them of all the times he taught in their temple courts without an incident. What is happening is the fulfillment of scripture. Jesus places his trust in God and allows the guard to arrest him.

Jesus Before the High Priest (26:57-68)

⁵⁷Those who arrested Jesus took him to Caiaphas the high priest, where the scribes and the elders had gathered. ⁵⁸Peter followed him from a distance as far as the courtyard of the high priest. He entered and sat down with the guards to see how this would end.

⁵⁹The chief priest and the whole Sanhedrin were searching for false testimony against Jesus so they might kill him. ⁶⁰They did not find any-- though many false witnesses came forward. At last two came ⁶¹forward saying, "This man said, 'I am able to destroy the temple of God and in three days rebuilt it.'"

⁶²Then the high priest stood up and said to him, "Do you have any answer? What is this that they testify against you?"

⁶³But Jesus remained silent.

Then the high priest said to him, "I charge you by the living God-- answer if you are the Christ the Son of God."

⁶⁴Jesus said to him, "Yes, it is as you say. But I say to you:
From now on you will see the Son of Man
Sitting on the right hand of power
And coming on the clouds of heaven.

⁶⁵Then the high priest tore his garments and said, "He has blasphemed! Why do we still need witnesses. See, you have just now heard the blasphemy. ⁶⁶What do you think?"

> They answered, "He deserves death."
> *67Then they spat in his face and struck him. Some slapped him*
> *68saying, "Prophesy to us, Christ--who struck you?"*

The first place Jesus is taken is to Caiaphas, the high priest. Archaeologists believe that Caiaphas and other religious leader lived across the Kidron Valley from the Mount of Olives on Zion's hill. Today this is located just outside of Zion Gate on the southeastern side of the Old City of Jerusalem. Church tradition has identified a house located around the church of St. Peter of Galicantu (the crowing rooster) as the home of Caiaphas. If this is true, and it very well could be, then the Jewish trial and confinement of Jesus the night before his crucifixion occurred here. Today you can walk through these ruins into a cellar (a water reservoir) that is identified as the place where Jesus was confined for the night. We do not know if this is the actual place where Jesus was imprisoned, but it is likely that Jesus spent his night in a cellar (a makeshift jail cell) underneath the house of Caiaphas guarded by the Jewish guard.

Much has been written about the trial of Jesus. It has often been described as a "mock trial," because the Jewish authorities did not adhere to many of the legal regulations of a fair hearing before the Sanhedrin. Today some scholars have labeled the Gospel writers as anti-Semitic because of their portrayal of the Jewish authorities at the trial and crucifixion of Jesus. But the early church had no reason to invent the inconsistencies of the Sanhedrin. Matthew was attempting to reach a Jewish audience with his Gospel. Why would he include facts that would incite them against the church if the facts were not true? Also, in the minds of the Gospel writers, everyone was guilty of the death of Jesus. To them, you and I who are 2,000 years distant from the event of the cross are just as guilty as any of the Jewish or Roman authorities. As Matthew describes the events of the trial of Jesus, he is not trying to assign guilt to the Jews or the Romans. He is accurately depicting how despised and hated Jesus was by the Jewish leaders. They wanted to rid themselves of Jesus. If they needed to cut a few legal corners, then they were willing to do that.

What illegal actions did the Sanhedrin take? (1) It was illegal for them to try a capital case at night. (2) The charge of blasphemy did not meet the legal criteria for that charge. To commit blasphemy you had to pronounce the name of God in your statement. (3) To execute someone the testimony of every witness had to agree. The Sanhedrin could not find even two witnesses that agreed. (4) The trial should have been held at the Royal Stoa in the temple area and not at Caiaphas' house. The Royal Stoa was the usual meeting place for the

Sanhedrin. (5) Jesus was not given a defense attorney. (6) A minimum of two days was required to decide a capital offence. The trial of Jesus was rushed through in one night.

Having said this, let me also note that the Sanhedrin was the most powerful ruling council in Judaism, and they had the power to cut corners where they saw fit. If they feared mob violence, then this would hasten their action. For them to execute Jesus before the Sabbath, they needed to try the case during the night and present it to Pilate the next morning (Friday morning). In their minds, their actions were appropriate. They were cutting corners that had to be cut to take care of a matter of supreme importance. This was a matter of national security, so the laws of a fair trial were secondary.

57 Matthew mentions that the high priest (a Sadducee), scribes, and elders met for the trial of Jesus. There is a noticeable absence of the Pharisees here. But the Sadducee sect dominated the Sanhedrin; therefore, it would be natural not to mention the Pharisees in the proceedings.

59-61 The Sanhedrin knew what they wanted to do–execute Jesus. But they did not have the power to execute criminals. Only the Romans could do that. So they had to take the case to the Romans. In a capital case, two witnesses were needed. They searched for false witnesses, but could not find any. Finally, two came forward with the charge, "Jesus said, 'I can destroy the temple and rebuild it in three days.'" This was enough evidence to push the trial on through to the conclusion they desired.

62-65 After the two false witnesses speak against Jesus, the high priest is ready to conclude the trial. He asked Jesus to answer the accusations leveled against him, but Jesus remained silent. Frustrated by Jesus' silence, Caiaphas cut to the heart of the matter, "Are you the Christ, the Son of God?" If Jesus said no, then the trial was over. If he answered yes, then they would charge him with blasphemy.

In the Greek, the answer of Jesus seems ambiguous, "you say." But most scholars note that the word "yes" is implied: "yes, it is as you say." His next statement leaves no doubt to his answer, "In the future you will see the Son of Man sitting at the right hand of the Mighty One and coming on the clouds of heaven." This is a Messianic reference. He was to sit at the hand of God, the place of power and honor.

The high priest took the statement of Jesus as blasphemy. He tore his garments to show his outrage and indignation. He asked the court to find Jesus guilty of the charge, and they concurred. Jesus was "liable of death."

67-68 As soon as the label of "blasphemer" was officially placed on Jesus, the Sanhedrin unleashed their fury on him. They spit in his face and struck him with their fist. They mocked him, punched him, taunted him, saying, "Prophesy, who hit you?" Then they would have placed him in a secure area for the night.

Peter Denies Jesus (26:69-75)

⁶⁹*Peter was sitting outside in the courtyard. And a servant girl came to him saying, "You also were with Jesus of Galilee."*

⁷⁰*But he denied it before all of them, answering, "I do not know what you are talking about."*

⁷¹*When he went out to the porch, another servant girl found him, and said, "This man was with Jesus of Nazareth."* ⁷²*And again he denied it with an oath, "I do not know the man."*

⁷³*After a little time passed, the people standing there said to Peter, "Certainly you are one of them, for your accent gives you away."* ⁷⁴*Then he began to curse and swear, "I don't know the man!" And immediately the rooster crowed.*

⁷⁵*Then Peter remembered what Jesus had said, "Before the rooster crows, you will deny me three times." And he went outside and cried terribly.*

All four gospels record the event of Peter's denial of Christ. I have always been impressed with how the Bible is willing to portray the foibles of its major characters. Peter is the unofficial leader and spokesman for the disciples. Yet here he denies Jesus. We should not forget that all the disciples denied Jesus. But Peter is singled out as an example from which we can all learn.

The Synoptics and John's Gospel differ in the order of the first two denials. We noted earlier a similar phenomenon in retelling of the testing of Jesus in the wilderness (Matthew 4). One retelling follows the chronological events as they occurred and the other follows a topical retelling. In the case of Peter's denial, it is difficult to determine which retelling is chronological and which is topical.

69-70 The first denial is prompted by an accusation from a servant. Peter, the rugged fishermen, shrinks before this lowly servant girl.

71-72 Another girl approaches him and accuses him of associating with Jesus of Nazareth. Peter again denies the accusation, this time adding an oath to his denial.

73-75 This third time, Peter's accent gives him away. Peter curses and swears in a vain attempt to keep his identity secret. After his third denial, the rooster crowed. This brings to Peter's mind the words of Jesus when he predicted his denial. Peter is cut by this and goes outside and weeps. Luke mentions that Jesus looked at Peter, inciting Peter's tears. Early church legend states that Peter never heard a rooster crow again without weeping.

Jesus Before Pilate (27:1-2)

27:1When the morning came, all the chief priests and elders of the people discussed together about Jesus and decided that he should die. 2They bound him and led him away, delivering him to Pilate the governor.

On Friday morning, the Sanhedrin met again to discuss what should be done with Jesus. After their discussion they handed Jesus over to Pilate. Pilate had the power to execute Jesus.

This discussion could have occurred at the Royal Stoa on the Temple complex. The Sanhedrin normally met here. Jesus would have been escorted from Caiaphas' house across a bridge into the temple area. We are uncertain where the events of Friday transpired. Some believe that Pilate was stationed at Herod's palace near the Jaffa gate, and some believe that he was at the Antonia Fortress overlooking the temple complex. Tradition places him at the Antonia Fortress. If tradition is correct, then the movements of Jesus on Friday would have been:

1. From Caiaphas' house to the Royal Stoa in the Temple complex.
2. From the Royal Stoa to Antonia Fortress to meet with Pilate.
3. From Antonia Fortress to Herod's Palace to meet with Herod.
4. From Herod's Palace to Antonia Fortress to meet again with Pilate.
5. Taken away to be crucified (either outside the northern gate of the city or on the Mount of Olives).

1-2 In Jesus' day Pontius Pilate was the Roman governor over Judea. Tiberius Caesar appointed him procurator in AD 26. Philo of Alexandria noted that his office was known for corruption, continual violence, harsh treatment of the Jews, offenses, numerous illegal executions, and harsh cruelty. Pilate cared little for the religious sensitivities of the Jews. He openly displayed pictures of the Emperor in Jerusalem. He took money from the temple treasury to build an aqueduct into Jerusalem. The New Testament testimony confirms this harsh picture of Pilate. He would have easily complied with the Jewish leaders to execute an innocent man on the charges of sedition.

Thus Jesus of Nazareth died outside the gates of Jerusalem suffering the most intense, shameful punishment devised by man.

Some scholars cast doubt on the manner in which the Bible portrays Pilate during the crucifixion narrative. They say that Pilate was too ruthless and unsympathetic to have acted as he did toward Jesus. For example, David Hill lists several Jewish sources that describe Pilate as cruel and violent, and writes:

> Even allowing for exaggeration in the Jewish works, their portrayal of Pilate is not easily compatible with the weak, vacillating (but fair) character portrayed in the Gospels. It is likely that the evangelists are guilty of whitewashing Pilate because of their desire to exculpate the Romans and put the full responsibility on the Jews for the death of Jesus.[20]

But scholars like Dr. Hill fail to note that there was no love lost between Pilate and the Sanhedrin. Pilate knew that the Jewish authorities wanted Jesus dead. He could have been sympathetic toward Jesus in order to upset the Jewish leaders.

The Suicide of Judas (27:3-10)

³*When Judas who betrayed him saw that Jesus was condemned, he regretted it and returned the thirty pieces of silver to the chief priests and elders, saying,* ⁴*"I have sinned by betraying innocent blood." They answered him, "What is that to us? See to it yourself."*

⁵*Judas threw the 30 pieces of silver in the temple and left. He went away and hanged himself.*

⁶*Then the chief priest took the 30 pieces of silver and said, "It is not lawful to put this in the treasury, since it is blood money.* ⁷*After discussing it, they took the money and bought the Potter's Field as a burial place for foreigners.* ⁸*This is why this field is called "A Field of Blood" to this day.* ⁹*This fulfilled the word of Jeremiah the prophet, which says:*

> *And they took 30 pieces of silver,*
> *The price on which a price is set*
> *Who the sons of Israel set a price,*
> ¹⁰*And they gave them for a Potter's field*
> *As the Lord commanded me.*

3-4 Some translations state that Judas "repented" for betraying Jesus. But a better translation would be "regret" or "to be filled with remorse." It is not the word used for repentance that leads to salvation. The story of Judas contrasts Peter's tears that led to true change with Judas' tears that led to his suicide.

5 Several inconsistencies between verse five and Acts 1:18-19 must be explained:

1. Matthew says the chief priests purchased the field, and Acts says that Judas bought it. But if the chief priests used the money that Judas returned, then it was the same as Judas buying it.

2. The naming of the Field of Blood seems to derive from two distinct ideas. Acts mentions the field was called Field of Blood because Judas died there. Matthew says the name came from the fact that the chief priests used blood money to buy the field. But these ideas are not mutually exclusive. The chief priests purchased the field and it was the same field where Judas committed suicide.

3. Matthew has Judas "hanging himself," and Acts records "he fell headlong, his body burst open and all his intestines spilled out." Some attempt to reconcile these two ways of dying by saying that Judas impaled himself on a spike that was hanging on a wall and his intestines fell on the ground. The word "hanged" is not normally used in this fashion. Others suggest that Judas hanged himself on a tree, but no one wanted to cut him down from the tree during the Feast of Unleavened Bread. Touching his corpse would have made them unclean. So he body remained hanging from the tree. It remained on the tree until it decomposed. Then the corpse fell to the ground and ruptured open. Traditionally, Judas is pictured as hanging himself on a tree by jumping out over a ravine. In time the branch broke and his body burst open. Since we don't know exactly how Judas died, any of these scenarios could have happened.

9-10 The "Potter's Field" could have been a field in the Hinnon Valley where potters dug clay from the ground. When this clay was depleted, the field was offered for sale. Matthew accredits this scripture to Jeremiah, when many scholars believe it is really taken from Zechariah 11:12-13. But Zechariah does not refer to a field. When we consider other passages in Jeremiah, Jeremiah 19:1-3 should be considered. Many of the motifs used in Matthew are seen here: a potter's jar, the Hinnon Valley, innocent blood, renaming the field. Matthew might have combined elements of Jeremiah 19:1-3 with Zechariah 11:12-13. As we have seen earlier, it was not uncommon for rabbis to do this with scripture.

Pilate Questions Jesus (27:11-14)

[11]*Then Jesus stood in front of the governor, and the governor asked him, "Are you the king of the Jews?"*

[12]*Jesus answered, "You say so."*

[13]*The Pilate said to him, "Do you not hear all the testimony they*

*make against you?" ¹⁴But he did not answer, not even a single charge. So the
governor was greatly amazed.*

Jesus now faces the Roman procurator Pilate. Pilate has the
power to free Jesus or to execute him. But Jesus does not protest his
innocence to Pilate. He accepts his fate.

Barabbas or Jesus? (27:15-22)

*¹⁵Now at the festival, the governor's custom was to release a prisoner
whom the crowd wished. ¹⁶There was at that time a notorious prisoner named
Jesus Barabbas.*

*¹⁷When the crowd gathered, Pilate asked, "Whom do you wish to be
released, Jesus Barabbas or Jesus 'Christon' (called Christ)?" ¹⁸For he knew
that it was out of envy that Jesus was handed over to him.*

*¹⁹While he was sitting on the judge's seat, his wife sent him word,
"Have nothing to do with that innocent man for today I have suffered greatly
in a dream because of him."*

*²⁰But the chief priest and elders persuaded the crowd to ask for
Barabbas and have Jesus killed.*

*²¹The governor asked them, "Which of the two do you wish to be
handed over to you?" They answered, "Barabbas."*

*Pilate said to them, "What shall I do with Jesus called 'Christ?'"
²³All said, "Crucify him."*

Although scholars have not found evidence of the tradition to
release a prisoner at this festival, there is no need to doubt the biblical record. Barabbas was an insurrectionist (*lestes*), probably a leader
in the first century zealots' movement—the type of leader that many
of the people wanted. The choice is between Barabbas the freedom
fighter and Jesus Christ who came to give spiritual freedom. The
people chose the freedom fighter.

The same word used to describe Barabbas was used to describe
the two thieves that died with Jesus on the cross. Their crime was
insurrection or high treason. They would not have been executed for
robbery, but treason was a capital offence. So the term "thief on the
cross," is better translated "insurrectionist on the cross."

Pilate Hands Jesus Over to be Crucified (27:23-26)

*²³Pilate asked, "Why? What has he done?"
The crowds cried out even more, "Crucify him!"*

*²⁴When Pilate saw he could do nothing, but rather a riot was
starting, he took water and washed his hands before the crowd saying, "I am
innocent of this man's blood, you see to it."*

²⁵*All the people answered, "His blood is on us and our children."*

²⁶*He then released Barabbas, and after flogging Jesus, handed him over to be crucified.*

The brevity of detail in the crucifixion story is amazing. Matthew writes, "After flogging Jesus, Pilate handed him over to be crucified." The punishment of flogging was the death of many men. A professional executioner used a cat of nine tails (*flagellum*) — a specially designed whip constructed by tying bones, glass and lead to the ends of strands of cord. This specially designed whip then struck the back, shoulders, and buttocks of the victim thirty-nine times (forty minus one). Since it was illegal to whip the victim over forty times, the soldiers would stop the beating at thirty-nine lashes, thus guaranteeing that they did not exceed forty. The first stroke of the whip would cause a welt to appear, after a few strikes, the wounds would open up, and by the end, skin and flesh would be in shreds, exposing the bones.

The Soldiers Mock Jesus (27:27-31)

²⁷*Then the governor's soldiers took Jesus into the Praetorium where they gathered the whole cohort around him. ²⁸They stripped him and put a scarlet robe on him. ²⁹They twisted a crown of thorns and placed it on his head. They put a reed in his right hand and knelt before him and mocked him, saying, "Hail, King of the Jews," and ³⁰they spat on him and took the reed and struck him on the head. ³¹After mocking him, they took off his robe and put his own clothes on him. Then they led him away to crucify him.*

A full Roman cohort was 600 men. The Praetorium is usually identified as a piece of pavement near Antonia Fortress (the *Lithostros*). The soldiers humiliated Jesus here. They paraded him around as a king, placing a scarlet or purple robe on his shoulders, a reed in his hand, and a crown of thorns on his head. The thorns were long, thin thorns that were indigenous to Palestine. Today the tree upon which they grow is called "the crown of thorns tree." The soldiers mocked Jesus and spat on him. They took the staff and beat him on the head with it, driving the thorns into his skull. At this point, blood gushed down his skull covering his eyes. When the solders finished, they stripped the robe off him. By this time, the wounds on his back had dried into the fabric of the robe on his back. Ripping the robe off his back would have reopened those wounds. Jesus suffered bitter pain even before he was placed on the cross.

The Crucifixion (27:32-44)

Have, have ye no regard, all ye
Who pass this way, to pity me
Who am a man of misery?

Ah! Sion's Daughters, do not fear
The Cross, the Cords, the Nails, the Spear,
The Myrrh, the Gall, the Vinegar

For Christ, your loving Saviour, hath
Drunk up the wine of God's fierce wrath;
Only, there's left a little froth,

Less for to taste, than for to shew
What bitter cups had been your due,
Had He not drank them up for you.

> *His Savior's Words, Going to the Cross*
> –Robert Herrick, 17th century British Poet

[32]As they went on, a man from Cyrene named Simon was forced to carry his cross. [33]They came to the place called, "Golgotha," which is "the place of the skull." [34]They offered him wine mixed with gall to drink. After tasting it, he did not wish to drink it.

[35]When they crucified him, "They divided his garments by casting lots. [36]They sat there and kept watch over him. [37]Over his head was placed the charge against him, "This is Jesus, the King of the Jews."

[38]Two rebels were crucified with him, one on his right and the other on his left. [39]Those who passed by insulted him shaking their heads [40]and saying, "You were going to destroy the temple and rebuild it in three days. If you are the Son of God, save yourself and come down from the cross." [41]Likewise the chief priests along with the scribes and elders mocked him, saying, [42]"He saved others, can he not save himself? He is the King of Israel? Let him come down now from the cross and we will believe him. [43]He trusts in God, let God deliver him now, if he wishes. For he said, 'I am God's son.'" [44]The rebels/insurrectionists who were with him also insulted him in the same way.

32 Prisoners were usually required to carry their own crosses, but Jesus was too weak from the brutal beatings to carry his cross all the way. Simon from Cyrene was compelled to carry the cross.

Mark notes that Simon is the father of Alexander and Rufus who are mentioned in Acts 19:33 as followers of Jesus. The inference is that Simon became a follower and so did his sons. After all, how can you carry the cross of Jesus and not become a follower?

33 The site of Golgotha, the Place of the Skull, cannot be identified now. It was located outside the city wall near a main intersection. The phrase "place of the skull" could be a descriptive term--a rock formation that looked like a human skull. Some translate this phrase back into Hebrew and derive a meaning of "the place of the head," referring to the place of the head of the altar of sacrifice. They then conjecture that Jesus was crucified on the Mount of Olives at the location where the priest sacrificed the red heifer on the Day of Atonement. This would have deep theological meaning, but it isn't clear from the text. Jesus could have been crucified at any public place outside the city walls of Jerusalem.

34 Why was wine mixed with gall/myrrh given to Jesus? This was a traditional medicinal preparation for easing pain. The myrrh would have made the wine stronger, but it would have been very bitter. Jesus tasted it and refused to drink it. Perhaps he was declining to drink this analgesic so as to be fully aware of the physical experience of his crucifixion.

35-37 Romans crucified criminals by tying their hands and feet or nailing them to a cross that was shaped like an "X," "T," or "t." That a charge was written over the head of Jesus implies that he was crucified on a "t" shaped cross.

The Death of Jesus (27:45-56)

⁴⁵*From noon until three in the afternoon, darkness came over the entire land.* ⁴⁶*About three o'clock Jesus cried with a loud voice, "Eli, Eli, lema sabachthani." This means, "My God, my God, why have you forsaken me."*

⁴⁷*When some who were standing there heard this they asked, "Is he calling Elijah?" *⁴⁸*Immediately one of them ran and took a sponge and filled it with sour wine. He placed it on a stick and gave it to him to drink.* ⁴⁹*The rest said, "Wait, let's see if Elijah comes to save him."*

⁵⁰*Jesus again cried out with a loud voice, and he gave up his spirit.*

⁵¹*At that moment the curtain of the temple was torn in two from top to bottom. The earth shook and rocks split.* ⁵²*Tombs broke open and many bodies of the saints who had died were raised.* ⁵³*They went out of their tombs and entered the Holy City and approached many.*

⁵⁴*When the centurion and those with him, who were guarding Jesus,*

*saw the earthquake and all that had happened, they were terrified. They said,
"Truly he was the Son of God!"*

 *⁵⁵Many women were also there, watching from a distance. They
had followed Jesus from Galilee to serve him. ⁵⁶Among them were Mary
Magdalene, Mary the mother of James and Joseph, and the mother of the sons
of Zebedee.*

45 In spring in Palestine, there are many days where you cannot
see a cloud in the sky. For darkness to come over all the land
from twelve until three was miraculous. Spiritual darkness had descended on the land and this was reflected by the physical darkness.

46 Jesus quotes Psalm 22:1. Jesus could have used the verse as a
cry of agony. Since Jesus took our sins, he had to be separated
from the Father. Perhaps this is what he meant by, "My God, my God,
why have you forsaken me." But when you look at the entirety of
Psalm 22, it is a hymn of trust. The Psalmist is placing his trust in God.
Perhaps Jesus had this in mind as he quoted Psalm 22:1.

48-49 One of those watching offered Jesus a drink of wine
vinegar from a sponge. It is unclear whether he wished
to mock or comfort Jesus. The rest are mocking him, but perhaps the
traditional astringent drink was offered to comfort Jesus, to help him
to rinse the taste of blood or bile from his mouth.

50 The death of Jesus is marked by one simple sentence, "And
when Jesus had cried out again in a loud voice, he gave up his
spirit." Death by crucifixion usually occurred by suffocation. As one
hung upon the cross, the lungs would cease to function and the blood
would become saturated with carbon dioxide. The body would long
for oxygen. To take a breath, you would have to push up with your
legs and fill your lungs. Since Jesus' feet were nailed to the cross, this
would be a very painful undertaking. It would be during this time
that Jesus would have made his seven statements on the cross. After
some time, the legs would begin to cramp and the pain from the nails
would be intolerable, then the victim would slump back down and
place the weight on the nails in his palms. He would begin to suffocate
again because he would not be able to breathe with the pressure on
his lung cavity. He would endure suffocation as long as possible, and
then reflexively lift himself back up by the nails in his feet. Often the
soldiers would hasten death by breaking the legs of the victim. If they
could not push up with their legs, then they could not breathe, and
would die quickly.

This is the type of agonizing death that Jesus endured. After such a painful ordeal, the Bible notes the death of Jesus simply as, "he gave up his spirit." Jesus who was in full control up to this point, in his arrest, in his trials, is still in control. He "gives up" his spirit.

51 When Jesus died the curtain of the temple was torn in two. The temple had an outer curtain and an inner curtain. The inner curtain separated the holy place from the most holy place. Matthew is referring to the temple curtain inside the temple. The temple curtain tore from top to bottom, signifying that God did the tearing. The curtain kept everyone away from the Holy of Holies where the presence of God resided. Only the high priest was allowed to go into the Holy of Holies, and he could enter only once a year. God now tears down this dividing partition. The presence of God is no longer separated from us. Everyone can now approach God.

52-53 Here are two very interesting verses. At the death of Jesus, tombs broke open and holy people rose from the dead in bodily form. They went into Jerusalem after Jesus rose from the dead, and appeared to many people. What in the world is going on here? Is it a scene from *Attack of the Zombies*? What can we learn here?

Did the dead rise when Jesus died and wait until the resurrection to enter Jerusalem? If so, what did they do in the interim? J.W. Wenham suggests an idea that I find acceptable.[21] When we read the passage we should place a full stop after the "tombs broke open." This completes a thought and begins a new thought. Thought number one, when Jesus died the earth shook, rocks split, and tombs broke open. Thought number two, bodies of many holy people came to life after Jesus' resurrection. Thus you have two distinct events—at the death of Jesus, tombs broke open; and at the resurrection of Jesus, holy people rose with him. The idea is that the resurrection of Jesus was such a powerful event that many holy people rose with him (whether their resurrection was to a natural body or a supernatural body is unclear), then they testified to the resurrection of Jesus in Jerusalem.

54 Matthew concludes his narrative of the crucifixion with the reaction of an eyewitness to the event. The eyewitness is the centurion who oversaw the execution. The Centurion exclaims, "Surely he was the Son of God!" What the Jewish authorities fail to see, the centurion sees. What Jesus' disciples have a hard time understanding, the centurion comprehends. The centurion sees with eyes of faith. This is a preview of the mission to the Gentiles.

The Burial of Jesus (27:57-61)

⁵⁷When evening arrived, a rich man from Arimathea came named Joseph. He was a disciple of Jesus. ⁵⁸He went to Pilate and asked for the body of Jesus. Then Pilate ordered for it to be given to him.

⁵⁹Joseph took the body and wrapped it in a clean linen cloth ⁶⁰and placed it in his new tomb, which was cut out of rock, and he rolled a huge stone in the door of the tomb. ⁶¹Mary Magdalene and the other Mary were there sitting opposite the tomb.

At that time of year sundown would have been around 6:00 p.m. The Sabbath would begin at this time. Since Jesus died around 3:00 p.m., Joseph of Arimathea had to act quickly to get permission from Pilate to bury Jesus and to conduct the burial before sundown.

The traditional site for the tomb of Jesus is the Church of the Holy Sepulcher in Jerusalem. In the first century, it was located outside the city and was a cemetery. I personally see no reason not accept this site as the most likely place where Jesus was buried. Joseph placed Jesus in his own tomb and sealed the tomb by rolling a large stone in front of the opening of the grave. Many tombs of this design have been uncovered around Jerusalem.

The Guard at the Tomb (27:62-66)

⁶²The next day--after the day of Preparation--the chief priests and the Pharisees gathered before Pilate saying, ⁶³"Sir, we remember that while the deceiver was still alive, he said, 'After three days, I will rise.' ⁶⁴Therefore command the tomb to be made secure until the third day. Otherwise, his disciples might steal him and say to the people, 'He has been raised from the dead.' This last deception would be worse than the first."

⁶⁵So Pilate said, "You have a guard of soldiers. Go make the tomb secure. You know how." ⁶⁶So they went with the guard and made the tomb secure by putting a seal on the tomb.

Remember that Matthew is addressing a predominately Jewish audience with his Gospel. Rumors of how the disciples had stolen the body of Jesus would have passed through Jewish circles for years after the resurrection. To answer this charge, Matthew includes in his Gospel a narrative describing how the Jewish authorities asked Pilate to post a guard over the tomb of Jesus for the purpose of making sure Jesus' disciples did not steal his body. Pilate refused to give his Roman guard for this duty. But he did instruct the chief priests that they could use the temple guard to watch the tomb. If the disciples did steal the body of Jesus, then they did it with the Jewish authorities' eyes wide open. Matthew is saying that it was the Sanhedrin that promoted a lie and covered up the truth.

The Resurrection (28:1-10)

I find that the Holy Week is draining; no matter how many times I have lived through his crucifixion, my anxiety about his resurrection is undiminished—I am terrified that, this year, it won't happen; that, that year, it didn't. Anyone can be sentimental about the Nativity; any fool can feel like a Christian at Christmas. But Easter is the main event; if you don't believe in the resurrection, you're not a believer.
                                      –John Irving, American writer

That Jesus succeeded in changing a snuffling band of unreliable followers into fearless evangelists, that eleven men who had deserted him at death now went to martyrs' graves avowing their faith in a resurrected Christ, that these few witnesses managed to set loose a force that would overcome violent opposition first in Jerusalem and then in Rome–this remarkable sequence of transformation offers the most convincing evidence for the Resurrection. What else explains the whiplash change in men known for their cowardice and instability?
                                      —Philip Yancey, **The Jesus I Never Knew**

¹After the Sabbath, at dawn on the first day of the week, Mary Magdalene and the other Mary went to see the tomb.

²Behold, a great earthquake began, an angel of the Lord descended from heaven, rolled back the stone and sat on it. ³His appearance was as lightening and his clothes as white as snow. ⁴The guards were afraid of him and shook and became as dead men.

⁵But the angel said to the women, "Do not be afraid, I know you are looking for Jesus who was crucified. ⁶He is not here, for he rose just as he said. Come see the place where he lay. ⁷Go quickly and tell his disciples–he has risen from the dead and is going ahead of you into Galilee. You will see him there." Indeed I have told you this.

⁸They left the tomb quickly. With fear and great joy, they ran to report this to his disciples. ⁹Jesus met them suddenly, saying, "Greetings!" They came to him, took hold of his feet and worshipped him. ¹⁰Jesus said to them, "Do not be afraid, go and tell my brothers to go into Galilee. They will see me there."

The resurrection is the most central and crucial event in all Christianity. It is what sets Jesus apart from other religious teachers. If Jesus rose from the dead, then his message is true. If he did not rise from the dead, then his message is a hoax. The resurrection made the difference in the disciple's lives. Before the resurrection they were a weak, faithless, defeated group. After the resurrection, they turned the world upside-down for Jesus. Paul said that if the resurrection were not true, then we as believers are above all men to be most pitied (1 Corinthians 15:19). Because of the resurrection, we can tap into the resurrection power of Jesus to change our lives. The resurrection is the pivotal event of Jesus' life.

When I was in seminary working on my master's degree, I had a New Testament professor who attempted to explain away all the miracles of Jesus as we came across them in the text. He explained that Jesus' walking on the water was an optical illusion. Many parts of the Sea of Galilee are very shallow and with the bright sun reflecting off the water it would look as if Jesus were walking on the surface of the water. He explained away every miracle in this fashion. But as we approached Easter, we came to the story of the resurrection in the text. I remember him saying, "I will explain away every miracle in the Bible except the resurrection. Because if Jesus did not rise from the dead, then we have no Christianity. If Jesus did not rise, then we have no hope of resurrection. As Paul said, 'we are above all men to be most pitied.'"

We were all a bit shocked at the professor's adamant attitude to the resurrection. One of my friends raised his hand and asked, "But professor, how is it that you can believe in the resurrection, and fail to believe the other miracles of the Bible? After all which is harder to believe, that Jesus rose from the dead or that he changed water into wine?" The professor had no answer to this except to restate his earlier claim, "If Jesus did not rise from the dead, then we have no Christianity." Even my liberal professor from seminary recognized the importance of the resurrection of Jesus.

1 "After the Sabbath" can also mean "late on the Sabbath." But since the women could not walk to the grave on the Sabbath, it is better to translate *opse* as "after." Also, the next phrase "at dawn on the first day of the week," makes clear that Matthew has Sunday morning in mind.

Many wonder why Jesus predicted that he would be in the earth "three days and three nights," when he was only in the grave three days and two nights. The answer is that in the Jewish mind a part of a day included the whole day (this is known as "inclusive" reckoning). If Jesus rose one hour after the Sabbath ended, then that would include the whole third day and night. In our Western mindset, Jesus went into the grave on Friday afternoon and rose Sunday morning that is three days and two nights. But by Jewish reckoning, Jesus was in the grave "three days and three nights."

Jewish tradition records that friends of the deceased would go to the tomb on the third day to make sure that the person was dead. After the predictions of Jesus, the women who followed Jesus had an extra reason to follow this tradition. Mark adds that they brought spices to anoint the body of Jesus. The women were going to pay tribute to Jesus. My question whenever I read this passage about the women going to the tomb is—Where are the brothers? Why is that only the women visit the tomb of Jesus? Brothers, let's make sure that we are not absent when it comes to honoring Jesus.

2-4 There was a violent earthquake and an angel appeared. This answers a question that is on the mind of many of his first century readers: Who moved the stone? The stones that sealed the tombs weighed hundreds of pounds and would have taken several men to move. If the guards had fallen asleep, how could they continue to sleep through the noisy process of the stone being moved? Matthew clarifies the matter: the angel moved the stone. I love the extra, added detail: the angel sat on the stone after he moved it.

The appearance of the angel caused the guards at the tomb to faint in fear. The Greek says they were paralyzed with fear and their expression was waxen and immobile–like they were dead. The angel rolls the stone away from the entrance to the tomb to prepare for the resurrection of Jesus.

We are not given details about the actual resurrection. I am always amazed at what the Gospel writers did not discuss.

5-8 John (John 20:12) mentions two angels where Matthew mentions one. This is not a contradiction. Where there are two angels, there is also one. Matthew focuses in on one of the angels, and John includes both of them in his account.

When the women meet the angel, the angel dispels their fear. He announces to them that Jesus has risen and they are to report to the disciples that he will meet them in Galilee. Matthew also includes an important detail, that the angel showed them the empty tomb. The women are the first eyewitnesses of the empty tomb. In the next few verses, they will be the first eyewitnesses of the resurrected Lord. Paul mentions that Peter was the first to meet the risen Jesus. But Paul is giving an abbreviated list. He might also have left the women off his list because theirs was not considered official legal testimony in the first century.

9-10 The women are the first to see the resurrected Jesus. They fall and worship him. Matthew notes that the women "clasped his feet." This is indirect evidence of the physical reality of the resurrection of Jesus. He was not a ghost; he was flesh. Jesus directs them to go and tell his disciples that he will meet them in Galilee.

Easter-Day

Thou, whose sad heart, and weeping head lies low,
Whose cloudy breast cold damps invade,
Who never feelist the sun, nor smoothist thy brow,
But sittist oppressed in the shade,
Awake, awake,
And in his Resurrection partake,
Who on this day (that thou mightist rise as he,)
Rose up, and cancelled two deaths due to thee.

Awake, awake; and, like the sun, disperse
All mists that would usurp this day;
Where are thy palms, thy branches, and thy verse?
Hosanna! Hark; why dost thou stay?
Arise, arise,

The Report of the Guard (28:11-15)

11While the women were going, the guards went into the city and reported to the chief priests everything that happened. 12After the chief priests met with the elders, they devised a plan to give the soldiers a large sum of money, 13saying, "You must say that his disciples came at night and stole him while we were asleep." 14If this report gets to the governor, we will satisfy him and keep you out of trouble. 15So the soldiers took the money and did as they were directed. This story is still told to this very day

Remember that Matthew is writing to a primarily Jewish audience. This is the audience that would have been influenced by the lies of the guards who circulated the story that the body of Jesus was stolen. Archaeologists discovered an imperial edict against tomb robbing in the city of Nazareth. This shows that tomb robbing was a problem in first century Palestine. So the story that was being circulated about the disciples was not that farfetched.

As an apologetic to that story, Matthew includes the true story. The guards were bribed by the chief priests to circulate a lie. This explains why the guards were still alive to tell the story. If the guards had really been asleep while on duty, they should have been executed. Why were they spared? They were spared because the chief priests

wanted them to circulate a false story accusing the disciples of stealing the body of Jesus. Matthew exposes the conspiracy and explains
why these guard who should have been put to death were allowed to
live.

11 Why do the guards report to the chief priests and not to Pilate?
Because they were a part of the temple guard and not the imperial guard. Pilate allowed the chief priests to post guards over the
tomb. The chief priests had posted their own guard for this job.

The Great Commission (28:16-20)

Jesus changed people. He changed their habits and opinions and
ambitions; he changed their tempers and dispositions and na-
tures. He changed their hearts. They were never the same after
they gave themselves up to him. God and humanity, the world and
duty, were different to them after they had looked steadily into his
face. Wherever he went, he transformed human lives. He transfigured human faces by cleansing the fountains of the heart. This is
greatness indeed.
                    –Charles Edward Jefferson, **Jesus the Same**

¹⁶*Now the eleven disciples went to Galilee to the mountain where
Jesus told them to go. ¹⁷When they saw him, they worshipped him, but some
doubted.*
        ¹⁸*Jesus came and spoke to them saying, "All authority has been
given me in heaven and on earth. ¹⁹Therefore Go! Go make disciples of all
nations! Baptize them by the authority of the Father, and the Son, and the
Holy Spirit! ²⁰Then teach them to obey all things that I have commanded you!
Be certain of this – I am with you always to the end of age."*

Matthew closes his gospel with the King giving a commission
to his subjects. Jesus declares the mission of his kingdom–to preach
the gospel to all nations. Much has been written in recent years about
mission statements. Companies form committees that meet for months
to develop their mission statement. Individuals are encouraged to
develop a mission statement. When I was working on my doctorate,
we spent an entire class developing a profile and a mission statement
for our churches. I found it a very boring class—because our profile
and mission statement had already been written. Our profile was
to be like the church of the Bible and our mission statement was to
preach the gospel to all nations. (Compare other forms of the Great
Commission, Mark 16:15-16; Luke 24:45-49; John 20:21; Acts 1:8).

Mission statements are not a new idea. Two thousand years ago Jesus, the King, gave a mission to his subjects. If we are still subjects of the King, then we must embrace his mission. What is your mission statement? Is it the same as your King?

The great commission occurred on a mountain in Galilee. There is no reason to assume that it was the same setting as the Sermon on the Mount or the Transfiguration. Mountains (high places) are often the setting for a revelation of God in the Bible. The post-resurrection ministry of Jesus is launched from the same place it began some three years earlier.

This great commission occurred in Galilee. It was not the last commission that Jesus gave to his disciples. I have heard it preached that Jesus ascended to heaven from Galilee after giving the great commission. It would seem that Matthew ends his Gospel this way. But Matthew doesn't mention the ascension of Jesus. We must look to the other Gospels to see where the ascension occurred.

When you study Luke's post-resurrection account, you see that after Jesus went to Galilee he returned to Jerusalem. Luke concludes his Gospel saying, "When he had led them out to the vicinity of Bethany, he lifted up his hands and blessed them. While he was blessing them, he left them and was taken up into heaven. Then they worshipped him and returned to Jerusalem with great joy. And they stayed continually at the temple praising God" (Luke 25:50-55). Luke places the disciples in the vicinity of Bethany in his Gospel. In Acts he specifies the exact location within Bethany, the Mount of Olives. Jesus ascends to heaven and Luke notes, "Then they (the disciples) returned to Jerusalem from the Mount called Olivet" (Acts 1:12).

Where was Jesus when he gave his final word to his disciples? He was on the Mount of Olives. Therefore, Matthew's version of the Great Commission was not the last charge that Jesus gave his disciples. It is probably the last charge that Jesus made to his disciples in Galilee. Matthew finds it to be the perfect way to end his gospel. Jesus ends where his ministry began. But it isn't really an ending. It is a beginning. A few weeks later, his ministry will begin for a second time. This time it begins through his disciples, and through them, Jesus will reach the world.

Most of the disciples worshipped Jesus when they saw him, but some doubted. Seeing Jesus after his resurrection was not a foolproof guarantee of faith. The person still had to open his heart to who Jesus was. Throughout the ministry of Jesus, his disciples struggled with faith. It would prove no different after his resurrection. Faith is something that has to be established, nourished, and re-established. The same is true in our walk with God today.

The great commission, Matthew 28:18-20, contains four "all's." Two of them are easy to see in the English and two are difficult to see. The easy ones to see are "all authority" and "all nations." The two that are difficult to see are "all things" ("to obey everything," NIV) and "all the days" ("always," NIV). Let's take a closer look.

1. "All authority has been given me on heaven and on earth." As the crowned king, Jesus has all authority. We know throughout Jesus' ministry he has displayed authority. He demonstrated his authority over sickness by healing various diseases. He demonstrated power over demons by healing the demoniacs. He showed power over nature by calming storms at sea. He had power over sin in that he could forgive sin (9:6). The crowds noted the authority of his teaching and how different that was from the teaching they commonly heard. So how does his authority differ after his resurrection?

His authority differs now not in its dynamic but in its scope. While Jesus was on the earth, he was bound to the earth. Soon he would go back to heaven. There he would reign again with his father. He can now speak of having all authority in heaven and on earth. This statement discloses two facts about Jesus. First, Jesus is the mediator between God and man. He died on the cross and his redemptive work was now over. Now everyone must recognize him as Lord. Jesus is king.

Second, Jesus had to learn obedience. When he came to the earth, he gave up a great deal. In heaven, Jesus had equality with God. But he did not consider this something to be grasped (Philippians 2: 5-11). He willingly gave up his position of authority in heaven to live with us. Now his position of authority in heaven has been returned to him. He is the crowned king who reigns over the heavens and the earth. The third volume of J.R.R. Tolkien's classic trilogy of Middle Earth is titled, *The Return of King*. This is an appropriate title to the ascension of Jesus into heaven. As he returns to heaven he returns as King—thus he has all authority on heaven and on earth.

2. We are to make disciples of "all nations." Jesus no longer sends his disciples just to the lost sheep of Israel. His mission has broadened and now includes "all nations." Just as Jesus' authority is universal, his mission is universal. Any church that embraces the great commission of Jesus must be a worldwide church. It is not enough to reach people just in the United States. It is not enough to just reach people that are like us, as in a white suburban church or a black intercity church. We must reach everyone.

I've had people say to me, "The mission field begins at home." If by this it is meant that we begin where we are and branch out from there, then "Amen." But too often what is meant is that we should reach people where we are and not worry about world missions. I believe that the mission field begins at home and extends to all nations. To truly reach people here, we must teach them that we are commanded to reach people everywhere.

The wording of the great commission in the NIV loses some of the nuance of the Greek. In the Greek it reads, "Therefore, Go! Go and make disciples of all nations! Baptize them by the authority of the Father, and of the Son, and of the Holy Spirit!" The real imperative of the verse is "to make disciples." The going and the baptizing are participles built around that imperative. Circumstantial participles that are dependent on an imperative carry the force of the imperative.[22] Jesus assumed that his disciples would be going. He had already ordered them to preach his word (4:19, 10:16-20, 13:38, 24:14). He also knew that the persecutions that he predicted were soon to follow and they would be forced to leave the land of Judea at that point. Also, how can you reach "all nations" without going? Jesus also assumed that they would be baptizing. He had already stressed the importance of baptizing in his ministry. You cannot make disciples without baptizing them. But the imperative force of "make disciples" is carried on to the participles — going, baptizing, and teaching.

Matthew mentions that we are to baptize in the name of the Father, Son, and Holy Spirit. "In the name of" means "by the authority of." This is not so much a formula that must be said exactly as it is written at each baptism; as much as it is a concept that the recipient of baptism must understand. Some contend that since the book of Acts mentions baptism in the name of Jesus that the formula said at baptism should be said only in the name of Jesus (Acts 2:38, 8:16, 10:48, 19:5). But Paul uses Trinitarian formulas in his writings (2 Corinthians 13:14; 1 Corinthians 12:4-6), and this formula is found in the *Didache*. This is a misunderstanding of what is being taught. Neither Matthew nor Luke states a formula that they expect everyone to repeat when they are baptized. They are giving a concept that should be understood. Baptism is through the authority of the Father, Son, and Holy Spirit with a special emphasis on Jesus because he paid the price with his blood that gives us forgiveness of sins. The early church bears evidence that both formulas were used side by side into the second century. I believe that one, both, or no formula can be stated at baptism as long as the recipient of baptism understands that what they are doing, they are doing by the authority of God, Jesus and the Holy Spirit.

Jesus placed the emphasis of his commission on "make disciples" (*matheteusate*). This is the imperative. You can go around the world preaching, but if you fail to make disciples, what have you really done? You can baptize whole villages, but if you fail to make disciples what have you really accomplished? The ministry of Jesus was to be a discipling ministry. You can't just baptize people and leave them to fend for themselves. They must be nurtured, matured, made into disciples. To disciple a person is to bring him under the Lordship of Christ, making sure that he or she is a follower of Jesus. This implies working with the person beyond the point of baptism. Baptism is the beginning of the journey. But the journey of discipleship is life long.

3. The third "all" is "teaching to obey all things (everything) that I have commanded you." "Teaching" is the third participle that is connected with the imperative "make disciples." The proper response of discipleship is going, baptizing, and teaching. R.T. France notes, "Baptizing and teaching" (v. 20) are participles dependent on the main verb, make disciples, they further specify what is involved in discipleship."[23]

We are to teach "all things" that Jesus commanded. This puts the emphasis on the words of Jesus. It is his message that we are to focus on.

4. We are to keep teaching disciples to obey until the end of "all days" (until the end of the age). This is the fourth "all" found in the great commission. Jesus does not forecast a time where obedience to his message will be unnecessary. Therefore, we must be careful to pass on the commands of Jesus.

Matthew concludes his gospel by giving the comforting promise of Jesus, "surely I am with you always to the end of 'all days' (the age)." Jesus' presence will be with his disciples. Matthew begins his gospel with Jesus being called Immanuel, God with us. He ends his Gospel with Jesus promising that he will continue to be with us. He is King. The King will be with us until the end of "all days." That is a comforting thought that disciples can carry wherever they go.

Practically Speaking ෫

The Great Commission

Jesus closes his ministry with the great commission. Matthew uses this as the closing statement of his gospel. What lessons can we learn from the great commission?

1. Jesus' plan was simple—to make disciples.

This was the plan of Jesus. His goal was not reach the whole world in his lifetime. His goal was to reach twelve men and teach them how to reach the world. He believed in the principle of discipling.

His commitment to the discipling principle becomes obvious when you see where Jesus spent most of his time in his ministry. If he wanted to reach the masses, why did he not go to Rome, Corinth, Athens, or Ephesus? Instead he spent most of his time in Capernaum–a small seaside village, the home of Peter and Andrew. When I visited Capernaum, I saw the synagogue where Jesus preached his first sermon. He would not have had a very large audience. Nazareth, his hometown, only had around one hundred people in it. The whole area of Galilee was small, not metropolitan at all. Jesus went there to make twelve disciples. At this point in his ministry, Jesus was not interested in preaching to large numbers of people. He was interested in reaching twelve hearts that would take his message to the rest of the world. His was a discipling ministry.

Jesus believed in discipling. How much do we believe in discipling today? We say that we are a discipling church. If someone looked at your life as the norm of your church, would they say we are a discipling church? Do you "teach people to obey?" Are you committed to discipling?

2. Walk in the steps of Jesus.

1 Peter 2:21 "To this you were called, because Christ suffered for you, leaving you an example, that you should follow in his steps."

Many say, "I wish I could go to Jerusalem and walk where Jesus walked." When I was in the Holy Land, one of my greatest thrills was walking where Jesus walked. I remember Sam Powell, an elder and evangelist in the New York church, saying before he left on a trip to Israel, "I don't care what we do over there, I just want to walk where Jesus walked." Sam tore a muscle in his leg before he left so he went on crutches. He hobbled where Jesus walked. But he made it over and experienced the wonder of being where Jesus lived.

The *Via Dolorosa* means "the way of suffering." The traditional site of the *Via Dolorosa* is a winding cobblestone street that twists and turns through an Arab market. Even though it is a traditional site with little left to resemble the first century street, there still exists a mystical aura as you walk where Jesus might have taken his steps.

Walking on authentic places where Jesus was is even more mystical and inspiring. As I've mentioned earlier, one of my favorite sites is the Garden of Gethsemane. Our family would go there for devotionals. You know it is the real site because it is on the Mount of Olives and mountains don't move. You could picture Jesus praying there with his disciples on the night he was arrested. It was incredible to be able to pray where Jesus prayed.

Another authentic site that I find inspirational are the steps on the southern side of the Temple Mount. I believe that the events of Acts 2 occurred on the steps of the Temple Mount. King Herod built these steps. Jesus and the early disciples would have used these steps to enter and exit the temple complex. Above these steps was Solomon's colonnade where the Apostles preached on Pentecost after the resurrection of Jesus. You can picture Jesus being there, and the early church beginning there.

But being where Jesus walked doesn't mean a thing if you don't try to walk in Jesus' steps every day. This is what Jesus really wants. One of the down sides to being in Jerusalem is seeing how people feel like a pilgrimage to Jerusalem is going to give them "good luck" spiritually. They kiss the place where the manger of Jesus was supposed to be. They kneel down and kiss the spot the cross was supposed to have stood. There are icons everywhere. They want a little holiness to rub off on them.

Jesus doesn't want to be remembered in this way. Jesus wants us to walk in his steps every single day. You can walk in the steps of Jesus wherever you live. You can walk in the steps of Jesus in a mall or in school or at work or in a hospital. You can walk in the steps of Jesus in New York, Hong Kong, Johannesburg, Sao Paulo, Sydney, or Moscow. It doesn't matter where you are. What matters is your heart.

How do we walk in the steps of Jesus? I wrote this devotional thought back in the early 1980s:

We walk in the steps of Jesus—
By making a new friend at work.
By helping someone get their groceries in their car at the supermarket.
By noticing that someone isn't at church and giving them a call to find out why.

We walk in the steps of Jesus—
By loving our children with an unconditional love. By making them feel like they are the most special children in the world.
By having marriages that shine. Marriages that say to the world–we are different

because we walk in the steps of Jesus.
By studying the Bible with someone this week.

We walk in the steps of Jesus--
By having a great time with someone this week.
By not giving into temptation.
By loving the unlovely
  Touching the untouchable
  Caring for those no one cares about
  Giving hope to the hopeless
And by taking salvation to all.

This is how we walk in the steps of Jesus.

          –GSK

Endnotes

[1] Philip Yancey, *The Jesus I Never Knew* (Grand Rapids: Zondervan Publishing House, 1995) pp. 187-188.

[2] David Hill, p. 332.

[3] Martin Hengel, *Crucifixion* (Philadelphia: Fortress Press, 1977).

[4] Ibid., p. 6.

[5] As quoted in Hengel, p. 25.

[6] Ibid.

[7] Hengel., p. 46.

[8] As quoted in Hengel, p. 90.

[9] Ibid.

[10] As quoted in Hengel, p. 92.

[11] Hengel., p. 94.

[12] Ibid.

[13] Ibid.

[14] See Carson, pp. 525-526.

[15] Carson, p. 530.

[16] Carson, p. 530.

[17] Gleason L. Archer, *Encyclopedia of Bible Difficulties* (Grand Rapids: Zondervan Publishing House, 1982), p. 376.

[18] Fritz Rienecker, p. 78.

[19] R. T. France, p. 375.

[20] Hill, pp. 347-348.

[21] See J.W. Wenham, "When Were the Saints Raised?" *Journal of Theological Studies* 32 [1981]: 150-152.

[22] Carson, p. 595.

[23] France, p. 141.

Appendix One
New Testament Chronology

6-4 BC   Jesus born

AD 26   John the Baptist begins his ministry

AD 27   Jesus begins his ministry

AD 30   Jesus dies, rises from the dead and ascends to heaven

AD 30   Pentecost, church begins

AD 34   Paul converted

AD 45   James written from Jerusalem

AD 47-48   First missionary journey

AD 49   Council of Jerusalem

           Galatians written from Jerusalem

AD 49-51   Second missionary journey

                  AD 50   1 Thessalonians written from Corinth

                  AD 51   2 Thessalonians written from Corinth

AD 51-54   Third missionary journey

                  AD 53   1 Corinthians written from Ephesus

                  AD 55   2 Corinthians written from Macedonia

                  AD 56   Romans written from Corinth on Paul's 3rd
                              visit there

AD 56   Paul takes collection to the church in Jerusalem

AD 56-58   Paul incarcerated at Caesarea

AD 59-60   Paul's journey to Rome

AD 60-62   Paul's first Roman imprisonment

           Philemon, Ephesians, Philippians, and Colossians written
           here

AD 62   Paul released from jail. He continues his mission work.

                  AD 63   1 Timothy written

                  AD 65   Titus written

                  AD 67   2 Timothy written

                  AD 67-68 Paul is executed

AD 62   James the brother of Jesus is stoned to death

AD 64   Rome burns by Nero's hand

AD 64   1 Peter is written from Rome

AD 65   2 Peter is written from Rome

AD 65-67   Nero executes Peter in Rome

AD 65   Mark is written from Rome

AD 67   Matthew is written from Palestine

AD 68   Hebrews is written from Palestine

AD 68   Jude is written from Palestine

AD 68   Luke is written from Rome

AD 68   Acts is written from Rome

AD 70   Destruction of the Temple of Jerusalem

AD 69-79   Revelation;1,2,3 John (possibly Gospel of John) are written

AD 90   Gospel of John written from Ephesus

Appendix Two
The Jewish Calendar

Sabbath:
Every Saturday the Sabbath was set aside as a day of rest. It began when the sun met the horizon on Friday evening.

Purim:
February-March. Celebrated deliverance of the Jews from the plot of Haman as recorded in Esther. It was a celebration of joy.

Passover:
March-April. The 14th day of Nisan. This was the oldest of the Jewish festivals. It celebrated the deliverance of the Hebrews from Egyptian captivity. The youngest member of the family asks, "What is so special about this night?" A narrative is told which brings the history of Israel to life.

Unleavened Bread:
April. This feast was celebrated immediately after Passover and continued for 7 days. During this feast the Jewish family was to remove all the unleavened Bread from the house. The Jews would remember the quick escape from Egypt during this feast.

Pentecost/Weeks:
May-June. This was celebrated 50 days after Passover. This was a thanksgiving festival for the harvest of early grain. The feast was celebrated by the making of loaves of bread.
The Jews also honored the Law and Moses on this day.

Atonement/Yom Kipper:
September/October. This was a day of fasting and the most holy day of the Jewish calendar. This was an important day for the High Priest. He would rise early and purify himself, pouring oil on his head. A bull was sacrificed on the great altar and its blood was sprinkled on the Ark of the Covenant in the Holy of Holies. This was the one-day of the year when the Holy of Holies could be entered and then only by the High Priest.

Tabernacles/Feast of Booths:
October–5 days after atonement. The feast of booths remembered the days when the Hebrews wandered in the wilderness for 40 years after

the escape from Egypt. It was a time of reflection and thanksgiving for the blessings of the year. They celebrated the protection of God during this feast. They also thanked God for the autumn harvest. They would build three sided tents in the yard to remember how God led them through the wilderness. They hung the first fruits (grapes) on the tents as a sign of thanksgiving.

Dedication/Festival of Lights/Hanukkah
December. This feast originated during the inter-testamental period (December 14, 164 BC). It celebrated the cleansing of the temple during the heroic activities of Judas Maccabeus. I Maccabees 4:56-59 and John 10:22-24 refer to this festival.

Note: Two things can be learned from the Jewish festivals.
1. You can see how important it was for Israel to commemorate the mighty acts of God so that they would not be forgotten. They would reenact the Exodus or the wilderness wanderings.
2. You can see that only one the holy days was a day of fasting. The rest were days of celebration and festivities.

Judaism in the day of Jesus:
In Jesus' day around 1.5 to 2 million Jews lived in Palestine. Around 4 million others were part of the Diaspora, Jews spread throughout the known world. 90% of the Jews of Palestine were the *Am ha-aretz* or the people of the land. These were poor people who scraped together a day-to-day existence. The other 10% were the political leaders and the landed gentry. The gap between the "have's" and the "have not's" was clearly marked in Jesus' day.

Jewish attitudes towards Rome:
The majority of the Jews paid taxes reluctantly. Most were hostile to Roman occupation. Judaism was a recognized (official) religion in Rome. The Romans could not set up their standards (the eagle) in Jerusalem.

Less than 40 years after Jesus, Jerusalem was razed to the ground because of civil unrest.

Bibliography

Aharoni, Yohanan. *The Land of the Bible: A Historical Geography.* Philadelphia: Westminster Press, 1979.

_____ and Avi-Yonah, Michael. *The Macmillan Bible Atlas.* New York: Macmillan, 1977.

Albright, W.F., and Mann, C.S. *Matthew.* The Anchor Bible, vol. 26. Garden City: Doubleday, 1971.

Allen, Willoughby, C. *A Critical and Exegetical Commentary on the Gospel According to St. Matthew.* Edinburgh: T. & T. Clark, 1912.

Archer, Gleason L. *The Encyclopedia of Bible Difficulties.* Grand Rapids: Zondervan, 1982.

Bacon, Benjamin W. *Studies in Matthew.* London: Constable, 1930.

Bammel, E., Editor. *The Trail of Jesus.* London: SCM, 1970.

Barclay, William. *New Testament Words.* London: SCM Press, 1964.

Barnett, Paul. *Is the New Testament History?* Ann Arbor, Mich.: Vine, 1986.

Bauer, W. *A Greek-English Lexicon of the New Testament and Other Early Christian Literature.* Translated and adapted by W. F. Arndt and F. W. Gingrich; second edition revised and augmented by F. W. Gingrich and F. W. Danker. University of Chicago Press, 1979.

Beare, F. W. *The Gospel according to Matthew: A Commentary.* Oxford: Blackwell, 1981.

Beasley-Muarry, G.R. *Baptism in the New Testament.* London: Macmillan, 1954.

Beasley, James R., et al. *An Introduction to the Bible.* Nashville: Abingdon Press, 1991.

Bettenson, Henry, Editor and Translator. *The Early Church Fathers.* Oxford: Oxford University Press, 1956.

Black, Matthew. *An Aramaic Approach to the Gospels and Acts.* Oxford University Press, 1967.

Blair, Edward P. *Jesus in the Gospel of Matthew.* New York: Abingdon, 1960.

Bloomberg, Craig. *The Historical Reliability of the Gospels.* Downers Grove, Ill.: InterVarsity Press, 1987.

Bonhoeffer, Dietrich. *The Cost of Discipleship.* 6th ed. London: SCM, 1959.

Bornkamm, Gunther. *Jesus of Nazareth.* London: Hodder and Stoughton, 1960.

Boyd, Gregory A. *Cynic, Sage or Son of God? Recovering the Real Jesus in an Age of Revisionist Replies.* Weaton, Ill.: BridgePoint, 1995.

Bromiley, G. W. *The International Standard Bible Encyclopedia.* Revised Edition. Grand Rapids: Eerdmans, 1979.

Brown, Colin, Editor. *The New International Dictionary of New Testament Theology.* Exeter: Paternoster press, 1975-1978.

Brown, Raymond E. *The Birth of the Messiah: A Commentary on the Infancy Narratives in Matthew and Luke.* Garden City: Doubleday, 1977.

Bruce, F.F. *I & II Corinthians.* The New Century Bible Commentary. Grand Rapids: Wm. B. Eerdmans Publishing Co., 1971.

_____. *New Testament History.* London: Pickering and Inglis, 1982.

Bultmann, Rudolf. *Form Criticism.* Translated by Frederick C. Grant. New York: Harper and Row, Publ., 1963.

_____. *History of the Synoptic Tradition.* Translated by J. Marsh.Oxford: Blackwells, 1963.

_____. *Theology of the New Testament.* 2 vols. Translated by K. Grobel. London: SCM, 1952-1955.

Carson, D.A. *The Expositor's Bible Commentary with The New International Version, Matthew.* 2 vols. Grand Rapids: Zondervan, 1995.

_____. *The Sermon on the Mount.* Grand Rapids: Baker, 1978.

Cranfield, C.E.B. *The Gospel According to St. Mark.* Cambridge: University Press, 1972.

Cullman, Oscar. *The Christology of the New Testament.* Translated by Shirley C. Guthrie and Charles A.M. Hall. 2nd ed. Philadelphia: Westminster, 1963.

Davies, W. D. *The Setting of the Sermon on the Mount.* Cambridge University Press, 1963.

Dibelius, Martin. *From Tradition to Gospel.* Translated by Bertram Lee Woolf. London: Redwood Press Limited, 1919.

Dodd, C.H. *The Parables of the Kingdom.* London: Nisbet, 1936.

Douglas, J. D. and Hillyer, N. (eds.). *New Bible Dictionary.* Leichester: InterVarsity Press, 1982.

Drane, John. *Introducing the New Testament.* San Francisco: Harper & Row, 1986.

The Early Christian Fathers. Edited and translated by Henry Bettenson. Oxford: Oxford University Press, 1956.

Finegan, Jack. *The Archaeology of the New Testament.* Princeton: Princeton University Press, 1992.

_____. *Handbook of Biblical Chronology.* Princeton: Princeton University Press, 1964.

France, R. T. *Matthew: Tyndale New Testament Commentaries.* Grand Rapids: William B. Eerdmans Publishing Company, 1985.

Fuller, Daniel P. *Easter Faith and History*. Grand Rapids: Eerdmans, 1965.

Gaebelein, Arno C. *The Gospel According to Matthew: An Exposition*. 2 Vols. New York: Our Hope Publications, 1910.

Geisler, Norman L. and Howe, Thomas. *When Critics Ask*. Wheaton, Ill.: Victor, 1992.

Grant, Robert M. *A Historical Introduction to the New Testament*. New York: Harper and Row, Publ., Inc., 1963.

Grasser, Erich. "Jesus In Nazareth.' *New Testament Studies*. 16 (1969-1970): 1-23.

Green, H. Benedict. *The Gospel According to Matthew*. The New Clarendon Bible. Oxford: University Press, 1975.

Guelich, R. A. *The Sermon on the Mount: a Foundation for Understanding*. Waco, Texas: Word Books, 1975.

Gundry, R. H. *Matthew: A Commentary on his Literary and Theological Art*. Grand Rapids: Eerdmans, 1982.

_____. *The Use of the Old Testament in St. Matthew's Gospel*. SNT 18. Leiden: E. J. Brill, 1967.

Guthrie, Donald. *New Testament Introduction*. Downers Grove, Ill.: Inter-Varsity Press, 1970.

_____. *New Testament Theology*. Downers Grove, Ill.: IVP, 1981.

Head, David. *Shout for Joy*. New York: The Macmillan Company, 1962.

Hendriksen, William. *The Gospel of Matthew*. Grand Rapids: Eerdmans, 1972.

Hengel, Martin. *Crucifixion*. Philadelphia: Fortress Press, 1977.

Hill, David. *The Gospel of Matthew*. New Century Bible. London: Marshall, Morgan, and Scott, 1972.

Jeremias, Joachim. *Jerusalem in the Time of Jesus*. Translated by F.H. and C.H. Cave. London: SCM 1962.

_____. *The Parables of Jesus*. S. H. Hooke, Translator. New York: Charles Scribner's Sons, 1954

_____. *New Testament Theology*. Part I. The Proclamation of Jesus. Translated by John Bowden. London: SCM, 1971.

King, Martin Luther, Jr. *Strength to Love*. Glasgow: William Collins Sons and Co., 1964.

Kingsbury, Jack Dean. *Matthew*. Philadelphia: Fortress, 1977.

_____. *Structure, Christology, Kingdom*. Philadelphia: Fortress Press, 1975.

Kittel, G. and Friedrich, G., Editors. *Theological Dictionary of the New Testament*. Grand Rapids: Eerdmans, 1964-1974.

Kummel, W.G. *Introduction to the New Testament*. Translated by S.H. Hooke. London: SCM, 1958.

_____. *The Theology of the New Testament*. Translated by John E. Steel. Nashville: Abingdon Press, 1973.

Ladd, G.E. *I Believe in the Resurrection of Jesus*. Grand Rapids: Eerdmans, 1975.

_____. *A Theology of the New Testament*. Grand Rapids: Eerdmans, 1974.

Lane, William L. *The Gospel According to Mark*. Grand Rapids: Wm. B. Eerdmans Publ. Comp., 1974.

Leon-Dufour, Xavier, Editor. *Dictionary of Biblical Theology*. Translated by Joseph Cahill. New York: Desclee Company, 1962.

Lohse, Eduard. *The New Testament Environment*. Translated by John Steely. Nashville: Abingdon Press, 1971.

Marshall, I. Howard. *Commentary on Luke*. New International Greek Testament Commentary. Grand Rapids: Wm. B. Eerdmans Publishing, Co., 1978.

McGarvey, J.W. *Commentary on Mark*. Delight, Arkansas: Gospel Light Publ. Co., 1875.

McKenzie, John L. "The Gospel According to Matthew." *The Jerome Biblical Commentary*. Edited by R.E. Brown, J.A. Fitzmyer, and R.E. Murphy. Englewood Cliffs: Prentice-Hall, 1968.

Moulton, J. H. and Milligan, G. *The Vocabulary of the Greek Testament, illustrated from the Papyri and other Non-Literary Sources*. 1930, reprinted Grand Rapids: Eerdmans, 1974.

New Dimensions in New Testament Studies. R. E. Longenecker and M.C. Tenney, Editors. Grand Rapids: Wm. B. Eerdmans Publ. Co., 1974.

Pritchard, James B. *The Harper Atlas of the Bible*. New York: Harper and Row, 1987.

Richardson, Alan D., Editor. *A Theological Word Book of the Bible*. London: SCM Press, Ltd., 1957.

Rienecker, Fritz. Translated by Cleon L. Rogers, Jr. *A Linguistic Key to the Greek New Testament*. Grand Rapids: Zondervan Publishing House, 1976.

Robinson, John A.T. *Redating the New Testament*. London: SCM Press, 1976.

Russell, D.S. *Between the Testaments*. Philadelphia: Fortress Press, 1960.

Schweizer, Eduard. *The Good News According to Luke*. Translated by David E. Green. Atlanta: John Knox Press, 1984.

_____. *The Good News According to Mark*. Translated by Donald H. Madvig. Richmond, Va.: John Knox Press, 1970.

_____. *The Good News According to Matthew*. Translated by David E. Green. Atlanta: John Knox Press, 1975.

Tasker, R.V.G. *The Gospel According to St. Matthew: An Introduction and Commentary*. London: IVP, 1961.

Taylor, Vincent. *The Gospel According to St. Mark*. London: Macmillan and Co. Ltd., 1953.

Tenney, Merrill C. *New Testament Survey, Revised*. Grand Rapids: Wm. B. Eerdmans Publishing Co., 1985.

Theological Dictionary of the New Testament. Gehard Kittel and Gerhard Friedrick, Editor. Geoffrey W. Bromiley, Translator. Grand Rapids: Wm. B. Eerdmans Publishing Co., 1968.

A Theological Wordbook of the Bible. Alan Richardson, Editor. New York: Macmillan Publ., Co., Inc., 1976.

Tolbert, Malcolm O. *Good News from Matthew*. Nashville: Broadman Press, 1975.

Wall, Robert W. "Divorce" in *The Anchor Bible Dictionary*, Vol. 2. New York: Doubleday, 1992.

Walvoord, John F. *Matthew: Thy Kingdom Come*. Chicago: Moody, 1974.

Wenham, J.W. "When Were the Saints Raised?" *Journal of Theological Studies* 32 [1981]: 150-152

Wilkinson, J. *Jerusalem as Jesus knew it: Archaeology as Evidence*. London: Thames and Hudson, 1978.

Wood, Clyde. *The Living Way Commentary on the Old Testament. Volume Two. Leviticus-Numbers-Deuteronomy*. Shreveport, Louisiana: Lambert Book House, 1974.

Yancey, Philip. *The Jesus I Never Knew*. Grand Rapids: Zondervan Publishing House, 1995.

Follow me, do not turn back.
Follow me, leave the dead to bury the dead.
Follow me, and I will make you fisher-men.
Follow me, take up my cross.

Where does He lead? Where is his path?
It leads to the leper–unloved, untouched, alienated.
It leads to the sinner–guilt-ridden, crushed, lost.
It leads to the poor–hungry, naked, sick, hopeless.
It leads to the Christian brother–weak, struggling, faithless.

No wonder I shudder, I hesitate, I draw back.
Who can follow in that path? Who can bear that cross?

"Lo, I am with you always!"
Dear Jesus, help my unbelief.

–GSK, late 1970s